SHABBOS
IN A
NEW LIGHT

MAJESTY, MYSTERY, MEANING

This unique work of genius proportions is incredibly rich in new ideas. It is a masterpiece of profound brilliance and beauty that will enable you to experience the lofty depths of the heightened sublime spirituality of Shabbos. Rabbi Hutner's inspiring and masterful thoughts bring the excitement, wonder and mystery of Torah study that satisfies our yearning for a deeper understanding of the uniqueness, mission and holiness of Israel.

Rav Hutner's profound, penetrating and creative analysis will transform your Shabbos experience and open your mind to the deeper meaning of one of G-d's most majestic, greatest and most valued gifts.

Shabbos is the dynamic spiritual engine that has assured the survival and spiritual development of the Torah nation through scores of generations of exile and persecution. Shabbos is the day that undergirds the spiritual creativity of the Jewish People. It inspires the continued upward progress of the Torah nation which will lead to the ultimate climactic triumph of the Messianic Era and the building of the Third Temple.

Through his creative and inspiring writing, Rabbi Hutner catapults us to understand Shabbos as the most significant transformational event of Jewish life. Shabbos capsulates all of Jewish history and yearning, it envelopes us with an experience of high spirituality and the aura of the Future Life. It transforms the material into the spiritual, and provides an experience of such heightened sublime spirituality that we are transformed and permanently elevated. Shabbos confirms for all times the uniqueness, mission and holiness of Israel. It is unlike any other day.

SHABBOS
IN A
NEW LIGHT

MAJESTY, MYSTERY, MEANING

As revealed through the writings of
RABBI YITZCHAK HUTNER
זכר צדיק וקדוש לברכה
**Author of Pachad Yitzchak,
Rosh Yeshiva Mesivta Rabbi Chaim Berlin,
Kollel Gur Aryeh and Yeshivas Pachad Yitzchak**

Interpreted and Adapted by
RABBI PINCHAS STOLPER

ספר פחד יצחק
מאת הוד כבוד אדוננו מורנו ורבנו
כש"ת מרן הגאון רבי יצחק הוטנר זצוקללה"ה
שער וביום השבת
דברי תורה בהלכות דעות וחובות הלבבות
בעניינא דשבת

The publication of Pachad Yitzchak in English is a non-profit venture.
To be able to continue to cover the considerable publishing costs, we
seek individuals who wish to become partners in this *meleches ha-kodesh*.
Please contact the author at the David Dov Foundation (see below).

Cover image was inspired by David Gilboa
Page layout and design by E. Chachamtzedek

FIRST EDITION: AUGUST 2009

PUBLISHED BY:
DAVID DOV FOUNDATION
603 TWIN OAKS DRIVE
LAKEWOOD, NJ 08701
732 370-6078; 732 232-3736

DISTRIBUTED BY:
ISRAEL BOOK SHOP
501 PROSPECT STREET
LAKEWOOD, NJ 08701
732 901-3990 FAX: 732 901-4012
isrbkshp@aol.com

Printed in China

CONTENTS

ACKNOWLEDGMENTS
AND APPRECIATION

SPECIAL THANKS ARE due to my Editor, a rare and outstanding *talmid chochom,* **Rabbi Yaakov Dovid Homnick** whose clarity of vision, brilliance, depth, insight, scholarship and sensitivity are awesome. This book could not have been published without his skilled editorial craftsmanship, whenever I was in doubt it was he who clarified, suggested revisions and shed light.

Much appreciation to Raizy Flamm for the extraordinarily beautiful cover, to Ruthy Ungar who typed and retyped the manuscript with skill and patience, to Esther Chachamtzedek who created the beautiful design of the body of the book, to Moshe Kaufman of Israel Book Shop who skillfully handled the distribution.

I recall with gratitude the inspiration and zealous devotion to Jewish tradition of my late parents, Rabbi David Dov Stolper, *ztz"l,* and Mrs. Nettie Stolper *a"h.*

No wife would have allowed her husband to turn the dining room table into a writer's habitat for months on end (I have two studies). I dedicate this volume to Elaine, my truest critic, whose patience and support made this volume possible. She personifies the nobility, *chessed,* dedication and insight of the Jewish wife, mother and grandmother. May we be worthy to merit the continued growth and achievements in Torah and *yiras shomayim* of our children, grandchildren and great grandchildren.

May the Torah learning engendered by this volume add *le'iluy nishmas* our daughter, *Malka Tova Bas Chaya,* and may her husband Rabbi Dr. Chaim Kaweblum and their children be comforted and enjoy Hashem's blessings for many years to come.

Songs and praises to the most Mighty and Kind, the *Ribono Shel Olam* Himself, Who has given me the *z'chus* to witness His miracles, to dwell in the tents of His Torah, and to be His agent in person and through my pen.

אני תפלה שכל הכי קרובים לרבנו זצוק"ל ורבים הם, וגדולים הם ממני,
ידעו שלא לכבודי קבלתי על עצמי את המשימה להוציא את מעיינות רבנו
חוצה ולהוציא לאור ספר שלם של כתבי פחד יצחק בשפה המדוברת כי אם
לכבודו, שהלא מורי ורבי הוא שהכניס אותי במחיצתו, ואין כבוד גדול מזה.

Pinchas Stolper
Kislev 5769/December 2008

This volume of Torah inspiration is lovingly
dedicated to the memory of our daughter

Malka Tova Kaweblum ע"ה

Malkie's wisdom, warmth and generosity was
devoted to inspiring, encouraging and teaching her
students, her five children, and scores of friends
and neighbors.

Malka Tova left an indelible mark on the lives of
countless others. Her courageous six-year battle for life
never tarnished her zestful love of life,
her warmth, her *emunah, bitachon* and *avodas Hashem.*

Malkie was the classic Woman of Valor,
a source of strength, counsel, guidance and love;
always giving, always devoted, always upbeat,
always selfless. Her suffering was with
"Ivdu es Hashem besimcha," serve G-d with joy.

תהא נשמתה צרורה בצרור החיים

DEDICATIONS

Sincerest gratitude to my friends and colleagues whose encouragement and support made the publication of this book possible:

Rabbi and Mrs. Kenneth Auman

Dr. Henry and Mindy Azrikan

Dr. and Mrs. Benjamin Befeler

Jack Belz

Dr. Ronald and Raina Berger
in honor of our son Avi
upon his graduation from Einstein Medical School

Rabbi Raphael B. Butler

Larry and Maureen Eisenberg
in celebration of our children Rebecca, Elisheva and Shlomo

Terry and Dennis M. Eisenberg
in honor of our children and grandchildren

Shelly and Joan Fliegelman

Drs. Avi and Elin Freilich

Howard Zvi and Chaya Friedman

Dr. Stanley and Marla Frohlinger
in memory of Malkie

Paul and Rachel Glasser
in memory of our parents,
Herbert and Charlotte Glasser, Ted and Leila Chernotsky

Rabbi Shlomo and Karen Hochberg
in loving memory of Joseph Ulevitch

Dr. David L. and Barbara Hurwitz

Lothar and Sue Kahn
be *matzliach*

Mr. and Mrs. Walter Kahn

Sarah and Steve Karp
with great respect

Arleeta and Ivan Lerner
with great respect

Dr. and Mrs. Noah Lightman

Vivian and David Luchins
in memory of Malkie

Joseph Macy
in memory of his wife Julia

In memory of our daughter Aviva Esther
by **Malka and Steve Miretzky**

Dr. and Mrs. Dovid Ogun
Your books are sweeter than honey

Harry and Helen Ostreicher

Stuart and Lisa Panish

Mr. and Mrs. Werner Rosenbaum
in memory of Max and Ilse Rosenbaum and
Leon and Helen Tempelsman

Mr. and Mrs. Levi Yitzchok Rothman

Lee C. and Anne Samson

Carmi Schwartz
keep producing your important books

Philip and Sylvia Spertus

Rabbi Ephraim Sturm

Leon and Helen Tempelsman

Dr. Barry and Shari Weinberger
in honor of our children, Simcha Leib and Ariella Rachel Krainczer,
Jason Craig, Aliza Pearl; and in memory of Malkie

Bennie and Shulamis Weinfeld
in memory of Avraham Pesach and
Hinda Weinfeld and Yehudah Leib Neidich

David S. and Grace K. Weil

Mr. and Mrs. Heshy Wengrow

Susanne and Michael Wimpfheimer
in honor of Jan, Orit, Barry, Shana, Gershon, Ahuva, Yair, Ariel, Avigayil, Noam,
Talia, Ayelet, Yonah, Maytal, Saadia, Adir, Adin and Amitai

Before you proceed…

SHABBOS IN A NEW LIGHT

MANY SHABBOS BOOKS are available, but very few deal with its message, challenge, goals and purpose. Through his rich, creative and inspiring writing, Rabbi Hutner catapults us to the opposite pole where Shabbos is understood as *the* most significant transformational event of Jewish life. Shabbos encapsulates all of Jewish history and yearning, it envelopes us with an experience of high spirituality and the aura of the Future Life. It transforms the material into the spiritual and provides an experience of such heightened sublime spirituality that we are transformed and permanently elevated. Shabbos confirms for all times the uniqueness, mission and holiness of Israel. It is unlike any other day. Shabbos is the dynamic spiritual engine that has assured the survival and spiritual development of the Torah nation through scores of generations of exile and persecution. Shabbos is the day that undergirds the spiritual creativity of the Jewish People. It inspires the continued upward progress of the Torah nation which will lead to the ultimate climactic triumph of the Messianic Era and the building of the Third Temple.

The theme of Shabbos concerns G-d's endless and enduring love for His people. This volume is an expression of pure love for Rav Yitzchak Hutner, whose brilliant, profound, piercing and creative intellect introduces us to his unique understanding of Shabbos.

These brilliant writings, which are offered in English for the first time, should not only be seen as original intellectual, spiritual, philosophical creativity, but as an effort to create a thought-provoking environment and framework for a more intense and meaningful observance and understanding of Shabbos, the central institution of Jewish life.

The lights of Shabbos are the lights of the final redemption; when properly understood and internalized, its lessons are essential to bringing the redemption. Shabbos is the grand miniature of the redemption.

SHABBOS: PACHAD YITZCHAK
INTRODUCTORY THOUGHTS

MOST PEOPLE DON'T read introductions but this one *is required reading* if you are to comprehend and appreciate these lectures. The power of this unprecedented study of Shabbos forcefully indicates that the depths of Shabbos extend far deeper than that which appears on the surface.

Hebrew, an extremely subtle, multi-meaning, precise, yet poetic language lends itself to far deeper nuances and meanings than does English. Some people therefore believe that Rabbi Hutner's deep thoughts can only be understood in their Hebrew original. This is in fact true for great Torah commentary in general and is especially so as regards Rabbi Hutner who was poetic, deeply intellectual, revealing and concealing at the same time. With this as a given, it is a matter of urgency that serious Jews study Rabbi Hutner's piercing analysis of Shabbos in English and internalize the many significant lessons that emerge. Rabbi Hutner's unique prognosis speaks volumes to each Jew's responsibilities during this critical historic period. The challenges facing Jewry make it imperative that thinking Jews be exposed to this unique classic of Torah thought that informs us that a sophisticated understanding of Shabbos is essential to our ability to initiate and maintain teachings and methods that are so urgently needed during these dangerous and precarious pre-messianic days.

People to whom I related that I had attempted an English language adaptation of *Pachad Yitzchak on Shabbos* often reacted that it was an impossible, almost undoable undertaking. This is so because Rav Hutner does not always reveal his meanings, expecting that his students, familiar as they are with his teachings on so many topics, would be able to make the necessary connections and associations.

Each of the countless times my editor and I reviewed the Hebrew text, we discovered additional depth that was not previously in evidence.

There is unquestionably yet more to be uncovered. No literary effort I have ever undertaken has been so overwhelmingly taxing, time consuming and difficult; yet so inspiring, enlightening and refreshing. At the outset of the labor I thought that I "comprehended" Rav Hutner's intentions, but I was mistaken. It was not until I attempted to transpose them into modern English with the goal that a broad public be enabled to understand the text, that I realized how subtle, inspiringly revealing and necessary were his words. If I had no goal other than to understand *p'shat,* the true meaning of the text, the entire daunting effort would have been worthwhile.

As noted above, English does not lend itself to the depth, majesty, poetry and subtlety of Rabbinic Hebrew. In style and presentation the objective of this volume is to provide the reader with an authentic, idiomatic English rendition of the Hebrew text which faithfully conveys our understanding of Rav Hutner's message. To quote the Talmud, (*Kiddushin* 49a) *"One who translates a verse literally misrepresents the text."* For this reason, whenever an editorial decision was called for, we opted for truth and clarity. Our intent is to be true to the message more than to the words, in order to plumb the timeless message of the most highly essential day in the life of the Jewish People.

If the reader feels that I have missed a point, or misread the text I will be delighted to hear from you, preferably in writing. I will study your proposal carefully.

ADVICE TO THE READER:

IF YOU SPEED READ, you will surely miss most of what is conveyed. It is essential that you read carefully and slowly, in order to comprehend and contemplate the message. You may discover that a second and third reading will uncover much that was missed in the first reading. These lectures can not be *"read"*. They must be *studied* by your mind and inner ear. They must be *"learned"* in the way we study the Talmud, for they reflect the holy thoughts of our Sages.

Note: Introductory paragraphs written in this typeface as well as text surrounded by square brackets are the comments and interpretations of the author.

ONE

The New Face of Shabbos

INTRODUCTION

S HABBOS BRINGS A "NEW FACE" to the world by revealing the purpose for which the physical world was created; namely, the virtue and spiritual achievement embodied in the Ten Commandments. This revelation, heard by three million Jews at Sinai, becomes meaningful to the extent that it is appreciated by the human mind.

Shabbos transforms Man into the key for discovering the inner light of G-d's Creation. On Shabbos Man takes on a "new face", an enlightened face, of his own.

Shabbos brings a new definition to the world, to mankind, to life and to the role of the human mind as the decoder, definer and manager of G-d's Creation.

SECTION I

ONE

"THOSE WHO TASTE SHABBOS merit life, while those who love its message have chosen greatness" (Shabbos liturgy, *Mussaf*).

Our appreciation of the 'message' of Shabbos is called love, while our appreciation of the essence of Shabbos is called 'tasting'.

This contrast in activity brings a contrast in actualization — in that the tasting of Shabbos is associated with 'life' while the love of its message creates a relationship of 'majesty'. This calls for an explanation.

TWO

DURING THE SEVEN FESTIVE days following the wedding of a bride and a groom, Seven Blessings — *Sheva Brochos* — are recited only when *panim chadashos* — 'new faces' i.e. new guests, have arrived at that day's festive dinner. Many authorities make an exception when the festive post-wedding dinner is on Shabbos, requiring the blessings even without new guests, because Shabbos itself is equivalent to 'new faces'. These authorities cite a Midrash as the source. The Midrash comments regarding the Song/Psalm of Shabbos: *"Mizmor Shir l'yom haShabbos, panim chadashos bo'u lekaan,"* i.e. "New faces have arrived" (*Tosfos, Kesuvos* 7b). Thus, the coming of Shabbos is equivalent to new faces coming.

[The Midrash, on a basic level, seems to be responding to the duplication of *"mizmor shir"*: a tune, a song. The explanation is that the Shabbos tune is becoming a song. The tune of the weekdays takes on a new face and becomes a song for Shabbos. *Mizmor* literally means a clipping or a snippet, when *mizmor* is used to describe music it implies a limited segment, while a *shir* indicates a larger composition, perhaps a symphony. – Ed.]

Both the *halacha* and its source present problems. What is the light that stamps the renewed sanctity of Shabbos with the imprint of *panim chadashos* — "new faces"? Furthermore, why is there no allusion to the "new faces" aspect of Shabbos in the blessings of Shabbos, when the Torah deals with the sanctity of Shabbos or when the Prophets discuss Shabbos pleasure? Only when we reach the Song of Shabbos in the Book of Psalms do we encounter such a reference. The hidden nature of this matter calls for a solution.

THREE

THE KEY TO THESE TREASURES is in the words of the *Gr"a* (The *Vilna Gaon*). *"Hashem is constantly engaged in the active renewal of His creation. The renewal of Creation on Shabbos was already prepared from the day before, and on Shabbos G-d rested even from that* (i.e. from renewal)" (*Aderes Eliyahu: Bereishis* 2:3). We see this in the verse, *"And He desisted from all His creativity."*

[This might appear to be a contradiction. However, this is the point of what follows. It is a paradox that G-d does not desist from active renewal in a concrete sense but in an abstract sense—by making the higher spiritual activity into the true goal of physical Creation. –Ed.] Here, as we said previously, lies the key to a fuller understanding of the Sanctity of Shabbos.

FOUR

SOMEONE WHO TRANSFERS FOOD from the indoors to the outdoors in a vessel on Shabbos, where the quantity of transferred food is less than the minimum required for desecrating Shabbos, is not guilty of wrongdoing, even as concerns the vessel (*Shabbos* 93b). The transfer of the vessel was peripheral to the transfer of the food. Although the act of transferring the vessel would ordinarily be a desecration of Shabbos, since the movement of the vessel was subordinate to the food, it cannot be considered a "purposeful activity." It is therefore not an act which contradicts Shabbos rest.

We have now arrived at our new insight, as follows. The distinction between the essential and the non-essential is not one among the many laws of Shabbos. Rather, it is a reflection of the inner workings of the resting of Creation.

To clarify this, let us look back at the Six Days of Creation that preceded Shabbos. During those six days, the Ten Divine Commands through which the Universe was created took effect. On the strength of those Divine declarations the natural laws governing the behavior of the entire universe were given form. Yet in all these Commands of the Six Days of Creation, the matter of Sanctity is not yet mentioned. Sanctity, in our present discussion, refers to the following: While during the Six Days of Creation the world itself came into being, it was not until Shabbos, the end-point, that the ultimate purpose of the Universe was brought into sharp relief (*Bereishis* 2:3).

"*Im lo brisi yomom voloyla, chukos shama'yim v'aretz lo somti.*" Were it not for G-d's covenant of Torah being studied day and night, Hashem would never have established the laws governing the heavens and the earth (*Jeremiah* 33:25). This covenant is the ultimate purpose of all the natural laws which govern the behavior of the world. These laws of heaven and earth were established by means of the Ten Commands through which the world was created and they, in turn, depend upon the Covenant i.e. the Ten Commandments through which the Torah was given. The Ten Commandments are the innermost aspect of the Ten Commands of Creation, expressing their ultimate purpose.

This is why *Vayekadesh* (and He sanctified) follows *Vayechulu* — (they were completed); the completion of the Six Days of Creation (*Bereishis* 2:1-3). After the Ten Commands, the time for the revelation of their *raison de etre* had arrived. On the Shabbos of *Bereishis,* the culmination of Creation, the light of the Ten Commandments shined forth so brightly that the Ten Commands of Creation were but a mere vessel, a sheath for that light.

The above primary-to-subordinate relationship defines the innermost workings of the resting of the Shabbos of Creation. That is, (Divine) resting does not require the effect of the Ten Commands of Creation to cease. Rather, the revealed light of the Ten Commandments (i.e. the sense that the purpose of Creation is Torah) shows that the Ten Commands function merely as their vessel; a vessel far less important than its contents. Measured against the Ten Commandments, the Ten Commands are as a utensil to its contents, like that which is peripheral to that which is central.

There is no need for the Ten Commands to cease functioning for Creation to be at a rest. As we have seen, any act deemed subordinate is not a contradiction to resting. This is what the resting of *Shabbos Bereishis* was; with the appearance of *kedushas Shabbos*, the sanctity of Shabbos, the entire universe was relegated to a subordinate position. The diminution of the physical world from a dominant to a subservient position is the resting of *Shabbos Bereishis*; the Shabbos of Creation.

Therefore, the constant active renewal of Creation is not a contradiction to the resting of Shabbos. The resting of Shabbos is a shift on a relative scale of values, not a total cessation of activity.

FIVE

IT IS IMPOSSIBLE FOR there to be a value judgment without the power of the mind, which alone can weigh and evaluate. No other human faculty can discriminate between primary and subordinate. Only after the proper measure of a thing has been taken can it be upgraded to a primary position or downgraded to a subordinate one.

Through the mind, which alone has the power to attach a subordinate value to something, the renewal of *Ma'aseh Bereishis* (Creation) on Shabbos can take place. The mind takes that renewal out of the class of deliberate work, permitting it to coexist with the cessation of work. Intelligence was not created until the last day of the Six Days of Creation: the Command of *"Let us make man"* (*Bereishis* 1:26) brought intelligence into the world. Until the arrival of man, no creature on the face of the earth possessed the power of intelligence.

We now return to the *Gr"a*, who says that the renewal of the Creation of Shabbos was prepared from *erev Shabbos*, the eve of Shabbos.

All the requirements of Shabbos are prepared on *erev Shabbos*. This applies here as well. The faculty which allows for the renewal of creation even on Shabbos does so by differentiating between the primary and the subordinate. This faculty, the intelligence, was made ready on the eve of *Shabbos Bereishis*.

SIX

THE TEXT OF THE *Shabbos Mussaf* prayer relates the concepts we have been discussing in a succinct way. *"Those who love its message have chosen greatness."* The message of Shabbos is precisely this: properly evaluating primary and subordinate, accurately weighing smallness of measure against greatness of measure. To show love for the message of Shabbos is to emphasize that which is great in measure, to have the mind see the relationship of the universe itself to the purpose underlying it as the relationship of subservience and smallness vis-à-vis dominance and greatness.

Evaluation (*ha'aracha*) is an anagram of determining superiority (*hachra'a*). The mind's weighing will lead to the mind's recognition of greatness. *"Those who love its message have chosen greatness."*

SECTION II

SEVEN

REGARDING SHABBOS REST, THE Divine command *"Let us make man"* (*Bereishis* 1:26), which formulated the power of intelligence, stands out from all other commands. (Divine) resting on Shabbos means subordinating the Universe to its inner purpose, it is impossible for the mind itself to rest. [This sentence means that because rest on Shabbos is accomplished by the mind's working, by definition the mind is not resting. –Ed.]

After all, it is the mind that performs the evaluation which assigns preeminence to the inner purpose of the world, thereby enabling Shabbos rest. The mind can distinguish between the world as we see it and its inner light, establishing their relative value — the one subordinate and the other primary. It notes the auxiliary status of the Ten Commands and their results and recognizes the dominance of the Ten Commandments as the ultimate purpose of the Universe. This comparative de-emphasis of the consequences of the Ten Commands *is* the resting of Shabbos.

Ironically, just when the commands of *Bereishis* are at rest the power of the mind reaches its zenith, its highest and most noble level. The resting of Shabbos is engendered by the power of the mind, so that on Shabbos when everything is resting the mind is creating.

"Let us make man" is the command that created the intellectual faculty. The same Shabbos rest that suppresses the possible supremacy of the world created by the Ten Commands accentuates the supremacy of the mind's power.

Thus, the command of *"Let us make man"* is that which stands out. During the Six Days of Creation it functions alongside the other commands. On Shabbos it stands apart, performing its most singular function, at the same time as the other commands are retreating from the foreground in anticipation of G-d's desisting from creativity. (Shabbos brings out the singularity of the intellect. As a result, the uniqueness of *"Let us make man"* among the Ten Commands is highlighted.)

EIGHT

WE ARE NOW FULLY prepared to understand why the Sages explained the blessing of Shabbos as *"He blessed it with the light of the face of man"* (*Bereishis Rabba* 11b) — in terms of the radiance of the human countenance. This appears to lessen the blessing of Shabbos. As stated in the Torah, the blessing is open-ended, while the light of the human face is just one small piece of Creation. It seems like the Sages took a broad blessing and shrank it to one particular case.

The explanation is as above. A man's face is the barometer of his intelligence. Here the subordination of the material clay to the light of intelligence is distinctly and measurably recognizable. *"The wisdom of the human enlightens his face"* (*Koheles* 8:1), the power of his intelligence is reflected in the glow of his face. The illumination of the face is caused by the mind shining forth in such strength that it penetrates the material flesh and envelops the face in the glow of intelligence.

The one place where this effect can occur is appropriately termed *"panim,"* face, for that word (*"penim"* in Hebrew means the inside) reflects the subordination of the external to the inner self, the corporeal to the light of intelligence. This subordination is the secret behind the glow that projects out to the face. That glow testifies that the body is secondary to the intellect, and the intellect is measured in relation to the body as a primary to a subordinate. [We can now understand why the human face is unique, how it reflects the soul and the Divine, how it is a demonstration of the uniqueness of man. – Ed.]

Shabbos rest is a major factor in forming the light of man's countenance. This rest reveals the ability of the intelligence to transcend the material world of the Commands of Creation, subordinating it to the Torah-light of the Commandments of the Tablets of Sinai. The clearest sign in the human body of the unique power of human intelligence is the "glowing face of man."

Just as Shabbos rest allows the mind to strip away the externals of the universe by revealing its inner qualities, it also allows the mind to pierce the outer shell of man to reveal his inner self.

The extra revelation of the inner person on Shabbos is through the glowing face. A person's face glows immeasurably brighter on Shabbos than it does during the weekdays.

NINE

"THE GLOWING FACE OF Man." The accent here is on both "face" and "Man." While Shabbos rest stops the functioning of the commands of creation, the command *"Let us create man"* is activated — and even intensified. The primary accomplishment of the command *"Let us create man"* was the creation of intelligence. Even in man himself the other human faculties are ancillary to his *unique* human quality, the power of intelligence: "the Man within Man." This subordination is the secret of the power and uniqueness of the glowing light of Man's face.

Thus, a person's face on Shabbos is the outward manifestation in the flesh and blood of man of the unique command *"Let us make man."* Shabbos rest causes the face to glow in a twofold manner: through the revealed interior piercing the exterior aspect of man, and through the intensification of the command *"Let us make man"* as the other Commands cease to function.

Note the sequence in the verse: *"Vayishbos… vayevorech"* ("Then He rested … and then He blessed").

While rest implies passivity, a cessation, blessing represents an addition. Ceasing and adding are generally seen as mutually exclusive. Therefore, our Sages explain this blessing as an increase in the 'light of the countenance of man'. Man's countenance is the one part of him where an increase in radiance is due to a stoppage — stopping the exterior from blocking the interior light. This radiance is magnified by nullifying subsidiary aspects to emphasize the primary, and quieting other worldly functions to highlight the primacy of the faculty of the mind.

Thus, the Sages interpreted *"Vayevorech"* — "And He blessed" — as a reference to the enhanced glow of man's face. This certainly does not confine the blessing to one of its particular aspects; rather, the increase in the 'light of the countenance of man' is the basis for the blessing and benefits flowing from the resting of Shabbos.

TEN

WE CAN NOW UNDERSTAND why the Sages used the following phrase in the prayer of Shabbos: *"The praiseworthiness of the Seventh Day is because it is (the time) when G-d rested from all His work."*

At first glance, we appear to be faced with regression in the enumeration of the virtues of Shabbos, for in specifying the levels of praise appropriate to Shabbos, we began with rest (*"To G-d Who rested from all creation," Sabbath morning prayer*). We went on to *"He ascended on the Seventh Day, and sat on His royal throne. With splendor He enveloped the day of Contentment. He declared the Shabbos Day a delight. This is the praise of the Shabbos Day, that it is (the time) when G-d rested from all His work."* Revisiting rest at the end after the preceding string of developments appears to be a regression. The explanation is as follows.

ELEVEN

OUR PREVIOUS DISCUSSION CONCERNING the glowing face on Shabbos helps us appreciate why the Song to the Shabbos Day stands out in comparison with the other days' songs. No other day's song refers openly to its day, while the Psalm for Shabbos proclaims itself to be the Song of the Shabbos Day.

The Song of each day corresponds to a Command, for each Command of Creation is unique to a specific day. The song appropriate to the creatures of each of the first six days remains locked inside them, because externally 'the world proceeds along its regular path' (i.e. lesser creatures cannot express their song). Only intelligence, inspired by holiness, can penetrate beneath the exterior to comprehend the Song intrinsic to the quality of each day. This faculty of the intelligence originated with Shabbos rest and its blessing.

Therefore, although the Song appropriate to each day is implicit in the day itself, the power that would reveal this inner song was not created on that day. No daily Song can openly declare itself to be the Song for that day, because the power to reveal the Song was not included in the creative Command of that day.

The Song of Shabbos is totally different. The resting on Shabbos brought about the blessing that made all the songs explicit. This was the power of intelligence inspired by holiness. This pierces the superficial aspect of a "world following its course," allowing the inner voice of the world to be heard. The nature of the Songs of *all* the Six Days of Creation is thereby understood — and revealed.

Naturally, then, the Song of Shabbos reveals its own identity as the Song of Shabbos. Just as the content of the song relates to Shabbos, the very ability to identify the inner Song of Creation relates to Shabbos. Thus, the song of Shabbos does not begin with, "It is good to praise G-d …" The song begins with the words *"Mizmor Shir l'Yom haShabbos"* (*Psalms* 92:1-2) — a Tune/a Song to the Shabbos Day, words that are an integral part of the song.

This is comparable to a minstrel who sings a song of joy over his ability to sing. The words *"Mizmor Shir l'Yom haShabbos"* (*Psalms* 92:1-2) are a song in themselves, a song over the power of Song to come into the open, something that could not occur until Shabbos.

TWELVE

THIS EXPLAINS THE FORMAT of the Shabbos prayer which concludes, "The Song of the Seventh Day on which (G-d) desisted from all His creative labors, and the Seventh Day praises and says, 'A tune/a song to the Sabbath Day. It is good to praise …'"

In other words, the praise of the Seventh Day is that it can praise itself, saying *"Mizmor Shir l'Yom haShabbos,"* 'A tune/a song to the Shabbos Day. As we previously demonstrated, the chapter in *Psalms* that opens with *"La'Hashem ha'aretz u'melo'ah,"* 'To G-d is the world and its contents,' cannot say of itself *"Mizmor Shir l'yom harishon,"*

'A tune/a song to the first day.' Only the chapter in *Psalms* of *"Tov l'hodos,"* 'It is good to praise,' has an integral introductory phrase, *"Mizmor Shir l'Yom haShabbos,"* 'A tune/a song to the Sabbath Day.'

All this derives from the fact that it was through the 'resting' of the extrinsic aspect of the world that the power of Song to advertise its own nature came about. This is what the Sages mean by saying, *this is the praise of the Seventh Day.* Since it was then that Hashem rested (thereby revealing the Song in Nature as explained) the Seventh Day itself praises, saying *"Mizmor Shir l'Yom haShabbos,"* 'A tune/a song to the Shabbos Day!'

THIRTEEN

WE RETURN TO THE Shabbos of the seven festive days of the bride and groom for whom we say Seven Blessings — *Sheva Berachos* — even without new guests, since Shabbos itself is considered a new face. This law derives from the saying of our Sages on the verse — *"A tune/a Song to the Shabbos Day — new faces have arrived."* We can now comprehend this in depth.

Nowhere but at the rejoicing of a bride and groom do 'new faces' obligate an increase of joy. This is because the primary cause for joy at a wedding is the fact that marriage is the breeding-ground of the new person. The rejoicing of marriage is over the joy of originating a new person. The arrival of a new person to participate in this joy is cause for further joy [because it underscores the premise of the entire party, namely that having new people in the world is a boon –Ed.], so we are obliged on his account to say Seven Blessings — *Sheva Berachos.*

The opinion that Shabbos itself obliges us to say the Seven Blessings — *Sheva Berachos* — is deduced from the Sages specifying "new faces" rather than saying simply a "new person." The deliberate choice of the phrase "new faces" tells us that the renewal of an individual's face is the equivalent of bringing in a new person.

FOURTEEN

JUST AS CHILDBIRTH ADDS a person in the Universe, a new light on a person's face expands the "person within the person" in his individual "small world". This augmentation of the light illuminating the face of man stems from the strength of the faculty of intelligence, which alone among the many powers of man belongs uniquely and exclusively to him.

Our Sages' phraseology taught that adding to the 'person within a person' is equivalent to the birth of a new person. It follows automatically that the presence of Shabbos itself obliges us to say the Seven Blessings — *Sheva Berachos*. The renewal of the 'light of the face of man' is the source of the Shabbos blessing, 'when He blessed man with the light of his face'. This renewal comes because ending the primary function of the other Commands intensifies the Command of *"Let us make man"*.

The central aspect of the blessing of Shabbos is that it is the time set aside — sanctified — for an addition to man's being, to his essential nature. This addition carries a twofold implication. An addition to the faculty (i.e. intelligence) that is uniquely man's in the realm of the individual, and the addition of man to the context of the Universe. The onset of the holiness of Shabbos can itself be considered as the origination of a new individual, entailing Seven Blessings — *Sheva Berachos* — at the joy of the union of the bride and groom. [Rabbi Hutner explained that the union of the two souls of the bride and groom into one soul represented the Creation of a new human entity. – Ed.]

Thus, the Sages derived the "new face" aspect of Shabbos specifically from the verse, *"Mizmor shir l'yom haShabbos"*. This association is based on the point of the verse as explained in the *Krias Shema* blessing of Shabbos. This verse tells us that the Seventh Day itself says praise, in contrast to the other days. This quality follows from the power to say Song that is unique to man, stemming from that addition to his being which originates on Shabbos.

The "new face" aspect of Shabbos is associated with this verse, for it is the Seventh Day which itself says *"Mizmor shir l'Yom haShabbos"* 'A Psalm/Song to Shabbos.' Only man enables that to occur. [In brief, the human being has the role of appreciating the spiritual purpose of Creation. This awareness is celebrated by song, itself a unique form of human expression. All of this shows the higher essence of man as the only creature who can identify and express the higher essence of the world. This gives man a "new face", his higher intelligence shining through. – Ed.]

FIFTEEN

WE NOW COME FULL circle, returning to the prayer which opened this lecture: *"Those who taste it merit life."* The attaining of life is associated with perceiving the taste of Shabbos.

Now we can appreciate the depth of this relationship. In *Parshas Bereishis* (Genesis), although life in general appears even before the creation of man, the word "life" is not mentioned until the creation of the soul of man. A close study of the *Ramban* in *Bereishis* is necessary in order to fully understand this matter, but the explanation of the *Ramban* is outside the scope of this lecture. Be that as it may, it is evident that the facet of life defined by the term "life" is devoted exclusively to man.

The Sages based the prayer of *'Those who taste it merit life'* upon this fact, explicit in *Parshas Bereishis*. Since the aspect of life defined by "life" is devoted exclusively to the essential nature of man, and since the blessing of Shabbos stems from an addition to that essential nature, to taste Shabbos *is* to be worthy of attaining that "life".

Now, the point changes based upon the subject. The attaining of "life" (*"they merited life"*) is for appreciating the taste of Shabbos *itself* while the choice of greatness comes from love for the *message* of

Shabbos. An appreciative perception of the addition to man's essential nature on Shabbos is what is meant by 'those who taste it'. Now we see that this addition to man's being is essential to the blessing of Shabbos.

At the same time, the choosing of greatness relates to distinguishing between the primary and the subordinate, to measuring the great against the small on Shabbos. These functions are *results* of the additional knowledge created on Shabbos. Achieving greatness therefore comes from loving the message of Shabbos while meriting "life" is related to appreciating the flavor of Shabbos itself.

"Those who taste it (Shabbos) *merit life, while those who love its message have chosen greatness."*

[An example might be the experience of marriage. The excitement the couple feel is a taste of their newly enhanced life. When they reflect upon the advantages of their new status, they realize that their choice has made them greater. – Ed.]

TWO

UNDERSTANDING THE DUALITY AND UNITY OF SHABBOS

HOW MAN CELEBRATES AND DIRECTS CREATION

INTRODUCTION

OUR SERVICE OF G-D is divided into two categories, which fall under the headings of "Love" and "Fear". All positive action and giving is part of Love. All self-restraint and withholding is part of Fear. Shabbos merges these two contrary impulses in a paradoxical yet cohesive way.

The moment celebrated by Shabbos is the completion of Creation, i.e. the place where expansive creativity gives way to constrictive restraint, through which G-d gave man the gift of a completed world. Thus, on Shabbos our behavior, emotion, intellect, even our physical enjoyment, always achieve a perfect balance between the impulse to grow and the need to rest [i.e. desist], the desire to understand and the acceptance of our limited understanding of G-d's world.

ONE

"WHOEVER NEGLECTS TO SAY 'True and certain,' *Emes ve'yatziv*, when praying in the morning and 'True and trustworthy,' *Emes*

17

ve'emunah, in the evening (both prayers immediately follow the *Shema*) has not fulfilled his obligation." (*Berachos* 12a) (*Rashi* explains that this requirement includes the entire text of the blessing that begins with *"Emes Ve'yatziv"* or *"Emes Ve'emunah"* and ends with *"Ga'al Yisrael."*). This is based on the verse, "to declare your love in the morning and your faithfulness in the night" (*Psalms* 92:3).

Rashi explains that the *"True and certain"* prayer is entirely devoted to the love G-d showered on our forefathers when He took them out of Egypt and split the Reed Sea. *"True and trustworthy"* includes our anticipation of the future fulfillment of G-d's promises to "redeem us from oppressive kings and tyrants, to grant us life, and to lead us to victory over our enemies."

While these prayers are said daily, they derive from Psalm 92, "A *Tune and a Song for the Shabbos Day"* where the verse "to declare Your love in the morning and Your faithfulness in the night" is found. The theme of kindness in the morning and faithfulness at night is present in both the root and its branches. The root forms part of the Song of the "Shabbos Queen," while the branches affect our daily behavior.

To explain this sequence, we must introduce the words of our Sages who note that Shabbos is filled with dualities (*Yalkut Shimoni* on *Tehillim* 92:2). The duality of the Shabbos observance is *shamor ve'zachor,* safeguard and remember. One of these words appears in each of the two texts of the Ten Commandments (*Exodus* 20:8 and Deuteronomy 5:12). The equivalent duality in the Shabbos Song is *"A Tune and a Song."*

To understand our Sages, let us investigate the implications of the dual nature of "safeguard and remember" and of *"a Tune and a Song."* In this way, we will identify the factors that constitute the duality of Shabbos.

We must first correct a misconception regarding "the awe of

Heaven." Even the publisher of a Kabbalistic work passed on this idea, mistakenly attributing it to an authoritative source. [The publisher of the Tomer Devorah quotes the following in the name of Rabbi Chaim Volozhiner. – Ed.] These are his words:

"It is easy to appreciate why the attributes of love, graciousness and compassion are found in man. This is due to his soul being a 'part of G-d' (Who has these qualities). There is only one thing that G-d demands of us that He Himself does not possess and that is the quality of awe. For G-d to be seen as demonstrating awe is inconceivable. Therefore the Sages said: "G-d has nothing in this world but the storehouse of the Awe-of-Heaven." All the other virtuous attainments and traits have their storehouses in Heaven."

The author of these words assumes that human awe cannot be patterned after any corresponding attributes of G-d. This is a serious error. In fact, the following is the universal rule: Every possible motif within man's service of G-d has a corresponding motif among G-d's attributes. Indeed the possibility of man's service of G-d is only because man is created in the image of G-d.

Could there then exist in man any movement in the service of G-d without a corresponding Divine attribute as expressed in G-d's behavior toward His world? There cannot.

TWO

HERE IS THE RESOLUTION: The *Ramban* in his commentary on *Yisro* (*Exodus* 20:8) writes that "love" generates our service to G-d in observing the positive *mitzvos*, while our observance of the prohibitions originates in the quality of awe.

The *Ramban* does not mean that the intellectual motivation for the performance of *mitzvos* is love while the avoidance of transgression is only motivated by fear. Quite the contrary. Just as love moves us to fulfill the will of our beloved, it inspires us to be careful not to act contrary to that will. Conversely, just as awe impels us to avoid things that are contrary to G-d's desires, it also constrains us not to be lax in fulfilling His will. The *Ramban* is referring to the spiritual forces that stimulate our positive or negative behavior in the service of G-d. There exist physical forces in nature that cause matter to expand; there also exist physical forces that cause matter to contract. Similarly, there are spiritual forces that cause expansion and others that contract or contain.

As regards the person who serves G-d, we see that love has an expansive effect. Love motivates man to act in honor of G-d, while awe causes man's psychic powers to contract as a way of advancing the honor of Heaven.

This is what the *Ramban* means when he says that love generates the fulfillment of the positive *mitzvos*. When powers of expansion stimulate one's soul, a force emanates from the soul that propels man in the direction of positive action. Awe, on the other hand, leads to the avoidance of sin. When inwardness rules a man's soul, his faculties are contained and an inactive state holds sway.

Elsewhere we explained why the term, "Awe of Heaven (*Yiras Shamayim*)" is used in place of "Awe of G-d's Name (*Yiras Hashem*)." There is no equivalent when speaking of love. Nowhere do we find the term, "Love of Heaven (*Ahavas Shamayim*)" used instead of "Love of G-d's Name (*Ahavas Hashem*)." This fact requires an explanation.

Our general effort to avoid the mention of G-d's actual "Name" and our constant use of euphemisms for G-d implies a withdrawal, a narrowing of the outgoing tendencies of the soul in a manner similar to the experience of the Sinai Revelation, where "they [the Jewish people] stood at a distance" (*Exodus* 20:15). This self-limitation is, in essence, the Awe of Heaven. Thus, to create symmetry between the phrase and its message, *Chazal* designed a way in which even the form of the phrase would constitute a performance of the *mitzvah* of awe. Using the term "Heaven" conveys a trepidation of saying "G-d."

It is for this reason that the quality of awe expresses itself in two ways; either as the "Awe of G-d's Name" or as the "Awe of Heaven," while the quality of love is stated *only* as the "Love of G-d's Name (*Ahavas Hashem*)." The Awe of Heaven is a quality of the soul which allows it to limit the universe for the sake of "the glory of Heaven."

THREE

THIS HELPS US FIND the quality of awe among the attributes of G-d as follows. The Sages (*Chagigah 12a*) explained G-d's name *Sha-dai* as a reference to, "*She'amar L'olamo Dai: G-d said to the world, 'it is sufficient'*." During Creation, the universe was in an expanding state until G-d declared its creative expansion to be sufficient, *dai*.

This is the characteristic of G-d's conduct of the world that corresponds to man's Awe of Heaven. Just as G-d acted to restrain further creativity in His universe to enhance the honor of Heaven, the person who serves G-d restrains his own inner world for the sake of G-d's honor. This limitation is called "*Yiras Shamayim*", the Awe of Heaven.

We are now able to shed light on the concept of the duality of the commandments of Shabbos. G-d's limiting of Creation is alluded to by both *"The heavens and the earth were completed"* (*Bereishis* 2:1,2,3) and *"the Lord ceased His creative efforts."* Without this behavior, the universe would have continued to expand and would never have attained completion. The verse *"and the Lord ceased"* therefore refers to G-d's command: "Enough/sufficient." As an immediate result of this command, the Seventh Day was sanctified with a holiness acquired through *limiting* creative effort.

Just as the universe was created through the declaration "sufficient," so too was the sanctity of Shabbos created through an act of sanctification based on "cease and desist, *dai*," i.e.: Creation is complete; it has attained its maximum allowable expansion. We now see that the positive motif of expansion and its inverse — desist from further expansion — are intertwined in bringing about the sanctity of Shabbos.

This is why remember (*zachor*) and safeguard (*shamor*) were said as one expression (*Rosh Hashanah* 27a). *"Remember"* includes the positive *mitzvos* of Shabbos, while *"safeguard"* includes the negative *mitzvos*. Both were said concurrently. This is the unique achievement of Shabbos, harnessing a functional duality, merging the expansiveness of love and the inwardness of awe into one creative force — to the point where the commandments rooted in love and the commandments rooted in awe could be expressed simultaneously. *Safeguard* and *remember* were linked to each other so that whatever is contained in one is contained in the other (*Berachos* 20b).

The sanctity of Shabbos suspends the *distinction* between the attributes of love and awe. It rests on the *combination* of expansion and compression, of love and awe. Those whose souls are totally dedicated to the service of G-d know this to be true in the deepest way. Indeed they can taste love in the restrictions of Shabbos and awe in the positive *mitzvos* of Shabbos.

This is what the Sages mean when they say that all aspects of Shabbos and her *mitzvos* are dual.

FOUR

NOW, WE CAN MOVE from the duality of the *mitzvos* of Shabbos to the duality of the Song of Shabbos: "*Mizmor Shir,* A Tune and a Song for the Shabbos Day."

Just as both expansiveness and limitation have a place in the emotional service of G-d, they also have a place in the intellectual service of G-d. For example, the *Maharal* (*Gur Aryeh/Bereishis* 2:5) states that one is forbidden to do a favor for someone who does not recognize the obligation of gratitude. This, despite the fact that we practice altruism in order to emulate G-d, and we note that He bestows much good even upon the ungrateful. This indicates to us that we are only obligated to emulate behaviors of G-d that follow a 'revealed' system (*Sotah* 14a, *Rambam Hilchos De'os* 1/5 and 6, *Pachad Yitzchok, Pesach* 18).

The mode of G-d's compassion that we can appreciate, and consequently emulate, is the intuitive path of "good for the righteous and suffering for the sinner" (*Berachos* 7a). His other way, of "good even for the sinner and bad even for the righteous", is not subject to imitation.

As the Torah says: "*The hidden ways are for G-d, our L-rd, but the revealed ways are for us and our children.*" (*Devarim* 29:28). This means that there is a Divine behavior we are required to imitate; that is the 'revealed' behavior, the one that follows the Torah's justice of reward for the righteous and punishment for the sinner. But there is also a Divine behavior to which we cannot relate, and which is consequently beyond our capacity to copy. This is the 'hidden' behavior of "good even for the sinner and bad even for the righteous", where its reasoning and purpose is not revealed to us.

As a result, our intellectual grasp of Divine ways creates a dual relationship, consisting of two opposite directions. One direction is a growing sense of connection which makes us want to emulate G-d. The other is a growing realization of His exaltedness which makes the idea of any genuine human association with Him seem impossible. The first describes the forward advance of the intellect; the second describes the intellect in retreat.

The first direction is the intellect's expansion, the second is its contraction. Thus the arena of intellect also features these two opposing movements, just as we found in the emotional sector, in the service of the heart.

We earlier referred to the two emotions of love and awe as expressions of expansion and contraction in the service of the heart. Now we encounter the intellectual counterpart, the difference between our intellectual approach to *"The hidden ways are for G-d, our L-rd"* and our intellectual approach to *"the revealed ways are for us and our children"*.

(It is worth quoting here the quatrain of Yehudah Halevi (*Collected Poems of Rabbi Yehudah Halevi, Volume II 121*):

> O, WHERE CAN YOU be found
> Your place hidden, concealed?
> O, where are You not found
> Your glory worldwide revealed?)

FIVE

THIS HELPS US UNDERSTAND the psalm titled *"A Tune, a Song for the Shabbos Day."* This is one of the few psalms whose contents contain no reference to the topic noted in its opening sentence. The first verse says *"A Tune, a Song for the Shabbos Day"*, while the balance of the chapter never once mentions Shabbos. It deals exclusively with G-d's conduct regarding, "when the wicked bloom like grass and the doers of iniquity blossom" (*Psalms* 92:8).

Although the *mitzvah* of joy on Shabbos is first explicit in the Prophets (*Isaiah* 58:13, see *Shabbos* 118b), it originates in the Torah, in *Bereishis*, where it speaks of the concluding moments of Creation. *"And G-d saw all that He made and it was very good, — and He ceased and He sanctified"* (*Bereishis* 1:31). We see that the rest and the sanctification of Shabbos came by way of the observation "it was very good," which relates to the entirety of Creation.

Just as our resting on Shabbos and our sanctification of Shabbos imitate the "resting" and sanctifying by G-d Himself on the Seventh Day of Creation, *Oneg Shabbos* (Shabbos pleasure) is our way of emulating the observation of "very good" with which G-d viewed His universe at the conclusion of Creation.

The Sages interpret *Vayechulu*, ("and they — the Heavens, the Earth, and all their components — were completed") metaphorically as in the completion of a residence (*Midrash Tanchuma Bereishis, Sheiltos of Rabbi Achai Ga'on*). They compare it to a king who, upon seeing the palace he built, acknowledges that it finds favor in his eyes. Just as he is pleased with it today, he says, "Would that it be G-d's will that this palace continue to bring joy all the days of my life!" (*Bereishis Rabba* 9:4)

This aspect of the appreciation of the universe lies at the heart of the word, *vayechulu*, "and they were completed," which introduces the sanctity of Shabbos. If a person is somewhat resentful concerning the way events unfold in the world, to that extent he lacks an appreciation of the sanctity of the Shabbos. (The more frustration and anger a person harbors concerning his own life, the less he really has Shabbos.)

SIX

THE DISCERNING READER WILL realize that the verse, "*it is good to praise G-d*", which follows immediately after the words, "*A Tune, a Song for the Shabbos Day*," is integrally related to the observation of "very good" found where Scripture discusses the sanctity of Shabbos. The mode of God's conduct that allows the sinner to receive goodness is intimately connected with the "very good" at the conclusion of Creation and the institution of the holiness of Shabbos (See *Bereishis* 1:31).

So long as an individual does not understand that the flourishing of sinners is for the ultimate purpose that "*their destruction will be forever*," his feeling of contentment toward the Author of creation is corrupted. His resentment darkens the "very good" that introduces the sanctity of Shabbos and celebrates the completion of the Divine palace. The Psalm explaining that the present flourishing of sinners leads to their ultimate destruction is the Song for the Shabbos Day: *"... A boor cannot know, nor can a fool understand this: When the wicked bloom like grass and the doers of iniquity blossom — it is to destroy them eternally" (Psalms* 92:8). The recognition of this fact *is* the joy of Shabbos, the Song of the Shabbos Queen. Only contentment remains, no resentment.

SEVEN

WE HAVE ALREADY SEEN how the duality of the *mitzvos* of Shabbos derive from the integration of the expansive "rise and do" expression of love with the contractive "do nothing," expression of fear. *"'Remember' and 'safeguard' were said simultaneously."* We have also seen how the two movements that constitute love and awe are among the emotional qualities of the individual who serves G-d and constitute the perception of connectedness with G-d on one hand, and the recognition of His exaltedness on the other.

We are now prepared to appreciate the duality of the Song of Shabbos, based on the foregoing discussion.

Just as the *mitzvos* of Shabbos are dual in that they include the two motifs fundamental to the service of G-d, so is the *Oneg*/satisfaction of Shabbos dual through the merging of these two motifs. While the *mitzvah* of Shabbos itself combines the impulses of expansion and contraction as they affect emotions of the heart and their resultant physical actions (love and awe, positive commandments and negative commandments), the mitzvah of *Oneg*/pleasure unites them as they affect our intellect and our beliefs (hidden and revealed, connection and remoteness).

As long as our acceptance of the 'hidden' Divine behavior of "the suffering of the righteous and the good awarded the sinner" is not as clear and straightforward as our acceptance of the 'revealed' Divine behavior of good for the righteous and suffering for the sinner, our soul cannot fully delight in the Shabbos. Thus, the two normally opposing motions of expansion and contraction that govern the intellect of the servant of G-d emerge as twins in the *mitzvah* of Shabbos joy.

[The last sentence might give a slightly inaccurate impression. It is not that the joy merges opposites in some new way similar to the merger within the intellect on Shabbos; it is that once the intellect accepts that the revealed system of reward and punishment is not contradicted by the appearance of happy sinners and suffering righteous people, then the person can appreciate all of Creation joyfully and pleasurably. – Ed.]

EIGHT

WITH THIS PROFOUND APPRECIATION of Shabbos pleasure, we can explain the twofold terminology used in the Song of Shabbos: "A Tune (*mizmor*), a Song (*shir*) for the day of Shabbos."

The phrase "*shirei zimrah*" (from the morning liturgy), means songs from which the praise of G-d emerges. In this context, *Zimrah* connotes praise. [Although zemer is usually taken to mean music, when used in a spiritual context it specifically implies a tune that gives praise. – Ed.]

However, the word *zimrah* has another meaning. It also means to prune, to separate from the life source, as in the *zomer* (pruning) which is included in one of the thirty-nine forbidden Shabbos labors. This usage is also found elsewhere in the Bible. The dual meaning of the root *z'mor* teaches that the height of praise comes when one admires the exaltedness of the object of his praise so much, that his own being seems inconsequential. He figuratively cuts down his own essence in the moment of praise.

Still, *Zimrah* does not refer to praise in a general sense. It specifically describes praise expressed in the form of a Song. While praise generally expresses a lower-ranking person's self-negation before his commander, *zimrah* as praise is an expression of pleasure during self-negation before the commander.

This enables us to see the difference between ordinary song and *zimrah*. In worship, Song expresses the pleasure of feeling connected and attracted to G-d. *Mizmor*, on the other hand, evinces the joy in sensing G-d's exaltedness and remoteness. Thus, the expression of pleasure and expansiveness in worship is the very content of *Shir/ song*, while the song that expresses pleasure at the self-limiting experience is called *mizmor*.

Based on our earlier understanding that the central point of Shabbos joy is the intermingling of these two types of pleasure, we can see that both *shir* and *mizmor* join together to constitute the Song of Shabbos as they form the single unit called the *Tune/Song* for the Shabbos Day.

The word *vayechulu* ("and they were completed") also has a dual implication. On one hand, it implies a state of completion. On the other hand, it implies a celebration of a joining together, like a wedding (*kellulos*). Shabbos rest derives from the conclusion of *Vayechulu*, while Shabbos pleasure derives from the celebration of the coming together of a completed world.

NINE

THE WORD *VAYECHULU* HAS an additional, third meaning. *Vayechulu* also implies consolidation and inclusiveness (*lichlol, hiskallelus*). That is to say, in each of the two original meanings there is an implicit reconciliation of opposites into an inclusive unit. Shabbos rest, the conclusion aspect of *vayechulu*, fashions a composite unit of expansion and contraction in our emotional qualities and our behavioral patterns (*remember* and *safeguard* said as one). Likewise, *Oneg Shabbos*, the festival aspect of *vayechulu*, creates an encompassing unit of expansion and contraction in our beliefs and our thinking (*mizmor* and *shir/song* sung as one).

The holy composer continues; he arranges his Song/Tune into two stanzas. The first is a Song of expansiveness. The second is a refrain of temperance. He begins: *"It is good to express gratitude to G-d and sing a mizmor to Your holy Name"* (*Psalms* 92:2). The same enjoyment that I feel as a perception of intimate identity with G-d, I also feel when I stand in wonderment at His distance.

"To recount Your love (chessed) in the morning and Your faithfulness at night." The Sages explain that *"chessed* in the morning" refers to prior redemptions (*Berachos 12a*), such as leaving Egypt. These are manifestations of the *tzaddik*, the righteous person, enjoying the good. The "faithfulness at night" refers to past and present states of exile. These are instances of the righteous who experience evil. The idea is to teach that whereas generally expressing the morning's love and the faithfulness at night are two separate categories of service to G-d — the first expansive through feeling connected, the second withdrawal through feeling overawed — they are unified in the Song of the Shabbos Queen.

For so long as "Your faithfulness at night" is not voiced in the same clear and self-evident manner as "Your love in the morning," the song of the Holy Shabbos cannot be heard. That song must fuse the intimacy of connection with the wonder of remoteness to form the *mizmor/shir,* the *Tune/Song.*

TEN

WE RETURN TO OUR point of departure, to the statement that "whoever neglects to say the '*True and certain*' prayer in the morning and '*True and trustworthy*' in the evening has not fulfilled his obligation."

Generally, the love of the morning and the faithfulness of night are divided between appropriately designated times — true and certain in the mornings, and true and trustworthy in the evening. However, in the structure of the sanctity of Shabbos, this distinction is dissolved, since all the affairs of Shabbos, both its *mitzvos* and its Song, are dual in nature. The sanctity of the Shabbos structure has the imprimatur of interweaving the two aspects of the duality into the single word, *Tune/Song.*

A close and careful perusal of the Psalm, "*A Tune, a Song for the Shabbos Day,*" in the context of our present discussion will be most enlightening to the reader who will find that these observations will explain it fully; for what we have been taught shines with the light of the sanctity of the Shabbos Queen.

THREE

THE ESSENCE OF SHABBOS IS DELIGHT

INTRODUCTION

THE PRIMARY MODE OF the Shabbos experience is oneg, delight, unlike Yom Tov which is characterized by simcha, joy. This is because Yom Tov celebrates points of victory in Israel's struggle through history while Shabbos anticipates how the world will be at the end of history, when all the hard-fought victories will become entrenched in the reality of mankind as part of universal everyday existence.

In intellectual terms, this means that the ideas the Jewish People have tried to teach the world throughout history will be fully accepted at the End of Time. The delights of Shabbos operate in an atmosphere of intellectual clarity that is similar to that future time.

There is a secondary element of joy in Shabbos, but it appears only at the moments of the initial arrival of Shabbos. We greet with joy the arrival of our day of delight.

ONE

"AND ON THE DAY *of your joy, and on your holidays, and on your New Moons, sound trumpets over your burnt-offerings and your Shlamim (peace-offering sacrifices etc.)" (Bamidbar* 10:10). The *Midrash Sifri* commented upon this: '*And on the day of your joy*, this refers to the Sabbaths.' We find in this segment that speaks of blowing trumpets a new subtitle for Shabbos, since 'the day of your joy' is certainly no more than a subordinate title for Shabbos.

[Editor's Note: The use of the English word 'subtitle' for the Hebrew word *kinui* is intended in the sense of a title given to a thing to express some lesser aspect of its nature rather than the primary or main aspect. The point here is that Shabbos is not mainly defined by joy. If it bears a title referring to its element of joy, that is a subtitle.]

Shabbos and Yom Tov are different regarding 'joy'; the explicit command on Shabbos is the *mitzvah* of *Oneg*/satisfaction while the explicit command of Yom Tov is the *mitzvah* of *Simcha*/joy. Thus, 'day of joy' is certainly not a primary title for Shabbos. Only in this particular context is Shabbos given the subtitle 'day-of-joy'.

Why specifically in this Torah segment dealing with the blowing of trumpets is Shabbos mentioned through a new appellation taking the place of its regular name?

To explain this, we need to grasp the distinction between the joy in (the Yom Tov *mitzvah* of) "*And you should be joyful in your holiday*" and the joy here in the phrase of "*the day of your joy*".

TWO

WE BEGIN WITH THE words of our great teachers on the verse of "*And G-d sanctified it* (Shabbos) ... " in the segment that begins with "*And they* (Heaven and Earth and all Creation) *were completed ... *" *Rashi* comments that this sanctification is achieved through *Mann* that did not fall on Shabbos. *Ramban* responds: 'The text does not give the impression of discussing something off in the future.'

In response, *Maharal* wrote that *Rashi* never meant to say the verse was referring to the future. The sanctification of Shabbos is definitely something G-d did immediately. The withholding of *Mann* on Shabbos (much later in history) is only cited by *Rashi* as a proof to the sanctification that is taking place now.

However, mention of a 'proof' in this context seems startling. Does the verse which declares G-d sanctified the Seventh Day need evidence and corroboration from other, later events?

THREE

RAMBAN EXPLAINS THE VERSE *"And G-d sanctified it* (Shabbos) ... " as a reference to the fact there is an 'extra soul' on Shabbos. We would like to explain this view within the limitations of our minimal grasp of these lofty matters.

We often note that the use of the same word in describing both holy and mundane concepts brings to a cognitive dissonance, eventually leading to mixups between holy phrases and mundane phrases. (See *Pachad Yitzhok Shavuos*, Lecture 4.) Here we have an example of concepts being confused and phraseology being transposed in this way.

The word *Sachar* is used in both the sanctified realm and the everyday realm. An employee receives 'sachar' (here meaning salary) for his work and a righteous person receives 'sachar' (here meaning reward) for his *mitzvah* performance. This double usage, one spiritual and one material, creates a tendency for conflicting visions within our concept of *sachar*/reward for a *mitzvah*. In truth, the concept of *sachar*/salary in the mundane realm is not related at all to the entity known as *sachar*/reward.

Any item in the world could be used to serve as salary. All the title 'salary' adds is a description of a particular form of transaction by which one person gives and another receives. When we say that an employee received *sachar*/salary, we are merely saying that something (money or a thing of value) changed hands from employer to employee for the purpose of paying for work performed. That object (or cash) exists independently, outside of the salary function it served in that transaction.

Being accustomed to using the Hebrew word *sachar* to describe both salary for employment and reward for *mitzvos*, we project the above image onto the concept of reward. We imagine that there exist in the spiritual worlds amazing pleasures and delights. When reward for *mitzvos* must be given, these pleasures and delights are then used (as currency) for that purpose.

This image of the reality of *mitzvah* reward is a distortion of that reality. If *mitzvah*-reward had its own word, we would not arrive at that distorted image. In truth, the pleasures and delights which serve as the currency for paying reward for *mitzvos* have no other existence outside of that function. When we speak of reward for *mitzvos*, we are not merely explaining a particular transaction of (G-d) giving and (righteous people) receiving. The process of rewarding *mitzvos* involves a new creation of pleasures and delights which have no identity other than being the prize for *mitzvah* performance.

It is not merely that these delights and pleasures are given and received under the heading of reward; they are defined as reward by their very essence. If you were to remove their characterization as reward they would return to nothingness. *Sachar*/salary/reward in everyday affairs is a particular way of acquiring a thing of value. By contrast, the concept of reward in holy terms involves the creation of a new unique entity (tailor-made for reward).

Now, the existence of all the worlds emerged from nothingness in the Six Days of Creation. Each form of existence emerged on the appropriate day. Which, then, is the day designated for the creation of this unique entity we call *sachar mitzvah* [defined as those pleasures and delights whose very creation is for the purpose of being delivered to the righteous as reward for *mitzvah* performance – Ed.]? Since the reward set aside for *mitzvos* is a separate reality, it must have its own moment of creation. Yet in the course of the Six Days of Creation we do not find that such an entity was created.

The explanation is based on the above. *Mitzvah*-reward was not created, nor fashioned, nor constructed, in the Six Days of Creation. It did not come into existence until the Seventh Day. This unique creation of *mitzvah*-reward is recorded in the Torah in the verse saying that G-d sanctified the Seventh Day. The real meaning of this act of sanctification is the creation of those unique pleasures and delights which exist only to serve as *mitzvah*-reward.

Indeed the Creation of all the worlds, measured against the creation of this form of existence to reward *mitzvos*, is seen as mundane by G-d, as it were. Therefore the creation of *mitzvah*-reward is an act of sanctification for Him.

In everyday matters, pleasures are divided in accordance with the capacity of the senses to receive. The pleasure of sounds are associated with the ear and the pleasure of sights are associated with the eye. In like manner, the pleasure and delights that constitute the reward for *mitzvos* call for the recipient to have a capacity for absorbing them. The name of this capacity for absorption is *neshama yesaira*, the expanded soul of Shabbos.

The soul itself came into being on the Sixth Day, as the Torah says explicitly, but the ability to absorb the pleasure of *mitzvah*-reward was not revealed until the Seventh Day. The capacity to absorb that pleasure could not be revealed before the pleasure had itself emerged from nothingness into reality on the Seventh Day.

This is what *Ramban* means when he says that the verse about G-d's sanctification of Shabbos refers to the formation of the expanded soul. Please understand this well.

FOUR

RASHI (*TALMUD BEITZAH* 16A) explains that the "extra soul" of Shabbos means a capacity to eat and drink (more than usual), thereby observing the *mitzvah* of Shabbos enjoyment. This gives us a new insight into the *mitzvah* to enjoy *Oneg*/satisfaction on Shabbos. The

satisfaction of Shabbos is itself connected to the reward for *mitzvos*.
Other *mitzvos* relate to their rewards in the following way: the *mitzvah* of today breeds the reward of tomorrow. However, the *mitzvah*
of Shabbos has the opposite relationship to its reward. Namely, the
existence of reward in the Future World engenders the *mitzvah* we
observe today.

Therefore, the fulfillment of other *mitzvos* does not require an
expanded soul, whereas the *mitzvah* of enjoying *Oneg*/satisfaction
on Shabbos can only be accomplished fully by our being given an
expanded soul.

[Shabbos is a foretaste of future reward. The problem is that
we live in the present, not the future. The future not only brings
new reward, it brings a new consciousness with which to absorb
that reward. Thus we need an infusion of that future sensibility,
'an expanded soul', to enable us to enjoy Shabbos fully. Since that
enjoyment is a *mitzvah*, we have the paradox of a *mitzvah* obligating
us to have a futuristic experience within the present, requiring a
special twenty-four-hour future-like soul-extension to enable us to
perform the *mitzvah* fully. – Ed.]

FIVE

THE TALMUD (*SANHEDRIN* 58A) says that a non-Jew ('son of Noah')
who refrains from work for a day deserves to die. The *Rambam* established this *Halacha* as applying to a non-Jew who created a private
religion (which includes a weekly day of rest).

This requires an explanation. If the problem is a general concern
about creating new religions, why would the Talmud choose to present this specifically in the form of declaring a Sabbatical day of rest?
Our earlier words provide an answer. The idea of a day of rest from
work is a general concept that demonstrates reward for keeping a set
of religious laws. Therefore the individual *mitzvah* that best expresses
the general concept of inventing a new religion is the establishment
of a Sabbatical day of rest.

[The English language, particularly in British usage, calls any vacation a 'holiday', suggesting an awareness of this idea that only holiness can earn a person a respite from work. – Ed.]

SIX

THE TORAH VERSE SAYS (that Shabbos should be kept) *"... because on that day He (G-d) rested from all His work"* (*Bereishis* 2:3). The *Vilna Gaon* (*Gr"a — Aderes Eliyahu*) notes the emphasis that G-d rested from *"all His work"*. As we know, even after the act of Creation, G-d continues to renew constantly, every day, the handiwork of Creation. This, then, is the meaning of resting from *"all His work"*. Not only did G-d desist from active creation in the sense of bringing things into their original existence, He even refrained from the work of daily renewal of the handiwork of Creation.

For us, this explanation requires its own explanation. Resting on Shabbos from the work of bringing Creation into existence, we can understand in terms of *"And they were completed... "* On Shabbos, no new commands were given for the purpose of adding new forms of existence within Creation.

But how can we understand that G-d rested on the first Shabbos — even from renewing the handiwork of Creation? After all, this work of renewing never stops for an instant, whether in the weekdays or on Shabbos. In Lecture 1, we identified the gem hidden in these words of the *Gr"a*. Our words there sizzle with the burning coal of the sanctity of Shabbos. Yet our discussion here enables us to express a synopsis using clearer language and more precision.

SEVEN

THE LAWS OF SHABBOS state: *"One who carries food* (from a private domain to a public domain), *less than the designated quantity, in a vessel, is not in violation — not only for the food but even for the vessel, because the vessel is subordinate to the food"* (*Shabbos* 93:2). [On the

food, his lack of a sufficient quantity is the basis for his acquittal.
–Ed.]

The physical act of carrying the vessel, when empty, to the public domain is considered a full violation of Shabbos. But if it happens to contain food, carrying the vessel is deemed subordinate to carrying the food. This removes carrying the vessel from the category of "a purposeful activity." It is no longer in violation of the cessation of work required on Shabbos.

There is new enlightenment implicit here, as follows. This legal classification of a primary act and a subordinate act is not one isolated detail among the multitude of laws concerning Shabbos, but in fact it reflects the innermost message of the cessation from work (by G-d) in the original Shabbos of Creation.

When the verse says G-d sanctified Shabbos, it refers to the creation of a new type of reality whose essence is the reward for *mitzvos*. In relation to this newly created reality, the creation of all other types of existence are secondary, just as a vessel is subordinate to the food it contains. Yes, the handiwork of Creation is renewed every instant, including Shabbos. The Divine 'rested' on Shabbos from renewing the world, in this sense: the appearance (inherent in the spirituality of Shabbos) of the existence of reward for *mitzvos* dwarfs the stature of all other forms of (physical) existence to a subordinate role, that of a mere vessel.

As explained earlier, no activity that is subordinate by definition can be seen as a contradiction to refraining from creation on Shabbos.

This is what the *Gr"a* meant when he explained that G-d's rest from 'all of His work' includes a 'rest' from the work of constantly renewing the handiwork of Creation. The sanctification of the Seventh Day introduces a shift in values when examining the various forms of existence. This new paradigm makes it possible for the work of renewing Creation every instant to continue even in the middle of the Day of Rest.

One who is alert to the nuances of Jewish thought will add this to the words spoken in Lecture 1; together, they provide great enlightenment for the spirit.

EIGHT

THIS GIVES US A palatable, reasonable understanding of the Torah section that describes the *Mann*. The Torah states that the lack of *Mann* falling on Shabbos is a proof of the gift of Shabbos itself: *"See that G-d has bestowed upon you the Sabbath"* (*Shemos* 16:29).

This seems astounding. Isn't the purpose of *Mann* to supply the nutritional needs of Jews in the desert? If there was some independent need to demonstrate the gift of Shabbos to this generation, why merge this with supplying food? After all, there are many actions performed by Heaven each and every day, and any of these could be suspended for Shabbos to demonstrate the gift of Shabbos. Why was this demonstration of the gift of Shabbos limited to the specific Heavenly activity of providing the *Mann* as food?

This is understandable in light of matters clarified in this lecture. The raining down of the *Mann* from the heavens to the earth is described by the verse as: 'Bread from the heavens.' As is written: *"(G-d says) I am now raining down for you bread from the heavens"* (*Shemos* 16:4).

This is intended to show that the *Mann* is excluded from the curse (upon earthly bread) of *"With the sweat of your brow you shall eat bread"* (*Bereishis* 3:19). Having bread in this world free of the curse requiring the sweat of one's brow; which can avoid the prerequisite of being farmed amid thorns and thistles — this is like showing a worker during the days of his employment an image of the salary that he will only receive at the end of the job.

This preview is a sort of halfway point between the essence of Divine *Avodah*/service and the essence of reward. On the one hand this preview relates to service, because it functions during the era of active service. On the other hand, it relates to reward, because it serves as a reflection and echo of future reward.

Here we encounter the inner message of the *Mann* stopping to fall on the Shabbos Day. The *Gr"a* taught, as explained above, that G-d resting on the Seventh Day of Creation includes even refraining from the regular work of renewing Creation (that is done every day).

If, despite this, we find no actual cutoff in the function of the handiwork of Creation on Shabbos (i.e. the world keeps running smoothly), it must be because the type of reality generated on Shabbos dwarfs the stature of the physical functioning of Creation and renders it subordinate.

[The renewing of Creation which allows the world to continue to exist obviously also happens on the Seventh Day. Yet it remains correct to say that G-d refrained from that process on Shabbos. He was doing it as a secondary function, not in its usual role as a primary function. This constitutes 'resting' from that work. –Ed.]

It follows that an entity midway between the reality of Shabbos and the reality of the Six Days of Creation cannot operate on Shabbos itself. Because it has a relationship to the reality of Shabbos, the holy day cannot dwarf its stature and demote it to the status of subordinate. On the other hand, because of its relationship to the days of work, Shabbos rest demands that it cease its functioning.

Indeed, the resting of Shabbos would have demanded that the entire reality of Creation be stopped, had there not been the alternative of allowing it to continue in a subordinate role. Therefore, the sun still shines on Shabbos and bread requiring the sweat of one's brow continues to grow on Shabbos — but the *Mann*, which needs only to be gathered, is forced to stop on Shabbos.

The Creation-decree of *"Let there be light"* and the Creation-decree of *"Let there be a firmament"* (*Bereishis* 1:3 and 1:6) still operate within their regular function on Shabbos, because there is a solution for them to function in a subordinate role (that constitutes a valid form of 'rest' for Shabbos). By contrast, the decree of *"I am now raining down on you bread from the heavens"* (see *Tosfos, Beiah* 2:b) cannot possibly operate on Shabbos because this bread is a preview (facsimile) for the essence of the reward. Reward can never operate in a subordinate status.

To restate the point: the cessation of work on the Seventh Day is described as rest 'from all His handiwork'. It is not only a rest from creating new reality but also from maintaining existing reality. The resting from maintenance is accomplished by consigning it to a subordinate status. The *Mann* cannot be lowered on Shabbos because it is not possible for *Mann* to have a subordinate status. The cessation from work on Shabbos precludes lowering the *Mann*, although it does not prevent the continued functioning of the light of day and the darkness of night. Please understand this well.

NINE

THE INTENT IS NOT that the *Mann* was "chosen" to provide a proof for the gift of Shabbos. Indeed the inverse is the case. For the purpose of providing nutriment to the generation of Jews in the desert, there was chosen a particular entity whose essence prevents it from existing on Shabbos. [They were given food that was too important to be subordinated. –Ed.]

(A deep and analytical thinker will be able to apply this principle in an analysis of the falling of the *Mann* on holidays.)

TEN

WE RETURN, WITH THIS in hand, to the words of *Maharal* on the Torah segment of *"And they were completed…"* [which includes the

phrase "And G-d sanctified it" concerning Shabbos, the Seventh Day
–Ed.] *Rashi* explained the verse *"And G-d sanctified it"* as referring to
Mann not falling on Shabbos. *Maharal* quotes *Ramban*, who says a
Torah verse would not be discussing some event far in the future. He
explains that *Rashi* agrees with the premise of *Ramban* but means
that the *Mann* not falling on Shabbos later is a proof to the sanctification done now.

[Not that the lack of *Mann* on Shabbos is the act discussed in
Beraishis, in which case the text would be describing a future event,
but rather the act of sanctification is a spiritual event which took
place at the completion of Creation. The later story with the *Mann*
corroborates *that* sanctification which took place at the beginning
of history. – Ed.]

Earlier we posed this question: does a Torah verse declaring that
G-d sanctified the Seventh Day require proofs and confirmation
from other events? The answer is now clear, based on the words of
this lecture.

Withholding the *Mann* from Shabbos teaches us the nature of
the very sanctification of Shabbos. Despite the workings of heaven
and earth continuing to operate, the particular act of lowering *Mann*
comes to a halt on Shabbos. This shows us the nature of the new
reality which grows out of the sanctification of Shabbos.

ELEVEN

THIS WILL EXPLAIN THE difference between the joy of *"the day of
your joy"* on Shabbos, and the joy of *"And you should be joyful on
your holidays"* of Yom Tov. But first we must outline the distinction
between the satisfaction (*Oneg*) of Shabbos and the joy (*Simcha*) of
Yom Tov.

[The word *Oneg* refers to a higher sense of pleasurable fulfillment, something like ecstasy. It is more than mere pleasure, which
is rendered into Mishnaic Hebrew as *hana'ah*. – Ed.]

TWELVE

TWO TYPES OF PLEASURE and delight are enjoyed by the intellect in the course of its service. One is the pleasure derived from the sense of great discovery that accompanies a new insight. The other comes from the sense of simplicity inherent in a particular insight. In most cases, these two sorts of pleasure are organized in the form of two vertical levels, one atop the other. The first level is the excitement of discovery when one's meditations yield the new insight. Only afterwards does a new process begin. It converts the prior sense of great discovery into a sense of simplicity and obviousness. This elevates the power of intellect while increasing the intellectual pleasure in that awareness.

Just as turning the surprising new discovery into an obvious truth greatly strengthens the power of intellect, converting pleasure-of-discovery into pleasure-of-simplicity greatly deepens the power of intellectual enjoyment and relish. [Although this idea may seem abstract, it is something we observe regularly. Watch a child's first delight in managing to ride a bicycle, albeit shakily. It is very exciting. Then watch when he becomes a smooth, casual rider and see the profound pleasure he takes in the mastery. – Ed.]

An example of this is found in the Midrash (*Vayikra Rabba* 16:B). It tells of a traveling salesman who advertised in the marketplace: "Who wants (a product that guarantees) life?" Everyone gathered round. Then he showed them the verse in Tehillim, *"Who is the man who wants life? Guard your tongue from evil"* (Psalms 34:13-14). When Rabbi Yanai heard that, he cried: *"I did not realize how simple this was."* Rabbi Yanai was saying that he had known the essence of the matter very well but had taken it to be a surprising insight. Now he felt he had grown a great deal, because what he had seen as a complex matter had been transformed into something simple and obvious.

The Midrash notes his "crying" (an emotional response) to convey that there was an increased pleasure and gusto in the deepening of his awareness from the level of the discovery to the level of the obvious.

THIRTEEN

THESE INSIGHTS GIVE US the phraseology for explaining the distinction between satisfaction and joy. The pleasure of appreciating the sense of discovery in the insight is called joy. The pleasure of appreciating the simplicity of the insight is called satisfaction.

This opens the door to a full appreciation of the joy of Yom Tov and the satisfaction of Shabbos. The following words will enable us to step inside this door.

FOURTEEN

IMAGINE THE FOLLOWING SITUATION. A person is exclaiming words of lavish admiration about the depth and sharpness of a particular idea, saying that it is genius-upon-genius. Then he concludes his remarks by adding this comment: *"Whoever does not understand this is a fool."* A remark like this would be astonishing. After all, there are many levels separating the simplicity only a fool could misunderstand and the complexity that represents genius-upon-genius.

How disturbing it is, then, to consider that precisely this expression is found in the chapter of *"A song, a tune, for the day of Shabbos"* in Tehillim. It begins by proclaiming: *"How great... how deep...* (are the deeds of G-d)!" (*Psalms* 92:6) At the end, it sums up: *"(Only) a shallow man would not know and* (only) *a fool would not comprehend this."* If in fact only a shallow man would not know, and only a fool would not understand, then where is the greatness and where is the depth?

FIFTEEN

TO ANSWER THIS QUESTION, we have to clarify the nature of the shallow man and the fool being discussed in the Psalm of *"A song, a tune, for the day of Shabbos"*.

As explained earlier, there are two different types of simplicity. There is a basic simplicity, where a thing is simple because it offers no special new insight. Then there is a profound simplicity, which comes after the understanding of the great new insight has deepened to the point where it has turned into simplicity.

Certainly, someone who cannot comprehend a simple thing is a shallow man and a fool. But each level of simplicity comes with its own (commensurate) shallow man. Each level of simplicity comes with its own (proportionate) fool.

A person who does not understand a subject in the category of basic simplicity is just an ordinary fool and shallow man. A person who grasps a particular idea as a special new insight but cannot process it to the point of simplicity, is a subtler sort of fool and shallow man. After all, someone who does not understand something simple is by definition a fool. But the level of foolishness is proportional to the level of simplicity.

This is the substance of the idea expressed in the Psalm of *"A song, a tune, for the day of Shabbos."* It describes a system whereby evil people can flourish like grass for the purpose of wiping them out forever at a point in the future when the righteous will flourish like date trees. Certainly this kind of system is great, deep and awesome to an enormous degree; there is no limit to the exaltedness of this tremendous insight into the way the world works.

However, the only reason this seems like a great insight is because we are still engaged in the period of service — *"Today is the time to do the mitzvos."* But in the period of reward — *"Tomorrow is the time to receive reward for them"* (*Avoda Zara* 3:a) — this great insight will turn into a piece of obvious information.

Consequently, inasmuch as Shabbos is the day on which reward was created, a day on which the "added soul" is born, a day that is a facsimile of the Future World, this becomes the song and the anthem of Shabbos: the description of the system in which the blooming of righteous people like date trees and evil people like grass is transformed from a surprising new insight into a simple, obvious fact.

The main message of *"A song, a tune, for the day of Shabbos"* is this: the greatness and profundity of G-d's actions and His thoughts/ plans (*Your actions are great; Your thoughts are deep*) are so thoroughly rooted in the spirit of Shabbos that they become utterly simple and obvious. To the point that someone who cannot understand and does not know these truths is a fool and a shallow person.

This shallow fool might well be a person of great spiritual and intellectual awareness. But if he appreciates the depth of Shabbos only on the level of a special insight, without a grasp of the utter obviousness of its truth, then, when it comes to Shabbos he is still only a foolish and shallow individual.

SIXTEEN

ALL THIS APPLIES TO Shabbos. However, we find no such phenomenon in relation to Yom Tov. After all, the events that generated the sanctity of Yom Tov are only in the category of *evidence* for a future in which the righteous person will bloom like a date tree, while the evil person blooms like grass. That is to say, the Exodus from Egypt is *evidence* for the future Redemption, the Giving of the Torah is *evidence* for the Torah of the Messiah, and the Clouds of Glory are *evidence* for the protection of the Jewish People for all eternity.

So long as we need proofs, we are still in the range of the special new insight. We have not yet arrived in the zone of the obvious. Any simple and obvious insight is exempt from the need for evidence and proofs, just as things identified by using physical senses do not require proofs and deductions. This is in line with our previous points. The essence of Shabbos is as a *facsimile* of a time that is all Shabbos. [A facsimile is defined in terms of the thing it represents, while a piece of evidence is not defined by the thing it proves. – Ed.] Whereas the essence of Yom Tov is only *evidence* for a time that is all Shabbos.

Through the perspective of Shabbos, the future *"time that is all Shabbos"* (Mishna *Tamid* 7:4) is seen as something obvious, while through the perspective of Yom Tov the future *"time that is all Shabbos"* can only be seen as a special new insight.

We established earlier that the pleasure of comprehending a special new insight is called *Simcha*/joy while the pleasure in apprehending its simplicity is *Oneg*/satisfaction. The conclusion is inevitable, and we proclaim it with vitality: "*Oneg*/satisfaction is for Shabbos and *Simcha*/joy is for Yom Tov."

SEVENTEEN

WE HAVE NOW CLARIFIED the great unity of the sanctity of Yom Tov with joy and the sanctity of Shabbos with satisfaction/*Oneg*. If despite all this we find a *single instance* where joy is cited as (part of) a descriptive term for Shabbos — as the Sages explained *"the day of your joy"* to refer to Shabbos — it is clear that this is entirely unlike the title of joy as applied to Yom Tov.

Linguistic sensitivity to the style of our Sages helps us discern that this difference arises from the very phrase of *"the day of your joy"*. There is no instruction here [to experience joy through joyful activities –Ed.] similar to *"And you should be joyful in your holidays"*. This is merely a recognition of an independent fact, that Shabbos is a day on which Jews have joy.

Here is a comparable example: a man received a very valuable painting, priceless beyond the range of wealth. He is filled with joy by this acquisition, despite the fact that the scene depicted in the painting may not be one of joy. The subject of the painting might be any theme in the world, yet receiving the gift of the painting causes joy for its owner.

Shabbos is a miniature of a time that is all Shabbos (*Berachos* 57b);

it is a portrait of satisfaction/*Oneg* rather than joy/*Simcha*. But we still experience joy in the fact that we merited to receive this portrait as a gift. The painting portrays satisfaction/*Oneg*; the gift of that painting is a cause for our joy/*Simcha*. (In this vein, the Sages instituted in the Shabbos prayer this precisely worded text: *"Those who keep Shabbos will be joyful in Your kingship."* Shabbos itself is not related to joy; it is those who keep it who are the joyful ones.)

EIGHTEEN

THIS DEFINES THE DISTINCTION between *"And you should be joyful in your holidays…"* and *"the day of your joy — referring to Shabbos"*. The joy of *"And you should be joyful in your holidays"* is thoroughly identified with the sanctity of the holiday. By contrast, the joy of "the day of your joy — referring to Shabbos" is a tangential element. The essence of Shabbos and the substance of the joy are not united.

Therefore, "joy" is not part of the main title of Shabbos; it serves only as a reference to a particular element in Shabbos or an adjective applied to Shabbos.

NINETEEN

WE CAN NOW CONCLUDE that despite the fact that on Shabbos we say *"Shabbos is not a time to cry out but a healing is soon arriving"* and on Yom Tov we say *"Yom Tov is not a time to cry out but a healing is soon arriving"* — the meaning varies between the subjects. On Yom Tov, the idea is that the sanctity of Yom Tov will overpower the illness and bring healing. Concerning Shabbos, the intention is that the essence of Shabbos leaves no room for illness to exist.

Seen through the prism of Shabbos the *"day that is all Shabbos"* (Mishna *Tamid* 7:4) is grasped in its simplest form; there is no room for illnesses or diminution of life. Whereas on Yom Tov the *"day that is all Shabbos"* is viewed as a great bonus, so healing comes in the form of a bonus as well, and the holiday can vanquish the illness.

(An analytical person should take note of the fact that the added offerings (*Mussafim*) of Yom Tov include a sin-offering (*Chattas*) while the added offerings of Shabbos do not feature any recognition of missteps at all.)

TWENTY

WE RETURN TO OUR starting point. We said that this innovation of appending the subtitle of "joy" to Shabbos was introduced especially in the Torah section dealing with the blowing of the trumpets (*Chatzosros*). This is because the blowing of the trumpets on holidays and the blowing of the trumpets in a time of crisis are both one *mitzvah*, as explained in the listing of *mitzvos*. In relation to both of these, the verse says: "…*and you shall be saved… from the hand of the attacker who is attacking you…*" (*Bamidbar* 10:9)

In terms of the essence of Shabbos there is no place for the existence of an attacker who is attacking at all. Therefore the mention of Shabbos in this Torah section is not in terms of its essence but in terms of its inauguration. The advent of Shabbos generates the subtitle of "Shabbos joy", as explained. We are joyful that Shabbos, the time of supreme satisfaction, is arriving.

Therefore it is specifically in the Torah segment dealing with the blowing of the trumpets that the new title of Shabbos as a time of joy is expressed.

TWENTY-ONE

"*AND ON THE DAY of your joy…* " This refers to the Sabbaths. (Midrash)

[Note: The final answer concerning the trumpets needs explanation. Rabbi Hutner proves that the essence of Shabbos cannot be expressed by a form of expression used in case of an attack. The essence of Shabbos is impervious to human attack.

This tells us what the trumpets of Shabbos are not, without clarifying what they are.

Perhaps Rabbi Hutner means that the trumpets are used to herald the arrival of Shabbos, thus speaking to the external joy we feel when Shabbos comes. Even when we blow trumpets over the midday sacrificial offerings, we are still engaged in greeting Shabbos, rather than experiencing its essence. – Ed.]

FOUR

THE JEWISH COVENANT WITH G-D

INTRODUCTION

SHABBOS IS A 'SIGN' of the Jewish Covenant with G-d because refraining from work is done to emulate, and thus model, G-d's rest at the close of Creation. The function of Shabbos is to serve as a declaration through the Jew's demonstration—to the effect that G-d created the world. A Jew behaving otherwise on Shabbos is by definition declaring otherwise.

These declarative acts multiply in significance when performed in the presence of ten Jews, who represent the idea of a Jewish community and nation. That nation has a mission to testify to G-d's truth.

Because Shabbos conveys an all encompassing testimony to the overall act of Divine Creation, the violation of Shabbos undermines the entire structure of Torah.

Once Shabbos testifies to the truth of Divine Creation, the goal of Creation becomes clarified, opening the door to the ultimate reward and pleasure of the Future World. The Jew who lives that testimony gets to enjoy a foretaste of that delight.

ONE

THE TALMUD (*BAITZAH* 16A) teaches: "Rabbi Yochanan said in the name of Rabbi Shimon ben-Yochai, All the *mitzvos* G-d gave to the

Jews He gave in public except for Shabbos, which he gave in private, as it says…" After a discussion, the Talmud concludes that this was said (not about the basic obligation of the *mitzvah* but) concerning the reward given for Shabbos observance or concerning the 'additional soul' of Shabbos.

In what way was the giving of Shabbos to the Jews private? This is not explained. After all, we find no difference in the way the *mitzvah* of Shabbos was revealed as compared to other *mitzvos*.

The following words will show precisely the location and nature of the privacy with which Shabbos was delivered.

TWO

WE BEGIN WITH AN enlightening insight into a major *Halacha* of Shabbos. There are only two *mitzvos* where a violator is immediately considered to have abandoned the entire Torah: idolatry and Shabbos (*Chulin* 5a).

[This is a legal category where a person is considered to have shown that he no longer considers Torah law to be binding; therefore he can no longer be trusted to fulfill Torah obligations properly. He is called a 'mumar', i.e. one who has switched allegiances away from the Torah. Generally, a person falls into this category when we observe a general disregard of all mitzvos. However, if he is seen worshiping idols or violating Shabbos publicly, we assume that he has rejected all of the Torah, even if we have not yet seen him commit other sins. – Ed.]

The Talmud (*Horayos* 8a) derives from a Torah verse that idolatry creates the presumption of abandoning the entire Torah. However, when it comes to Shabbos, no reason or source is mentioned in the Talmud as a basis for the public violator to be subject to the same presumption. *Rashi* (Talmud *Chullin* 5a) offers an explanation: one who profanes Shabbos appears to be denying the act of Creation.

This is not readily understandable. If so, when a person neglects to perform the positive commandment of the Pesach offering (Paschal lamb), shouldn't we say that he is rejecting the entire Torah because he appears to be denying the Exodus from Egypt?

The *T'shuvos Hageonim* [letters written by scholars in the period shortly after the Talmud was completed – Ed.] offers an alternate explanation. Since Shabbos is called a 'sign' (a signal or pact between the Jews and G-d that He created the world in six days), a violation of Shabbos negates that 'sign', an act which is equivalent to the complete rejection of Torah (*Shemos* 31:17/*Eiruvin* 9b).

However, this also seems inadequate, in that *tefillin* and circumcision are also (identified in the Torah as) 'signs', yet when one neglects to perform those *mitzvos* he is not presumed to be rejecting the entire Torah.

THREE

LET US CLARIFY, AS FOLLOWS. Shabbos is a 'sign' in a unique way, not shared by other *mitzvos* such as *tefillin* and circumcision which also function as 'signs' (*Shemos* 13:9/*Bereishis* 17:11). When we identify various *mitzvos* as 'signs', we mean that they are a symbol for a covenant that G-d has entered into with the Jewish people. The content varies depending on the subject.

Regarding *tefillin* and circumcision, the meaning of the 'sign' is contained within their own identity. [They are mitzvos which are a 'sign' of something important in Judaism. But that sign is expressed within that individual mitzvah act. – Ed.]

By contrast, the meaning of the 'sign' of Shabbos is not contained in the act of desisting from work, taken by itself. Instead, a person's refraining from work reflects the Divine act of "desisting from work and refreshing the spirit" (*Shemos* 31:17). Consequently, the rest of Shabbos is an act of testifying to the event of Divine rest in Creation.

Because we were chosen to deliver this testimony, Shabbos functions as a 'sign' of G-d's covenant with Israel. [Please ponder the fact that we say "And they (the heavens and earth) were complete..." (in the synagogue on Friday night) while standing in pairs, we are observing all the laws of testifying. As the scholars of truth phrased it: 'Shabbos is called a testimony' (*Tur Orach Chayim* 26:8).]

Thus, the 'sign' that is an element of refraining from work on Shabbos is actually built on the motif of testimony that is present in Shabbos.

Tefillin on a person's head and the circumcision on a person's body represent 'signs' of his covenant with G-d, without clarifying some prior event that underpins this covenant.

By contrast, the 'sign' aspect of Shabbos provides a clarification of an event that precedes this covenant. Since we are the ones clarifying this event (of G-d creating, then desisting), the very fact that this testimony is entrusted to us serves as a 'sign' of the covenant between G-d and the Jewish People.

Since refraining from work on Shabbos is a method of delivering true testimony, it follows that violating Shabbos is a method of delivering false testimony. This is what *Rashi* meant when he said that an act of violating Shabbos is the equivalent of a denial of the act of Creation. We were troubled by that; after all, if someone does not bring the Pesach offering, do we brand him a denier of the Exodus from Egypt?

Now we appreciate that *Rashi* is saying that this is a result of the mission of testimony built into Shabbos observance. This makes any act of violating Shabbos into a form of false witnessing concerning the original act of Creation by G-d. Please understand this well.

FOUR

HAVING ARRIVED AT THIS point, we are able to say the following. Ten Jews gathered in one place are called an *Eidah* (a testimonial congregation) (*Megilah* 23:b). This is because the very existence of the Jewish community testifies to the truth of G-d's covenant with Israel. And every gathering of ten Jews constitutes a defined congregation within the collective of the Jewish People (*Sanhedrin* 39a).

Such a congregation is called *Eidah* (related to *Eid*, meaning witness). Any gathering of ten Jews is graced by the Divine Presence because of its role in the collective testimony of the Jewish People — concerning G-d's covenant with that People (*Yeshayahu* 43:12, also *Yalkut Shimoni*). Consequently, an act of violating Shabbos in the presence of ten Jews is seen as a denial of the testimony provided by that *Eidah*/congregation.

Violating Shabbos in private is false testimony about the Divine Act of Creation; violating in public adds to this, because the presence of the public magnifies this false characterization of events. The presence of the public changes it from a mere lie into a lie that confronts the truth and denies it. The violation of Shabbos in public, in the sight of a congregation of Jews, is a public declaration that the testimony of truth from G-d's *Eidah* is a falsehood. Denial of the true testimony of a Jewish *Eidah*/congregation makes its author a *mumar* who has abandoned the entire Torah.

This is what the Geonim meant when they wrote that one who violates Shabbos is considered to have rejected the entire Torah because Shabbos is called a 'sign'. These words were troubling to us, because *tefillin* and circumcision are also identified as 'signs' [without sharing this law of being identified with the entire Torah – Ed.].

The answer lies in these very words. The 'sign' quality of Shabbos is based on the element of 'testimony' within Shabbos, as explained.

By extension, negating the 'sign' of Shabbos in plain view of an *Eidah*/congregation of Jews is judged as setting up a second testimony contradicting the first one [which is provided by the presence of ten Jews keeping Shabbos – Ed.]. Denying the fundamental testimony of the Jewish Shabbos is a rejection of the entire Torah.

SEE *SHULCHAN ARUCH YOREH DEAH* (2:5): "One who has switched (from the Torah) to idolatry or one who has switched to violating Shabbos in public, or one who has defected from the entire Torah (i.e. we witness him violating all the other laws) besides these two sins, is considered to be like a Gentile [i.e. he has lost his presumption of trustworthiness as a Jew –Ed.]."

In the comments of Rabbi Akiva Eiger, (beginning with *Chutz Mishtayim Ailu*) he writes: "This (law that violating all *mitzvos* besides the two big ones is considered a rejection of the entire Torah) is based on the words of Rabbenu Yerucham.

On the simplest level, this is provable by the fact that if it were not true, and a person were only considered to have defected from the entire Torah if he actually violated all of the Torah, then he would in any case have been designated as having defected, based on idolatry or Shabbos violation. It must be that when we say that a person has rejected the Torah by violating all of it, we mean all of it besides the big two.

Still in all, I have a question. Maybe one is only deemed to have defected from the entire Torah if he violates all the *mitzvos* including Shabbos, excepting only idolatry. It's just that he violates Shabbos in private, because in order to be deemed to have defected based on the violation of Shabbos alone, it is necessary to do so publicly."

Having clarified the need for 'public' violation of Shabbos, we are prepared to elucidate this *Halacha* (and answer the question of Rabbi Akiva Eiger), as follows. Remember, the reason Rabbi Akiva Eiger offered for this law is only a proof that such is the case, it does not provide any logical rationale for this concept of the entire Torah "besides" for the big two.

Instead, the rationale for this law is as follows. Generality and specificity are two descriptions that contradict each other. One entity cannot be both general and specific within the same aspect. There-fore, once the *Halacha* has determined that one who has defected in the area of idolatry has defected from the entire Torah, then when expressing a defection from the Torah, idolatry represents the entirety of the Torah. Once it has this general role, it is no longer an individual item within the general category of "all the Torah".

This, then, is the rationale of the "besides". The general aspect of Torah encompasses the subjects within Torah as individual parts of that generality. Once we say that idolatry becomes an encompassing representation of the entire Torah, we can no longer see idolatry as one individual point within Torah.

Saying that idolatry is a way of violating the entire Torah at once means that the entire Torah does not include idolatry as an individual point.

The same rule and the same standard can be applied to Shabbos violation. Shabbos serves as a general concept that encompasses the entirety of Torah, so it can no longer be one of the individual details of Torah. When it says that all the smaller violations add up to a general defection from Torah, that must mean all the smaller ones without Shabbos.

Earlier we explained that Shabbos has this universal capacity because it is a testimony. Our desisting from work on Shabbos has the effect of serving as a witness to Divine Creation, which is regarded as an encompassing expression of Torah rather than a detail within Torah.

However, when it comes to affixing the category of *mumar*, the false testimony delivered by violating Shabbos is not sufficient (to indicate that he has abandoned all of Torah); there must be an active denial of the true testimony. This is why the Shabbos violation must take place 'in public' for us to assign the status of having completely abandoned the Torah.

It turns out, then, that doing this act 'in public' does not in any way accentuate the quality of Shabbos being considered a general violation. Had the sin of Shabbos violation not been considered a general undoing of the Torah, the fact that it was done in public would not in any way alter that calculation and render the person a *mumar*.

In fact, changing his behavior from an act of false testimony to an act of contradicting true testimony would not contribute to making this a more general sin in any way.

The whole point of omitting Shabbos (from the list of violations needed to prove abandonment of the entire Torah) was based on Shabbos being a general sin. The violation being 'in public' neither adds to, nor subtracts from, the quality of Shabbos being viewed as a general sin.

It is now clear that the distinction between private and public violation only concerns the abandonment of Torah through Shabbos violation. But when it comes to the rule that all the violations besides Shabbos add up to a rejection of all of Torah, there is no difference between public or private violation. The violation of Shabbos, public or private, cannot play the role of an individual sin within a cumulative perspective of Torah. The general is not the specific.

SIX

UNTIL THIS POINT, WE have introduced our presentation by explaining a major *Halacha* of Shabbos. Now we enter the body of the presentation.

SEVEN

IN THE SHABBOS MORNING blessing prior to the recital of *Shema*, we say: *"He made glory a mantle for the Day of Serenity, He declared enjoyment for the day of Shabbos."* The enjoyment "He declared" and for glory "He made a mantle". Thus, enjoyment relates to declaration, or naming, while glory relates to donning a mantle. We are now prepared to explain this network of relationships.

There is a well-known phrase by the holy masters and scholars of truth: "Nothing in the realm of good is higher than *Oneg* (enjoyment/ecstasy) and nothing in the realm of evil is lower than *Nega* (leprosy/plague)."

[This is intended to be an anagram. In Hebrew the words Oneg and Nega have the same three letters. By a slight rearrangement within a group of just three letters it is possible to move from the highest experience of good to the lowest experience of evil. The message here is to be very careful, because there can be a fine line between the highest good and the lowest evil. –Ed.]

The connection of letters in the Holy Language (Hebrew), comes about by assembling things through wisdom. In fact, the structure of words in the Holy Language parallel reality, rather than merely acknowledging it. Thus, the words *Oneg* and *Nega*, which have the same letters but in a different sequence, show two opposing lines in a common area, like the maxim that "to know two opposites is to have one piece of knowledge". In brief, the polar opposite of *Oneg* (enjoyment) is called *Nega* (leprosy).

We see from this that leprosy is at a greater extreme of opposition to enjoyment than is death itself. On the other hand, we all know that "flesh for flesh, or all that a man has, he would give for the sake of his life". It is certainly possible that if a person had the choice, he might choose to endure leprosy over death, in which case death is really a lower form of bad than leprosy. Still, the words of the scholars of truth are true in relation to the inner depths of the effect on sanctity of these experiences of *Oneg* vs. *Nega*.

EIGHT

THE TALMUD (*KIDDUSHIN* 39B, *Chullin* 142a) teaches: Reward for *mitzvos* does not exist in this world. "This world" excludes two other states of being which, although they are different from each other, have in common the fact that they are not a part of 'this world' when it comes to the reward for *mitzvos*.

There are two states of being in which there is reward for *mitzvos*. One is in *Gan Eden* (Paradise/Heaven), where the souls of the righteous sit and take enjoyment from the glow of G-d's Presence. The second takes place in this world after the Resurrection of the Dead, in a time when "the Earth will be filled with knowledge". The main difference between these is that in the former state the enjoyment is not being absorbed into the form of man (with body and soul), because only souls sit in *Gan Eden* (Heaven). A soul removed from its body does not constitute a human form, because a human being consists of the combination of body and soul.

By contrast, the latter state of being, in this world after Resurrection, features reward absorbed by an intact human form. It is the Earth [consisting of people with bodies and souls – Ed.] that will be filled with knowledge, not just souls as in *Gan Eden* (Heaven).

"Today to do them, tomorrow to receive reward" (Talmud *Eiruvin* 22a). Each individual has his own 'tomorrow' (in Heaven after death). Universal mankind also has its 'tomorrow'. [In this world, after Resurrection, when "the Earth will be filled with knowledge" (Isaiah 11a). –Ed.]

The 'tomorrow' of the individual does not relate to the human form of that individual. Because the reward only reaches his soul. By contrast, the universal 'tomorrow' is delivered to mankind in its human form. The whole point of that 'tomorrow' is that those who slumber in the earth shall arise (so the body can participate in receiving its just reward).

Since the fate of the individual is always auxiliary to the fate of the universe, the primary 'tomorrow' of receiving reward is the 'tomorrow' of mankind at large, in which reward is delivered to the full form of man, combining a body and a soul.

The fact is that the purpose and essence of the existence of enjoyment is for rewarding *mitzvos*.

When we speak of enjoyment taking place in *Gan Eden* (Heaven), that is only a borrowed term to dramatize a point. The essential concept of enjoyment does not conform at all to the enjoyment that is experienced in *Gan Eden* (Heaven). On the contrary, enjoyment (in its purest form) is distinct from the pleasures and pampering of *Gan Eden* (Heaven). It involves a flow of vitality delivered to the human form combining a body and a soul.

This only applies to the post-Resurrection world for mankind in general, not to the pleasure that souls receive in *Gan Eden* (Heaven). That is merely personal reward, the 'tomorrow' of the individual. Therefore it is said: "Nothing in the realm of good is higher than *Oneg* (enjoyment) and nothing in the realm of bad is lower than *Nega* (leprosy)." They carefully said leprosy, not death. This can be understood as follows.

Just as the apex of good, enjoyment, refers to that flow of liveliness that is drawn into and is maintained within a body-and-soul human form, so, too, the nadir referred to here, must be the greatest absence of vitality that can be experienced by a human form.

Leprosy is the absence of life in the affected area, appearing on the body of a living person, as the verse says: "Do not be like a dead person …" (*Bamidbar* 12:12) The state of death, by contrast, cannot occur in a human form that combines a body and a soul. [Once death arrives, the soul is severed from the body, so this element of 'bad' is not experienced by a body and a soul together. – Ed.]

Oneg/enjoyment can only be experienced by the human form combining a body and a soul; its opposite on the bad side must be the experience of the absence of life — within a combined body and soul. Therefore, leprosy is cited here, not death. "Nothing in the realm of good is higher than *Oneg* and nothing in the realm of bad is lower than *Nega*."

ONIGHTTEXT

NINE

AT THIS POINT, WE can glean a meaningful insight into the depth of
'Shabbos pleasure'. There are two categories of 'tomorrow' included
in '*tomorrow* (is the time) to receive reward'. There is the 'tomorrow'
of each individual person and the 'tomorrow' for all of mankind.

The impact of Shabbos extends to encompass both categories of
'tomorrow'. On one hand, Shabbos is a foreshadowing of the 'time
that is all Shabbos' (*Berachos* 57b). This is the effect of Shabbos in
the framework of the general 'tomorrow' of the post-Resurrection
world.

On the other hand, we find that Shabbos halts the functioning of
Gehinnom (*Bereishis Rabba* 11:6) [i.e. the punishments of Hell are
suspended each week for the twenty-five hour period of Shabbos
– Ed.] This is the effect of Shabbos within the personal 'tomorrow'
of each individual.

It was explained earlier that the true 'enjoyment' (*Oneg*) of Shabbos applies only to the state of man combining a body and a soul.
Thus, the root of Shabbos enjoyment cannot be in the reward for
mitzvos received by souls in *Gan Eden* (Heaven, since no body is
present). That experience is only called 'enjoyment' (*Oneg*) as a borrowed term. Instead, the main root of Shabbos is in its foreshadowing
of the encompassing 'tomorrow' [within this world, because that
state includes both a body and a soul – Ed.].

However, since in a secondary way the pleasure of *Gan Eden*
(Heaven) is called 'enjoyment', the range of Shabbos expands beyond its essential home in the general 'tomorrow' of mankind into
the boundaries of the personal 'tomorrow' of the individual. It can
achieve within the realm of personal reward-and-punishment the
suspension of *Gehinnom* (Hell).

We now can taste the sweetness of the beautiful poetry in the
Shabbos prayer: *"He made glory a mantle for the Day of Serenity, He*

declared enjoyment for the day of Shabbos." The glory of Shabbos is in the fact that all the judgments [i.e. negative phenomena that are a result of judgments and punishments for sin –Ed.] are removed, and even *Gehinnom* is suspended.

However, that is only a 'mantle' of glory for the sanctity of Shabbos. And every garment must have a body to dress. The main body — the main narrative — of the sanctity of Shabbos is its fore-shadowing of the 'time that is all Shabbos' after the Resurrection of the Dead.

The functioning of Shabbos within the personal 'tomorrow' is only a mantle for its main function in the universal 'tomorrow'. The actual affixing of a name (for Shabbos), which expresses the essence of a thing, is directed at 'enjoyment'/satisfaction. 'Enjoyment' by man with a body and a soul. Such reward is only in the universal 'tomorrow' (and not in the personal 'tomorrow' after death).

"He declared enjoyment (as a name for) for the day of Shabbos" (*Yeshaya* 58:13). Enjoyment is the main body, the main theme, of the sanctity of Shabbos. This body has a mantle of glory. That garment is the suspension of the functioning of *Gehinnom* over the course of Shabbos. That effect of Shabbos in the boundary of the personal 'tomorrow' is only a garment of glory adorning the effect of Shabbos in the boundary of the global 'tomorrow'. That is why we say that *"He made glory a 'mantle' for the Day of Serenity"*.

TEN

WE RETURN TO THE concept of Shabbos serving as testimony. Shabbos is 'called' a testimony. The emphasis here is on the word '*called*', as in a name. In other words, the act of witness in Shabbos is part of its essence, unlike the glory which is only a garment, a mantle, for the sanctity of Shabbos.

The aspect of testimony becomes the 'name' of Shabbos, similar to the aspect of enjoyment, about which the liturgy states, '*He declared enjoyment (as a name for) the day of Shabbos.'* A 'name' refers to the essence of a thing, not to its garments.

In Scriptural texts we never find Shabbos having any other name added, besides the name, 'enjoyment' (as in *"You should call Shabbos enjoyment"*). We must then say that the name of 'testimony' being appended here to Shabbos is not a new name, but an outgrowth of the name that we find in Scripture (namely, *oneg:* 'enjoyment,' pleasure, satisfaction).

How does the name 'testimony' grow out of the name 'enjoyment'?

ELEVEN

AMONG THOSE WHO SERVE G-d intelligently there is a famous maxim: Our acts contradict our knowledge.

After all, our intellect encompasses many areas of the obligation of man in this world, and we have extensive knowledge of the paths of spiritual growth. If all our broad knowledge were actualized, we would be completely righteous individuals, filled with love of G-d, fear of G-d and connectedness to G-d. Since we do not become complete tzaddikim, it must be that somewhere deep within us some barrier is blocking the light of our knowledge from affecting the roots of our actions. Therefore it is said: Our acts contradict our knowledge.

The deep thinker will detect here the root of the nugget of wisdom that *Maharal* often repeats: '*Adus* (testimony) has the same letters as *Da'as* (intellect).' [In Hebrew, *adus* and *da'as* are an anagram, spelled with the same letters arranged differently. – Ed.]

Many activities and actions contradict our knowledge, but there is one activity which must be performed hand-in-hand with that knowledge. The slightest lack of coordination with the intellect deprives this particular activity of its vitality and negates it completely. The name of this activity is bearing witness.

The essential reliability of the witness is based on his reporting with the maximum precision possible, according to the best of his knowledge. This is the uniqueness and the essential weight of the recital of testimony, the fact that it escapes from the vise of the awful contradiction that exists between our intellect and our activities.

Thus, the holy construction of words in our holy language determines that the letters of 'testimony' and 'intellect' must be the same. This should be well-understood.

TWELVE

THIS CONTRADICTION BETWEEN OUR actions and our knowledge applies only to the man engaged in the service of G-d. The man of *"Today, to do them"*. But the man engaged in receiving reward, the man of *"Tomorrow to receive reward"*, is one about whom it is written that "the earth will be filled with knowledge", i.e. there will be no corner of the human personality that will not be governed by knowledge.

Here we have arrived at the place from which the concept of 'testimony' in Shabbos flows from the concept of 'enjoyment'/'satisfaction' in Shabbos.

Identifying Shabbos as a time of enjoyment refers to the goodness and liveliness that overflows from the encompassing 'tomorrow', which can be received only by man in his unique structure that combines body with soul. This very human form in its future state ('tomorrow') is exempt from any contradiction between knowledge and action.

Which of our present actions can come closest to that future form of man where there is no contradiction between action and knowledge? The answer is 'testifying'.

Thus, it is appropriate for the sanctity of Shabbos, which foreshadows that state of mankind in which action and knowledge are not in conflict, to be identified as the sanctity of 'testimony'.

'*Adus* (testimony) contains the same letters as *da'as* (knowledge).' 'And you should identify Shabbos as (a time of) enjoyment.' 'Shabbos is called a testimony.'

THIRTEEN

THE END OF THIS lecture now connects with its beginning. We began with the statement of Rabbi Shimon ben-Yochai that Shabbos was given to Israel in private. At that point we asserted that in the course of the lecture we would identify the location and the nature of this privacy in the gift of Shabbos. Now we have arrived at that point.

See *Rambam* at the end of his work (*Yad Hachazaka, Hilchos Melachim*), where he states that it is not worthwhile to try to figure out the exact details of the state of affairs at the End of Days. A person should not spend much time analyzing the exact meaning of the Midrashic statements dealing with this subject; rather, he should believe in the concept (of a Messianic era) in a general way. Analyze *Rambam*'s words well.

We learn from these words of the *Rambam* that the study of Torah which deals with the End of Days is to be approached differently than studying Torah in general. Generally, a person's engagement in Torah study must include the clarification and analysis of all the details. As our Sages say, (the level of knowledge should be that) 'If a person asks you, you should not stammer', 'The words of Torah should be sharp in your mouth' (*Kiddushin* 30a).

However, when dealing with the End of Days, the Torah teaches that we only have access to a general overview of the matter. It is not appropriate to attempt to analyze the details with precision. (This new insight has been discussed in our Bais Medrash in a number of different ways.)

On any subject dealing with *mitzvos,* the Torah aims for "…you should not stammer" so that the words should be "sharp (in your mouth)". Yet this turns out to be the boundary line. The engagement with the Torah dealing with *mitzvos* of *"Today to do them"* is on one side, and the engagement with the Torah dealing with the arena of *"tomorrow"* is on the other.

In the first group (Torah of 'today'), the approach is to be "sharp"; in the second (Torah of 'tomorrow') the approach is to "not spend much time analyzing details of Midrashic information". This is the borderline between the Torah of our current time of *mitzvah* performance and the Torah that deals with the End of Days.

When it comes to the *mitzvah* of the enjoyment of Shabbos, this border is muddied. This *mitzvah* is unique because it incorporates the 'tomorrow' of receiving reward in the midst of the 'today to do them'. The enjoyment of Shabbos is but a shadow of the all encompassing 'tomorrow'.

From the perspective of the *mitzvah* of the enjoyment of Shabbos, it would seem that the Torah that relates to the End of Days should be absorbed into the regular system that applies to the entire Torah, and there, too, we should aspire to the standard of "sharp". In response, we have the amazing new idea pronounced by Rabbi Shimon ben-Yochai, that Shabbos was given in private, and the Jews were not informed in advance concerning its reward.

Although Shabbos is no less revealed than the other *mitzvos* in the Torah — in fact, there is no level of Revelation in other *mitzvos* whose equivalent is not found in the *mitzvah* of Shabbos — there is still a deep sense of privacy in Shabbos. The same status may apply to other *mitzvos* and to Shabbos, yet in relation to Shabbos it must be considered 'privacy'.

Usually, the fact that the reward is not known is not seen as privacy within the structure of the *mitzvah,* because reward is something that exists outside the body of the *mitzvah* itself. By contrast, not revealing the reward for the *mitzvah* of Shabbos is, in a sense, hiding the face of the *mitzvah* itself. Consequently, this is taken to be a notable factor of privacy unique and specific to the Shabbos Queen.

[Since reward is woven into the essence of this *mitzvah*, because Shabbos is a foretaste of the End of Days within our own lives, it would have been more natural for the reward of Shabbos to be revealed. Keeping it concealed introduces a certain 'privacy', a sense of hiddenness, within the fabric of Shabbos. – Ed.]

Thus, the intention of this lecture has been accomplished. We have identified both the location and the nature of this 'privacy' in the structure of Shabbos.

ADDENDUM TO CHAPTER 4

ONE

IN TALMUD *SANHEDRIN* 78B, we find the following statement: "Moshe knew that the wood-chopper was eligible for the death penalty, as it states that 'its (Shabbos') violators must surely be put to death'. What he did not know was which form of death penalty should be used to kill him."

[This is a reference to the story in *Bamidbar* Ch. 15, where Jews discovered a man chopping wood on Shabbos and brought him to Moshe. The verse states that Moshe did not know what to do with him, until G-d spoke to him and said the man should be stoned. This opinion in the Talmud believes that Moshe never doubted that the man must be put to death; he was merely seeking clarification as to the proper form of execution. – Ed.]

The *Tosfos* commentary, beginning *Lo Hayah Yodeah*, says the following: "*Although an unspecified death penalty is asphyxiation* [i.e. there is a principle that wherever the Torah says the punishment is death but does not elaborate, we assume it to refer to death by asphyxiation – Ed.], *he (Moshe) logically compared him to an idol worshiper, who is killed by stoning, since one who violates Shabbos in public is like one who denies the essence of Judaism, inasmuch as he denies the act of Creation."*

In his *Gilyon Hashas* commentary (published in the margin of the Talmud), Rabbi Akiva Eiger asks as follows: "This seems problematic to me, because according to this, Moshe's doubt applied only to one who (like the wood-chopper) violated Shabbos in public, because that is a denial of the essence of Judaism. How do we know, legally, that one who violates Shabbos in private is to be stoned? Maybe the fact that the wood-chopper was stoned proves only that G-d agreed with our teacher, Moshe, in this reasoning, which applies only to a public violator, leaving us with no source for stoning a private violator."

TWO

IN RESOLVING RABBI AKIVA Eiger's question, the following seems a reasonable approach.

The "House of Stoning" for carrying out the death penalty was situated outside the 'camp'. [Although stoning calls only for a hill about twelve feet high and a flat area adjacent to it, with a collection of boulders and stones handy, the Sages referred to the designated area as a "House of Stoning". The Talmud in *Sanhedrin* (42b) teaches that this stoning area must be set up outside the 'camp', i.e. outside the residential areas of a city. – Ed.]

There is an exception in the case of a person being executed for idol worship. Such a person is stoned in the gate of the city where he committed the act, as the Torah verse says openly: "And you should take that person out ... to your gates ..." (*Devarim* 17:5)

Thus, if the execution of the Shabbos violator was a subset of the law to stone idol worshipers, as assumed at this stage of *Tosfos'* reasoning, the stoning would be carried out at the gate of the city where that person committed his violation of Shabbos. After all, according to this reasoning, the only source for the stoning of a Shabbos violator is the stoning of the idol worshiper.

When the Torah, in the story of the wood-chopper, reports that the law of executing a Shabbos violator was clarified to Moshe, it is clear that the sentence was a stoning outside the camp. The Torah says explicitly, "Pelt him with stones … outside the camp" (*Bamidbar* 15:35). G-d's clarification of the verdict for the woodchopper shows that the stoning of a Shabbos violator is its own separate category, not a subcategory of stoning an idol worshiper.

Once the Shabbos violator has his own legal category with stoning as its sentence, there is no longer any basis for considering a difference between a private violation and a public violation. He is a Shabbos violator, and his stoning is called for by the Torah on the basis of that identity, not as a type of idol worshiper. This resolves the question raised by Rabbi Akiva Eiger.

THREE

HOWEVER, SEE TALMUD *YEBAMOS 48b*, in the commentary of *Tosfos* beginning *Zeh Ger Toshav*. These are *Tosfos'* words: "*Rashi* explains, that he [the Convert-Resident] accepted upon himself not to worship idols, and violating Shabbos is like worshipping idols [so there is an implied acceptance of Shabbos observance by the Convert-Resident]."

[The Convert-Resident, *Ger Toshav*, undergoes a partial conversion sufficient to allow a non-Jew to reside in Israel when the Temple is standing and Jews have a sovereign government. This person commits to abandoning idolatry in all its forms. *Rashi* understands the Talmud to say that the Convert-Resident must observe Shabbos as an extension of his commitment to reject idolatry. – Ed.]

Here we see explicitly that the equivalence of Shabbos violation to idol worship does not differentiate between public and private violation. Otherwise, the implied acceptance of Shabbos by the Convert-Resident would have included only public observance.

Since *Rashi* and *Tosfos* did not distinguish, the understanding is that the Convert-Resident is obligated to observe Shabbos even in private. Thus, even violation of Shabbos in private is equal to idol worship. This fits with the main text of Chapter 4, which explained that what is added by public Shabbos violation is a greater negation of the 'testimony' of the Jewish congregation through Shabbos observance.

The essential element of heresy in Shabbos violation is what gives it the legal status of an idolatrous act. There is no difference between a private or public violation.

FOUR

THERE STILL REMAINS SOME need to reconcile the individual applications of this principle. Because when it comes to the Convert-Resident, we assume that violating Shabbos, even when done in private, is the equivalent of serving idols.

Whereas in relation to the death penalty of stoning for Shabbos, we were prepared to distinguish between private and public violation (considering only public violation to be equal to idolatry), as the language of *Tosfos* in Talmud *Sanhedrin* indicates, and as Rabbi Akiva Eiger — in the course of asking his question — understood *Tosfos'* intention.

FIVE

How to Enjoy the World

INTRODUCTION

THE CREATION OF MAN on the Sixth Day altered the essence of everything that existed previously. Man's expansive intellect and vision encompasses all of Creation as a whole, establishing Creation as a unified entity.

When a Jew devotes his Shabbos to enjoying the world, he is confirming that G-d's world is a wonderful place. He mirrors the enjoyment G-d Himself had when everything was completed at the end of the Sixth Day.

This perception of Creation on Shabbos stimulates our intellect, extending our horizons. We develop the ability to define things from an immensely broader perspective.

ONE

THE *MITZVAH* OF SHABBOS satisfaction is presented in the Torah as an act of identification, *"And you shall call the Shabbos a delight"* (*Yeshayah* 58:13). The *mitzvah* of Yom Tov joy is presented as a directive (to engage in an activity): *"And you should rejoice on your holy day"* (*Devarim* 16:14).

It's important that we understand why the *mitzvah* of *oneg Shabbos*, Shabbos satisfaction, was not presented as a direct action

73

imperative, *"v'hisanagta"*, "You should take enjoyment," similar to *"v'samachta"*, "You should rejoice" (which is used for *Yom Tov*).

TWO

THE RECITATION OF *'SHEMA'* on Shabbos and during the week is the same *mitzvah*, but the blessings preceding the *'Shema'* on Shabbos differ from the weekday blessing. The blessing *'Yotzer ohr'* ('He created light') of the Shabbos liturgy contains subjects not mentioned in the weekday *'Yotzer ohr'* blessing. Obviously, the sanctity of Shabbos makes these additions compulsory.

This explains the additions, since the increase of sanctity on Shabbos causes an increase in praise to G-d. But how are we to understand the omission of a particular mode of praise to G-d from the Shabbos *'Yotzer ohr'* blessing? We refer to the praise that expresses, *"How numerous are Your creations, G-d!"* This is part of the weekday blessing, but appears to have been deliberately omitted from the Shabbos blessing.

THREE

THE SYNTHESIS OF TWO ideas forms the basis for this omission. We will analyze each idea individually.

FOUR

ON EACH OF THE SIX Days of Creation, G-d declared, *"it was good"* (*Bereishis* 1:21). This declaration appropriately follows the command of creation particular to that day. On the fifth day, objects created that day merited both the assessment of *"it was good"* and a special blessing for those objects. That declaration was made directly after the act of creation and before the blessing. The *"it was good"* declaration referred to that which was created on that day, and the blessing directed at those items was deliberately placed afterward.

On a basic level, this declaration appears to serve as an introduction to the blessing. Without the *"it was good,"* those items would have been unworthy of blessing.

However, on the sixth day its creations received a blessing, and G-d also declared *"it was very good"* (*Bereishis* 1:31). But we find the order reversed, with *"it was very good,"* following the blessing. This suggests that on the sixth day, in contrast to the previous day, the blessing is the introduction to the declaration. Without the blessing the *"it was very good"* declaration would remain premature.

In short: on the fifth day, without *"it was good"* there would have been no blessing, but on the sixth day without the blessing there would have been no *"it was very good"*.

FIVE

THE UNDERSTANDING IS AS follows. In the first five days of creation, we find no common thread uniting the different creations of each day. Moreover, there was clearly no unifying element enabling them to coalesce into an organic whole.

Only on the sixth day did something arrive that tied together all that was created into one structure. This emerges from the verse that commands Adam, *"fill the earth and subdue it"* (*Bereishis* 1:28). The integrity of the total creation was established through the command to man to subjugate it. From that moment, all categories of being share the following common denominator: they are all in man's domain, they were all designated for man's use.

Now we realize that the verse — *"G-d saw all that He had made and it was very good"* (*Bereishis* 1:31) — relating to the sixth day uses *"all"* not in a quantitative sense but in a qualitative sense. The verse does not describe an accumulation of individual isolated objects, but describes a gestalt, an entity that took form as individual elements coalesced into an integrated structure. The verse *"G-d saw all that He had made,"* said on the sixth day, teaches us that G-d now views all the parts of His creation in their relation to a whole, not as the isolated self-contained units they appeared to be earlier.

This explains why the order on the sixth day is the reverse of the fifth day. It is true that on the fifth day the *"very good"* declaration serves to introduce the blessing. Without that declaration the events of that day would not merit a blessing. But the object of the *"very good"* on the sixth day necessitates a reversal of the order. Since the *"very good"* declaration on the sixth day refers to *"all that He (G-d) made"* — a universe newly viewed as a unity — and since this view takes place only after the blessing specifying the placing of creation in man's hand (this supplies the unifying factor for all classes of being) the blessing *must* precede the *"very good"*. The order of the sixth day must be the reverse of what it was on the fifth day.

This is the first of the two concepts we discussed previously. We will now examine the second concept.

SIX

RABBI ACHAI GAON SAYS in his *Sheiltos* (1): *"Members of the House of Israel are obligated to rest on the Shabbos Day, for when G-d created His world He created it in six days and rested on the Seventh Day (Bereishis 2:2); He blessed and sanctified that day like one who completed the labor of constructing a house and declared a holiday. As people say: 'the completion party of the house.' So too does the verse state, 'And G-d ceased on the Seventh Day.'"* [The reader is urged to see the remarkable words of Rabbi Achai Gaon to their conclusion.]

When we rest on Shabbos, we are placing ourselves in correspondence with G-d, Who decreed rest for Himself. This we see from the verse, *"He rested and relaxed"* (*Shemos* 31:17) (spiritually of course). One might think we only imitate G-d when we perform the *mitzvah* of resting and relaxing, but not when we perform the *mitzvah* of Shabbos satisfaction/pleasure (*oneg Shabbos*), there being no specific verse linking our satisfaction to G-d's. This is an uncomfortable thought — because pleasure is the most vital aspect of Shabbos. How could it be that our reflecting G-d's efforts on Shabbos does not include our special *mitzvah*-obligated satisfaction (*oneg Shabbos*)?

To dispel this faulty understanding of Shabbos, Rabbi Achai Gaon wrote that *va'yechal* — and He completed — is to be interpreted as the celebration of completing a house, the pleasure and satisfaction of a "house dedication". G-d not only ceased work and "rested" on the Seventh Day, He also took pleasure and satisfaction. On the Seventh Day, Hashem took occasion to delight in His universe, celebrating the completion of "His house".

Just as our rest on Shabbos emulates G-d's desisting from creation, our taking pleasure and satisfaction on Shabbos emulates His satisfaction upon seeing His world completed. Our Sages compare this allegorically to the situation of a king, who, enjoying the completion of his palace exclaimed, "if only the palace were to find favor in my eyes always as it does today." So Hashem exclaims about the completed universe, *"I hope the palace will always find favor in my eyes as it does today."*

SEVEN

CLEARLY, THE PLEASURE HASHEM found in His universe on Shabbos could only have come about after He saw *"all that He created"* and He found it to be good. It is *"all,"* the all-encompassing view of the universe, that consolidates every aspect of being into a structure worthy of the name "palace". As we said earlier, *all* is used here not to denote quantity, but in its qualitative sense; to describe a gestalt, not an accumulation of isolated objects.

It follows that the pleasure Hashem declared for Himself on Shabbos is over the completion of an effort. *Oneg,* pleasure, resulted only after everything that had been created on the preceding days became intertwined and revealed as an integrated structure we can now describe as a "house".

EIGHT

THIS EXPLAINS THE OMISSION in the blessing *"Yotzer ohr"* (He created light) on Shabbos. The same blessing for the weekdays states, *"how numerous are Your creations, G-d!"* Yet the Shabbos version deliberately omits it.

What appears to be an omission is in reality an addition. Appreciating a multitude of separate objects calls for a quantitative view of reality. Such a view has no place in the *"sanctification of Shabbos"* and the *"Shabbos pleasure"* scheme of things. Shabbos pleasure can only be derived from a qualitative appreciation of creation, where the many facets of creation are perceived as integral parts of a single whole, to be described in terms of greatness, not in terms of number.

One may apply the adjective "many" to a collection of unaligned points, but once the points join to form a line, the line must be measured in terms of its magnitude, not in terms of its quantity. The aggregate measure we might apply before the alignment is replaced by a measure of magnitude after the alignment.

This principle applies equally to our praise of Hashem. During weekdays (our frame of reference being *"that He made"* not *"all that He made"*) we speak of reality in terms of quantity and we observe *"how numerous are Your (G-d's) creations"*. On Shabbos, in contrast, when Hashem declared the celebration for His completed palace, the pleasure that follows is a result of consolidation and coherence. We place ourselves in correspondence to Hashem and omit any reference to quantity. Instead of saying *"How many are Your creations"* we proclaim *"How great are Your creations,"* as is written in the Psalm/ Song of Shabbos (*Tehillim* 92:6).

On Shabbos, when we appreciate the pleasure of combining and joining together, we take the measure of the universe on a standard of magnitude. This transition from a measure of quantity to a measure of magnitude is reflected in the *Yotzer ohr* blessing of Shabbos. The omission from that blessing of *"How numerous are Your creations"* (*Psalms* 92:6) is balanced by the insertion of the praise: *"His greatness and His goodness fill the universe."* This shows explicitly the substitution of greatness for quantity in the *Yotzer ohr* blessing of Shabbos.

NINE

LET US DEVELOP THIS line further. This *oneg*/pleasure of completion has an offshoot. It is a broadening of the intellect in line with the comment of the Sages that a pleasing residence broadens a man's "sense of perspective." This means that when the pleasure of a beautiful residence extends through the person's mind it strengthens his power to recognize importance and assign honor (*Berachos* 57b).

This effect may be felt in either a sacred or a profane manner. To the secular individual, the pleasure of a beautiful residence will heighten his sense of self-importance until he is in extreme danger of falling into a destructive grip of arrogance. However, to the individual who lives a life of holiness, the pleasure of a beautiful residence will heighten in his mind the relative importance of sanctity and the glory of the soul, so he is quite likely to raise his level of "cleaving to Hashem."

It therefore follows that the honor of Shabbos is contained in the pleasure of Shabbos. The pleasure of Shabbos is the pleasure/satisfaction of the completion of the universe, making it into a pleasing residence. A pleasing residence broadens one's mind. This sharpens one's appreciation of relative values, helping a person to properly assign honor.

This also explains the following *halacha* regarding Shabbos pleasure. *"Anything done for the sake of Shabbos honor, slight though it may be, represents a fulfillment of the obligation of Shabbos pleasure"* (*Shabbos* 118; *Tur, Orach Chaim* 242).

Honoring Shabbos is a fulfillment of the Shabbos obligation of pleasure because enjoying the pleasant residence that is the universe expands the mind and strengthens the sense of honor. It stands to reason that this expansion should itself be a fulfillment of the *mitzvah* of Shabbos pleasure. Although the heightened sense of perspective is not identical to pleasure, but follows in its wake, it becomes a fulfillment of the Shabbos pleasure obligation.

Nothing similar can be said concerning the joy of Yom Tov. Nowhere do we find that honor is equivalent to joy on Yom Tov. In fact, exactly the opposite is true. On Yom Tov we are instructed that the means of attaining joy differ according to the individual. Children are happy with sweets, while for women finery and ornaments are more in place (*Rambam Hilchos Yom Tov*). In sum, the *mitzvah* of Shabbos pleasure may also be fulfilled through a heightened sense of perspective, though this is not the direct equivalent of pleasure; the joy of Yom Tov can only be fulfilled through something identified as a medium of joy.

We now return to the problem with which we began. We took note of the seemingly anomalous way the *mitzvah* of Shabbos pleasure was phrased — it was presented as an act of definition rather than as an imperative of direct action. There is no verse *ve'hisanagta,* "and you shall enjoy pleasure," with respect to Shabbos that is the equivalent of *vesamachta,* "you shall be happy," with respect to Yom Tov.

TEN

TO GIVE SOMETHING A name is to articulate the quality that pinpoints that thing's essential identity. The imperative to give Shabbos the name *oneg*/pleasure is to create a framework within which pleasure emerges as the primary aspect of Shabbos. This may well be accomplished even if the framework is structured as a consequence of pleasure, not identical to pleasure itself. The *mitzvah* of Shabbos pleasure may be fulfilled through the heightening of perspective.

When perspective is born of the satisfaction of a pleasing residence, the pleasure is not actively present anymore. Rather, it operates subliminally to produce the heightened perspective. Since the obligation of Shabbos pleasure is performed even when pleasure itself is not openly present, the *mitzvah* takes the form of an act of naming.

In other words, Shabbos is to be described as pleasure, and pleasure operates on two levels. At times it operates overtly, when the individual actually feels a sense of pleasure. At times it operates below the surface, when the individual gains heightened perspective as its result.

The joy of the festival, on the other hand, which can only be sustained through something clearly identified as an avenue of joy, is presented as an imperative of direct action. The verse therefore says *"and you shall rejoice in your festivals"* with respect to festival joy, while with respect to Shabbos the verse says: *"and you shall call the Shabbos a pleasure"*.

SIX

How Shabbos and the Mishkan Direct Our Lives

INTRODUCTION

THE JEW REFRAINS FROM building the Mishkan [Tabernacle] on Shabbos because G-d stopped creating the world on Shabbos. This shows Man's perception that the entire world is a Tabernacle, a place built to serve G-d.

This awareness affects our attitude toward work in the weekdays as well. All our mundane activities are now directed to the higher purpose of serving G-d.

ONE

"IF YOU RESTRAIN YOUR feet on Shabbos and refrain from pursuing your business on My holy day... and honor it by not engaging in your regular activities, your ordinary needs and mode of speech, if you call Shabbos a delight, and honor G-d's holy day, then you will delight in G-d..." (*Yeshayahu* 58:13)

Of all the many precepts pertaining to Shabbos, these were selected as prerequisites for the reward of *"then you will delight in G-d."* This particular choice seems astounding. The laws enumerated in this verse are among the least severe of the regulations that govern Shabbos. In fact, it seems to be a deliberate listing of the most lenient laws of Shabbos. It is highly perplexing to discover that the *"then you will delight"* reward is specifically associated with these milder obligations.

TWO

THE GREAT ASSEMBLY INSTITUTED a prayer relating to the *mitzvos* of Shabbos which has no counterpart in any other *mitzvah*. The *Mincha* prayer of Shabbos contains this phrase: *"May Your children recognize and know that their rest derives from You."* No other *mitzvah* is accompanied by a request that Jews come to recognize that the *mitzvah* derives from G-d.

THREE

WE APPROACH THIS AS FOLLOWS.

The Torah often refers to an elective activity as if it were an imperative. When this occurs, the Sages go to pains to discover the implications of that language. This situation recurs most frequently concerning Shabbos. The Torah speaks many times of the activity and labor of the six weekdays in obligatory terms — as in *"Six days shall you work"* (*Shemos* 20:9) and similar verses — even though this *"work"* is discretionary. [There is no obligation to work in the weekdays if one doesn't need the money, yet the Torah uses language that sounds like an instruction to work all six days and rest only on Shabbos. – Ed.]

Some *Rishonim* maintain that this terminology used in this connection stems from the obligation imposed by the verse to *"Know Him in all your ways,"* (*Mishlei* 3:6). Or, as the Mishna puts it, *"Consecrate all your activities to Hashem"* (*Avos* 2:12).

Man's non-obligatory activities are being described in imperative terms so all of man's actions should be brought under the heading of service to G-d, in accordance with *"Know Him in all your ways."*

The problem is that the verse opens with the six weekdays and concludes with Shabbos. How does this verse retain its integrity and express a unified thought? There is no apparent reason why the *"Know Him in all your ways"* mode of service to G-d and the obligation to observe Shabbos should be contained in one verse.

How does being aware of G-d in all of life's workaday activities connect with serving Him through Shabbos rest?

FOUR

THE *MITZVAH* OF SHABBOS rest as defined in the Torah, is an act of placing ourselves in correspondence with G-d. Just as G-d decreed rest for Himself on the Seventh Day, He decreed rest for us.

If so, a clear contradiction presents itself. G-d ceased His activity of creating the universe, yet our rest is not legally structured to reflect resting from creating a universe, but in totally different terms. Shabbos rest is defined by identifying the thirty-nine types of labor (and avoiding such labor needed in the construction of the Tabernacle). This would appear to undermine the very foundation of our rest, which is a process of emulating the rest of G-d. How do we emulate His rest by withdrawing from the labor of constructing the Tabernacle?

The resolution is clear. G-d's creation of the heavens and earth means one thing: He devised a setting from which man would serve Him. For Jews, the world is nothing but the place to serve G-d. Our involvement in the building of the Tabernacle was to construct a place to serve Him. The construction of the universe and the construction of the Tabernacle share common ground — one is an edifice built by G-d to enable man to serve Him, the other is an edifice built by man to be able to serve Him. This reality enables the 'rest' of Hashem to be reflected in our rest.

As the Torah specifies: *"Do not engage in any labor, because G-d created Heaven and Earth in six days and rested on the Seventh Day"* (*Shemos* 20:10). G-d "rested" from constructing a setting for Israel to serve Him, so must Israel rest on the Seventh Day from constructing a setting designated for serving G-d. The structure erected by G-d is called the universe, the structure erected by man is a Tabernacle. The difference in name does not detract from the resemblance in concept.

FIVE

THUS, WE LEARN THAT Shabbos rest is meaningful because the entire universe is designated as a place exclusive to serving G-d. If a single point of the universe were excluded from serving Him, the creation of Heaven and Earth would no longer correspond to the erection of the Tabernacle. This would deprive our Shabbos rest of its most elemental aspect, making rest from the construction of the *Mishkan* analogous to G-d's resting from the construction of the Heavens and Earth.

Appreciating the universe as a place designated exclusively to serve Hashem is achieved through the obligation in the verse, *"Know Him in all your ways."* The purpose of this obligation is to eliminate the possibility of anything in the universe being precluded from the service of Hashem. It follows that Shabbos rest is contingent on a *"Know Him in all your ways"* world-view.

This condition is not external to Shabbos rest nor is it incidental to Shabbos; it is intimately and directly bound to Shabbos rest; indeed, it forms the very foundation upon which Shabbos rest is based.

SIX

THE *RISHONIM* TAUGHT THAT the verse *"Six days you shall work"* describes man's non-obligatory activities in imperative terms in accordance with the obligation imposed by *"Know Him in all your ways."* We commented earlier that this verse, which closes with the Shabbos rest obligation, appears to lack continuity. There seems to be no clear connection between the *"Know Him in all your ways"* obligation and the *mitzvah* of Shabbos rest.

We now see that the *"Know Him in all your ways"* of the six weekdays is the sine qua non of the *mitzvah* of Shabbos rest. Without *"Know Him in all your ways"*, our Shabbos rest would in no way parallel G-d's rest. Shabbos is built upon this parallel.

SEVEN

THEREFORE, THE REQUEST THAT *"Your children will recognize and know that their rest derives from You"* is specifically associated with Shabbos. No similar request exists for any other *mitzvah*; we do not request that Jews recognize and know that *tzitzis* or *succah* derive from G-d.

Our request means the following: Jews rest from the labor of constructing the *Mishkan* and G-d rests from the labor of constructing Heaven and Earth. Beecause this can seem to be a discrepancy we request that G-d's children recognize and know that their rest derives from Him. This is why this request only appears in connection with Shabbos.

EIGHT

LET US DEVELOP THIS line of thought further. *"He who toils on erev (the eve of) Shabbos is able to eat on Shabbos"* (*Avodah Zarah* 3a). These words teach that the honor of Shabbos and the pleasure of Shabbos are proportionate to the toil of the six weekdays.

Since our Shabbos rest is built on the entire universe being an arena for serving G-d — where nothing exists that is not included in service to Him — it follows that the honor and pleasure of Shabbos should also extend over every aspect of our Shabbos existence.

However, the actual *mitzvos* of Shabbos, desisting from labor, delighting in and honoring Shabbos; exclude certain areas of our life on

Shabbos. Walking, speech and similar actions, for example, are not governed by 'rest', 'honor' or 'pleasure'. It would appear as though the scope of Shabbos misses a broad area.

The answer is clear. Aside from the rest, honor and pleasure *mitzvos* of Shabbos, there is also an obligation to be different. Every aspect of our behavior on Shabbos should differentiate from the normal pattern of the week, beyond the differences included in the obligation of pleasure and honor.

Your meal schedule should be different on Shabbos; your walking should not be usual, nor should your speech be ordinary. No area of life is exempt from the 'be different' regulation. Clearly, any component of an activity can be altered and varied in some way, so that it is performed with a different nuance.

The obligation to modify our behavior on Shabbos completes the parallel between the range of Shabbos and weekday toil. [In the weekdays, all work is for G-d; on Shabbos, all experience reflects a state of sanctified rest. –Ed.] In essence, Shabbos rest reflects a time of receiving reward — for "weekday" work. The rule to treat all Shabbos experiences differently completes the atmosphere of reward that is Shabbos.

It stands to reason that the reward for the *mitzvah* of Shabbos should be based on those factors that extend the honor and pleasure of the Shabbos Day, the "reward" of the day, into every area of experience.

This is exactly what the Prophet is saying: *"If you restrain your feet on Shabbos and refrain from pursuing your business on My holy day… and honor it by not engaging in your regular activities, your ordinary needs and modes of speech… then you will delight in a flow of beneficence from G-d."* We found it astonishing that the verse should limit itself to those Shabbos obligations that are dealt with most leniently. Why should the *'then you will delight'* reward be based specifically on smaller regulations? Now the answer to this question is self-evident. Although the items enumerated are not among the more severe obligations of Shabbos, they represent, as a package, the obligation to alter our life-style on Shabbos.

'If you restrain your feet on Shabbos': your manner of walking on Shabbos should not be as it is during the week. *'By not engaging in your ordinary mode of speech'*: your pattern of speech on Shabbos should be different than during the week. It is this obligation that uniquely effects the symmetry between the honor and pleasure of Shabbos and the toil of *erev Shabbos* (i.e. the six days of the week).

SEVEN

SHABBOS AS THE TASTE OF THE MESSIAH AND THE RESURRECTION

INTRODUCTION

THE COMMANDMENT OF SHABBOS was not only taught verbally to Moshe as part of the giving of Torah; it was also handed to him physically as part of the giving of the Tablets of Stone.

This linkage ties Shabbos to the power of Torah to elevate even the inorganic stone of the Tablets. Thus, Shabbos foreshadows and anticipates the restoration of the dead to life in the Resurrection.

This is not only an anticipation of the world after the Messiah; it even brings us a taste of the world after the Resurrection of the Dead.

ONE

THE SHABBOS MORNING LITURGY includes this phrase: "[*Moshe should rejoice with his gifted portion, because You called him a loyal servant. A glorious laurel you placed on his head, when he stood before You on Mount Sinai;] and two Tablets of stone he brought down in his hand, and there was written in them (the obligation of) keeping Shabbos*."

This stanza begins with the high achievement of our teacher, Moshe, who was called a loyal servant, who received a glorious laurel,

91

and it was he, the very same, who had the Tablets lowered into his hands by G-d. As a conclusion of this, it says: "…and there was written in them (the obligation of) keeping Shabbos." It seems clear that this phrase is intended to continue and expand the description of the levels of attainment reached by Moshe.

This seems hard to understand. How does Shabbos being written into the Tablets enhance Moshe's attainments? Shabbos in the Tablets appears to be no different than the other commandments in the Tablets. In short, Shabbos being mentioned in the Tablets does not appear to indicate the greatness of Moshe any more than the very fact that he received the Tablets.

TWO

IT IS EXPLICIT IN the Torah that the delivery of the Tablets to Moshe came *kechaloso*, "when He finished speaking to him" (*Shemos* 31:18).

The Sages added this observation: the word was written without the "*vav*" vowel, enabling it to be read variantly as *kekalaso*, "*like His bride*". They derived the following: "*Just as a bride is adorned with twenty-four ornaments, so, too, a Torah scholar should be adorned with, and knowledgeable in, the twenty-four books of Scripture*" (*Rashi* and *Midrash Tanchuma: Ki Sisah:* 16).

Hearing these words should unleash a storm in one's heart. Are not the twenty-four books of Scripture part of the entirety of Torah? Do we need an explanation, complete with an analogy (to a bride's ornaments), in order to obligate a Torah scholar to know those books? And what is the comparison to the twenty-four ornaments of a bride?

Furthermore, this is taught specifically at the moment Moshe is being given the Tablets. How does this relate more to the giving of the Tablets especially, more than to the giving of Torah in general?

All of this tends to block us from the light that emanates from these words of our Sages. The purpose of this lecture is to remove this blockage, so we can be receptive to absorbing these words of the Sages.

THREE

LET US BEGIN FROM the most fundamental phenomenon in Creation. A world exists, and a person exists within that world. About the world it merely says *"that it was good"* (*Bereishis* 1:4). About man it says: *"… all that He had made, and it was very good"* (*Bereishis* 1:31). This shows us how man achieves goodness. He encompasses within himself and connects to his personhood all the parts of the world. As was said to Adam, *"Fill the land and conquer it"* (*Bereishis* 1:28).

The elevation of the world occurs by virtue of furthering its connection with the image of man. [This seems a very strong conclusion from the above. If man's role is to bring the world towards him, this movement of the world towards man should serve as an elevation for the world itself. –Ed.]

Now, the way in which plant and animal life connect to the image of man is through the system of providing food and clothing. [See Talmud *Bava Kamma* 71b-72a, where we find the following statement.] Rav Nachman said, *"The reason why I was not able to answer your (Halachic) question last night was because I had not eaten any beef from an ox"* (*Baba Kama* 71b also 72a). In other words, the life force within the flesh of the ox was converted within Rav Nachman to the vitality of clear thinking in Torah matters.

Since minerals (in Hebrew, *domem*, i.e. all inorganic substances, such as stone, metal, etc.) are not included in either food or clothing (early commentators debate the status of salt), they must find other pathways through which to connect to the image of man. One of the most established methods is through the use of precious stones and diamonds as adornment and jewelry. The beauty of the human countenance is enhanced by a certain evocative quality with which those minerals are endowed.

In the hierarchy of Creation the level of the mineral is lower than the levels of plant and animal life. Consequently, the most outstanding example of the human countenance drawing to itself the lower orders of Creation — is the beauty of jewelry and ornaments.

We know too that there is a special relationship between jewelry and the countenance of a bride. The blessing we recite on a bride (at the wedding) says that G-d "is forming the human being" (*Kesuvos* 8a). After all, the power of the bride lies in the fact that she will, in the future, bring out from within her body a new face with a human image (i.e. a child). Therefore it is appropriate for the human image as expressed in the countenance of the bride to be adorned with precious stones and jewelry.

A countenance that wears a piece of jewelry is announcing and saying: "See my power and effectiveness. I am even able to attach to myself all the lowest levels of Creation, elevating them to where they serve to provide additional beauty for my sake." This is the special uniqueness of ornaments and jewelry designed for the countenance of the bride.

FOUR

UNTIL NOW, WE HAVE been discussing the analogy of the bride's jewelry. Now, from the example to its subject.

A Torah scholar (*Talmid chacham*) is someone who knows the Torah. The substance of this knowledge is expressed in its ability to make *Halachic* decisions. We know (Talmud *Horayos* 4a) that when a law is explicit in the Torah, citing it — or getting it wrong — does not count as a "decision".

In such a case, there is no obligation to bring the cow that is offered when the community sinned as the result of a matter being misleadingly decided. [When the Sanhedrin realizes that it erred in an earlier ruling, and most of the community sinned as a result of that ruling, a cow is offered as an atonement. However, this applies only when the error was in deciding an application of a law, but if they miss an explicit verse, then no atonement is possible. – Ed.]

Any matter that is openly explained in the *Chumash* does not require a 'decision', because all it needs is for someone to 'go and read it in school'. If you can 'go and read it in school', that removes it from the arena of Halachic 'decisions'. Superficially, we might have deduced from this that the knowledge of 'go and read it in school' (i.e. Scripture) might not be part of the profile of a Torah scholar. Because the main essence of a Torah scholar is his ability to render Halachic decisions, and the knowledge of 'go and read it in school' matters are removed from the arena of such decisions.

But this would be an entirely incorrect conclusion. Indeed the knowledge of the 'go and read it in school' material, when it is incorporated into the profile of the Torah scholar, becomes bone of his bone and flesh of his flesh, constituting an established element within the overall completeness that is the profile of the Torah scholar.

Still in all, this only holds true for *knowing* the 'go and read it in school' part of Torah. Despite the fact that this knowledge does not relate directly to *Halachic* decisions, it still calls for the use of intellect and good sense.

However, the *halacha* says that a person who reads the Written Torah must recite the blessings upon the Torah even if he does not understand what he is reading (See *Shulchan Aruch Harav, Yoreh De'ah, Hilchos Talmud Torah* 2:12). Only in relation to the Oral Torah must one comprehend the words in order to make a blessing. This seems to mean there is a level of real Torah which stands entirely outside of the boundaries of the profile of a Torah scholar. That profile calls for intellect and good sense, but the level of reading words of Torah without understanding has no relationship at all to intellect and good sense. In which case it would seem that this level of Torah has no purpose whatsoever for a Torah scholar.

Yet in truth this is inconceivable. Here, the analogy of the bride with her ornaments enters the scene. It is there to show that just as man must encompass all the aspects of Creation, the Torah scholar must encompass all the aspects of Torah. Now, the knowledge of how to read the letters, with no comprehension of their meaning, represents the equivalent within speech of the mineral within Creation. (In the language of the scholars of Truth [i.e. Kabbalists – Ed.], the assembly of letters to fashion words is called: *stones building houses*.)

The ornaments of the bride show the power of the human countenance to draw to itself even the lowly level of inorganic matter. So, too, the Torah scholar must prove that he can include in his "speaking in Torah" even the inorganic portion of the power of speech. Namely, the knowledge of the letters without understanding their meanings.

This applies to the obligation to know the twenty-four books of Scripture. Because a book includes writing. And writing includes letters. The presence of a letter in Torah includes the circumstance of its being read without comprehension. Letters without comprehension are the inorganic element within the power of speech. Their role in the profile of a Torah scholar is identical to the role of inorganic stones in enhancing the countenance of a bride.

FIVE

THIS OBLIGATION FOR A Torah scholar to know the twenty-four Holy Books was presented separately from the general giving of Torah. It was presented with the giving of the Tablets. That linkage was surprising in our eyes. Why connect the knowledge of the twenty-four books of the Written Torah with the delivery of the Tablets in particular?

But now, prepare your mind to appreciate the sweet taste of honey in the following delightful words that explain this linkage.

Had the Ten Commandments not been written in the *Chumash*, and their only appearance would be in the Tablets, they would have been exempt from the rule that phrases from the Written Torah are not to be taught orally (*Gitten* 60b). Indeed, the entire categorization of the Ten Commandments as part of the Written Torah is because they can be found in the *Chumash*.

By the same token, had that been the case, they would not have received the categorization of Oral Torah that may not be written (ibid.). Because the Tablets are not subject to this division between "Written and Oral".

The elements of written-ness and oral-ness within the Tablets are at a perfect equilibrium. This is because the distinction between "Written and Oral" only applies in regard to something defined as Torah to be studied. The Tablets, however, were not given for the purpose of study. Instead, they were placed in the Ark and ensconced in the Holy of Holies, a place where no human may enter. [The point of this theoretical exercise—"what if the Ten Commandments were only in the Tablets?"—is only to establish that items written in the Tablets are not considered Written Torah on that basis. Only things written in the Torah scroll are legally considered to be Written Torah. Things in the Tablets combine the essence of both Written and Oral Torah. –Ed.]

Therefore, the obligation of the Torah scholar to know the twenty-four Holy Books was specifically said in connection with the delivery of the Tablets. Because the innermost purpose of this knowledge of Holy Books by a scholar is to connect the Written part of Torah with the sharply mastered Oral Torah. This obligation to bring the surface Written Torah together with the in-depth Oral Torah is very much one with the delivery of words of Torah in a form that does not distinguish between its Written and Oral component [i.e. the Tablets, which equate the Written and Oral by placing both beyond the range of study, as above –Ed.].

In fact, this type of equivalence has no source in Torah except in the Two Tablets of the Covenant. Then the obligation of the Torah scholar to master the twenty-four books of Holy Scripture is attached and fastened to the delivery of the Tablets in particular.

LET US LAY OUT another version of that approach, but from a deeper perspective. It was said of the Jews hearing the Ten Commandments: "My soul went out when He spoke" (*Shir Hashirim* 5:6). The Sages explain that with each utterance from G-d at Mount Sinai, the souls of the Jews flew away and left their bodies until G-d revived them with a restorative dew (*Shabbos* 88b). What is this restorative dew? It is not something extraneous that comes from outside the Commandments. Rather, this dew was hidden in the substance of the Ten Commandments. As we find the Sages saying: "*A dew of Torah will resurrect him*" (*Kesuvos* 111b).

The Commandments themselves are the restorative dew that resurrected the Jews after their souls left their bodies. After the soul left the body when G-d spoke, their bodies became the equivalent of inorganic stone, and the dew within the Commandments themselves brought them back to life. This power is unique to the Ten Commandments, and is not found in other words of Torah.

The division between the effect of the Ten Commandments and the effect of other words of Torah can be characterized in this way: the effect of other words of Torah relates primarily to the faculties of intelligence and awareness, while the effect of the Ten Commandments expands to include even the body when it is in an inorganic state.

This is in keeping with the aphorism: whatever is more exalted is capable of lowering itself further.

SEVEN

WE USE THE SAME expression when referring to the Tablets as when referring to the entire Torah, using the word *Mattan* (Giving) equally for both, calling one *Mattan Torah* (Giving of the Torah) and the other *Mattan Luchos* (Giving of the Tablets); still, the meaning changes depending on the subject.

The Giving of the Torah refers to giving through speech. *"And G-d spoke to Moshe"* — that is the classic phraseology of the Giving of the Torah. But the Giving of the Tablets refers to giving through a physical act. *"And He gave* (handed) *to Moshe"* (*Shemos* 31:18) — that is the classical phraseology of the Giving of the Tablets. *"And He spoke"* — the Giving of the Torah. *"And He gave* (handed)" — the Giving of the Tablets.

This distinction in the manner of the giving conforms to the different ways in which these two gifts function.

The Ten Commandments, which are able to extend their impact to reach even the inorganic body, are fittingly delivered by a physical act (of handing over the Tablets), because acts are done by the inorganic physical mass of the body. By contrast, the other words of Torah, which primarily operate in the zone of the intellect, are fittingly delivered in the mode of speech, inasmuch as speech is an expression of intelligence.

The same rule and the same standard applies to the difference between the surface upon which they are inscribed. The writing surface for the Torah scroll is the leather of a living creature, whereas the writing surface of the Tablets is stone, which is never anything but a mineral.

This is the deeper version of what was explained earlier in Segment 4. The delivery of the Tablets incorporates the inorganic into the realm of words of Torah. It also features the ability of the words of Torah to affect the inorganic body. Specifically at the time of this delivery, we encounter the vision of the enhanced beauty of the bride whose countenance is framed with the inorganic adornments of precious stones and jewels.

EIGHT

IT IS FASCINATING TO consider that this entire vision of the enhanced beauty of the bride through her jewelry arises from the reading of the word *kechaloso* ("when He finished") as *kekalaso* ("like His bride"). The simple meaning of this verse is: *"And He gave to Moshe when He finished speaking to him."* In other words, after the giving of the Torah through speech was finished (*"when He finished speaking"*), the giving through a physical act began. When He finished speaking, there were "given" to Moshe two Tablets of stone. "Given" refers to a process of passing from one hand to another.

Thus, the word *kechaloso* on the simple level refers to a transition. It went from giving Torah through speech and writing on the parchment of a living thing to a giving of Torah with a physical act of passing and handing an inorganic object. How beautiful and appropriate it is, then, that this transition features the light of the beauty of the bride that bursts forth from her countenance framed with precious stones!

Please understand this well, because it is not possible to be more explicit than this in a written work.

NINE

WE NOW DRAW THIS line of reasoning further. When the Sages coined the phraseology describing the greatness of Moses in the liturgy of the *Shacharis* (morning) prayer of Shabbos (*Moshe should rejoice...*), they were not satisfied to use the language of the verse in the Torah that describes giving of the Tablets: *"And He gave (handed) to Moshe..."* Instead, they stood and they honed and they coined and they sealed the following: *"... and two Tablets of stone he brought down in his hand."* They specifically said "brought down in his hand".

Why? Because the ultimate achievement of the delivery of the Tablets was that it constituted a giving of Torah through a physical act rather than through speech. This added level of lowering Torah into his very hand represents the profound concept that the Torah in the Tablets is able to affect even the inorganic body. A physical act is performed with the inorganic physical body while (the delivery and reception of) speech is an expression of intelligence and thought.

TEN

WE ARRIVE AT THE explanation of the conclusion of the stanza that begins "*Moses should rejoice …*" and ends as follows: "*… and there was written in them* (the Tablets, the obligation of) *keeping Shabbos, and so it was written in Your Torah.*"

These words show that there is an advantage to the sanctity of Shabbos by Shabbos being mentioned in the Tablets. Exactly what is this advantage? What would Shabbos have lacked had it been written only in the *Chumash* (and not in the Tablets)?

To understand this, let us sharpen our awareness of the sanctity of the Holy Shabbos. Without the sanctity of Shabbos, the dividing line between the current world and the future world would have been complete and total. Either this world or the next world (but never both at once). The sanctity of Shabbos represents the creation of a new entity known as "a facsimile of the future world" (*Berachos* 57b). Still, there are very many levels and aspects to the future world. When we say that Shabbos serves as a "facsimile of the future world", that does not tell us how much of an aspect of the future world is being achieved, or what level of the future world Shabbos portrays as a "facsimile".

Torah follows a system of truth (*Avodah Zarah* 4b). We can judge the level of any holiness that appears in the Torah, in proportion to the level of the location where it was presented. The same rule and the same standard applies to the sanctity of Shabbos. Since the sanctity of Shabbos is written into the Tablets, we know the power of the "facsimile of the future world" that is in Shabbos. It reaches all the way to the dew of resurrection with which the dead will eventually be brought back to life. That dew of resurrection relates to the giving of the Tablets [because the Ten Commandments had the capacity to revive the Jews whose souls had departed their bodies – Ed.].

Since the "facsimile of the future world" in Shabbos is included in the Tablets, then this "facsimile" must be in accordance with the level of sanctity that was achieved in the giving of the Tablets. Therefore we know that the "facsimile of the future world" of Shabbos is even a facsimile of the time of the Resurrection of the Dead.

This explains the conclusion of the stanza: *"Moshe should rejoice… two Tablets of stone he brought down in his hand and there was written in them (the obligation of) keeping Shabbos."*

Since the two Tablets of stone were lowered into "his hand", Torah was being given through a physical act affecting the inorganic body. Not merely a giving over through speech which only operates upon the intellect. Because of this, these words of Torah have in them the dew of resurrection that is able to revivify even the inorganic body. Thus, the "facsimile of the future world" in Shabbos is even a facsimile of the time of the Resurrection of the Dead.

ELEVEN

WE CAN NOW CONNECT the end of this lecture to its beginning. *"Moshe should rejoice with his gifted portion… and two Tablets of stone he brought down in his hand, and on them was written* (the obligation of) *keeping Shabbos."* These words were troublesome to us: what added greatness of Moshe is expressed in the fact that Shabbos was inscribed into the Tablets? What is the difference between Shabbos being in the Tablets and the other nine Commandments being in the Tablets?

What we have explained clarifies this as well. The lowering of the Tablets into the hands of Moshe was repeated twice, the first set of Tablets and the second set of Tablets. Neither of them have survived in our possession. The first were broken (*Shemos* 32:19) and the second were hidden (*Horiyos* 12a; Tosefta, *Sotah* 13:2). But since G-d will return them to us in the future world and Shabbos is a facsimile of the future world, we can experience, even now, in each Shabbos, a facsimile of the Tablets being given all over again.

This is the advantage in the greatness of Moshe that is couched in the fact that the keeping of Shabbos is written into the Tablets. It demonstrates the power and durability of the lowering of the Tablets by Moshe, that even after they were broken and hidden — we still achieve a "facsimile" of those Tablets being brought down in each and every Shabbos.

TWELVE

"TWO TABLETS OF STONE he brought down in his hand, and there was written in them (the obligation of) *keeping Shabbos."*

EIGHT

The Role of Shabbos Pleasure in Bringing the Future World

INTRODUCTION

IN SEXUAL TRANSGRESSIONS, THE Torah counts having pleasure as equivalent to a physical act. This is because the procreative act brings the world towards its future, and the future is a world defined by pleasure rather than action.

On Shabbos the experience is similar. We live in a facsimile of the future world, so that a day of experiencing pleasure becomes as fulfilling as a day of high achievement.

ONE

AT THE END OF THE middle blessing of the Shabbos prayer, a segment begins: *"Show favor to our (day of) repose..."* It concludes: *"...and bequeath to us with favor Your holy Sabbath."*

Asking to receive Shabbos with favor would seem to be a rephrasing of the request to "show favor to our repose". Could it be the same request is being made twice in one paragraph?

Actually, there is an outward distinction between the two. The second relates to Shabbos in general, asking G-d to *"bequeath to us with favor Your holy Shabbos"*, while the first relates specifically to resting on Shabbos, asking Him to *"show favor to our repose"*.

We must still ask: what is this second form of showing favor that is directed more to the aspect of resting on Shabbos than to the general substance of Shabbos?

TWO

IN *PACHAD YITZCHOK* FOR Pesach (Lecture 54), we cite the words of *Ramban* in *Yisro* that the root of all positive commandments is Love (of G-d) and the root of all negative commandments (prohibitions) is Awe (of G-d) (*Shemos* 20:8).

In this connection, we wrote (Segment 3) the following:

"This is the root of the idea that "Remember" (Shabbos) and *"Keep"* (Shabbos) were expressed simultaneously [in the Ten Commandments] as one utterance (*Shemos* 20:8 and *Devarim* 5:12) (*Rosh Hashanah* 27a). *"Remember"* includes all the positive commandments of Shabbos and *"Keep"* includes all of its prohibitions.

They were expressed as one because the uniqueness of Shabbos is that "all its affairs are in duplicate" (See *Yalkut Shimoni Tehillim* 92:1).

[The Midrash points out that Torah phrases discussing Shabbos, such as "remember" and "keep", tend to come in pairs. The Midrash then notes that all human engagement with Shabbos, such as breaking bread on two loaves for the Shabbos meal, comes in pairs. –Ed.]

Shabbos blends into one the expansive power of Love with the constrictive power of Awe. Thus, all the positive commandments of Shabbos, rooted in Love, and all the prohibitions of Shabbos, rooted in Awe, can be expressed in one utterance.

Furthermore, *"remember"* and *"keep"* are legally linked, so that whoever is obligated in one is obligated in the other. In the sanctity of Shabbos, the usual division between Love and Awe is negated. It is only through the blending of expansiveness and constrictiveness that the sanctity of Shabbos is constructed."

See that lecture in depth, because these words are explained there fully.

Extending that point, the lecture goes on to say:

"Those who serve G-d soulfully feel a clear, deep awareness that in the prohibitions of Shabbos they also experience a taste of serving G-d through Ahavah/Love."

Many people ask for an explanation of this difference in the sensation of honoring prohibitions in reference to Shabbos. They mainly seek to comprehend the actual experience involved. How could a person taste the expansiveness of "get up and do" while engaged in avoidance, in "sit and don't act"?

To calm the turbulence in the hearts of those questioners, let us begin as follows.

THREE

MANY LAWS OF THE Torah require a physical act as a precondition. For example, if one sinned without doing a physical act, he does not bring a sin-offering (*Toras Kohanim; Vayikra* 1:2).

However, referring to sexual prohibitions, the Torah convicts *"the souls that do the* (prohibited) *act"* (*Vayikra* 18:29), even though the female did not perform a physical act [because her role is deemed in Halachic terms to be physically passive –Ed.].

This is explained in the words of our great scholars (*Tosfos* in Talmud *Bava Kamma* 32a) as follows: *"The Torah is deeming the pleasure involved to be the equivalent of a physical act."*

Nowhere else in the Torah do we find such a concept, that taking pleasure is the equivalent of a physical act. This law is limited to sexual offenses, based upon the following profound understanding.

"Today is for doing them (mitzvos) *and tomorrow is for receiving their reward."* (Talmud *Avoda Zara* 3a)

We see here a distinction between a time called "tomorrow" and a time called "today". "Tomorrow" is reserved for receiving reward. "Today" is reserved for the burden of effort.

Indeed we find another difference between the time of "tomorrow" and the time of "today". Today is a world that is temporary. Tomorrow is a world that is enduring. Thus, all future time after the era of "today" is part of "tomorrow" (*Berachos* 57b).

We can now postulate that the world of physical action is temporary, inasmuch as "doing them" only occupies the realm of "today". By contrast, the world of pleasure is enduring. This is because reward occupies the realm of "tomorrow".

[The idea is that all action relates to the part of history that requires a person to act in the present so as to earn his future reward. Action is a significant concept only in an era or a state of being where one is assigned to achieve and fulfill his destiny through action.

Conversely, taking pleasure is a process of receiving, placing the person in a position of being rewarded, a state that reflects the character of a future world rather than the reality of the current world.

Thus, when we encounter action in a future world, it is a carry over experience that really does not relate to that time. And when we encounter pleasure in the present, it is a spillover of an experience whose true home is only in the future world. – Ed.]

This describes an outright division between the temporary world and the enduring world. But it is possible to make relative distinctions in these terms as well, by saying this: The closer you are to the realm of the eternal and enduring, the closer — in direct proportion — you come to the domain of pleasure.

The world of eternity is the world of pleasure.

FOUR

AMONG THE MANY ACTIVITIES of this fleeting world, the one that comes closest to the realm of eternal existence is the act of procreation. Because only through having children can the "eternity" of the species or the individual be accomplished.

The act of procreation comes so close to the realm of eternity that it enters entirely into the realm of pleasure. The rule is: the domain of the power of pleasure is in the world of eternity.

The essence of the act of procreation places it in the domain where pleasure is the governing power. Within this domain, pleasure is the defining element. Consequently, when it comes to this act, the Torah considers the taking of pleasure as the equivalent of acting.

[In essence, we are treating the experience of procreation as being based in the future more than in the present. In the future, pleasure is significant, action is not. Thus, paradoxically, in assessing liability for a sexual prohibition in the current world, we use the standard of taking pleasure in place of the usual standard of physical action. – Ed.]

Up to this point, our terminology was taken from the future. Now let us explain this concept using terminology taken from the past.

Two things occurred to man in the beginning of his existence. Death was decreed upon him. And he was banished from the Garden of Eden.

This indicates that a life in paradise and the absence of death are ideas that naturally link up to form one cohesive reality.

Since procreation is done to escape the decree of mortality, it is natural that the enjoyment and pleasure are basic to the act. Thus, in matters relating to the process of procreation, the Torah considered the taking of pleasure to be the equivalent of a physical act.

[NOTE: This idea is presented here very tersely. Some might benefit from a more detailed explanation, as follows.

When life exists without death, there is no reason for the world to be anything but paradise, a source of all things that enhance life. Once death is introduced, life turns into a thing with limits and shortcomings; not all experiences are pleasurable.

However, there is a "solution" to death even in our present reality. A person keeps himself alive and immortal by generating a child who carries a part of his life forward in time. Having children insures his future, making him immortal, thus affecting and redefining his present life as something that will not really die, and consequently is a pleasurable existence.

The act of procreation is pleasurable, because it changes the father's life from a dying receptacle for pain to a living receptacle for pleasure. In relation to this act, the Torah equates taking pleasure with performing a physical action. – Ed.]

The same rule and the same standard applies to the sanctity of Shabbos. The most outstanding thing about Shabbos is that it is a facsimile of "tomorrow" functioning in the midst of the world of "today".

We are now arriving at a deep understanding of why *Oneg*/enjoyment is a mitzvah requirement on Shabbos (Rambam, *Hilchos Shabbos* 30:1). Enjoyment experienced on Shabbos is not merely enjoyment on a particular day. It ultimately expresses the idea that enjoyment is the essence of Shabbos.

On this day, the distinction between pleasure and action is removed. In the currency of Shabbos sanctity, the Torah equates pleasure with action.

(Analyze carefully the verse that says *"to do (make) the Shabbos"* (*Shemos* 31:16). Although it refers to resting on Shabbos through refraining from action, the Torah calls it "to do", similar to the phrase *"And the souls that do ..."* [in reference to sexual violations], where the Torah considers pleasure equivalent to action.)

FIVE

THIS CONTAINS THE ANSWER to calm the turbulent hearts of those who asked earlier: "How does one taste some expansiveness of 'get up and do' in the course of a self-restricting moment of 'sit and do not act'?"

In observing Shabbos, even the prohibitions operate within the parameters of *Ahavah*, the service of G-d through Love. This factor is unique and strictly limited to the prohibitions of Shabbos.

The sanctity-of-the-day inherent in Shabbos creates a reality of "pleasure-equals-action". So, too, in the obligations of the heart that apply to Shabbos, the barrier that usually separates "get up and act" (positive commandments) from "sit and don't act" (prohibitions) is eliminated.

[Note: This phrase, "obligations of the heart", is central to all of the volumes of this work, which are described as works dealing with "laws of opinions and obligations of the heart". It is a way of describing the inner experience that is appropriate to the performance of mitzvos and living a Jewish life in general. –Ed.]

Indeed the definition of an "act" on the day of Shabbos is essentially different from the definition of an "act" during the six days of activity.

Once the barrier between "get up and do" and "sit and don't act" is eliminated, even the prohibitions of Shabbos are assessed within the context of (the service of) *Ahavah*/Love.

That elimination of the barrier between "get up and do" and "sit and don't act" on Shabbos, is included in the phrase of the Sages: *"Remember"* (i.e. observe the positive commandments of Shabbos) and *"Keep"* (i.e. observe the prohibitions of Shabbos) were expressed simultaneously as one utterance.

[To review, here is the logical sequence.

In the future, the world is a place for pleasure, not action. Since Shabbos is a microcosm of the future, it is structured as a day for pleasure. On this day, taking pleasure is the equivalent of a physical act.

The fact that action is a function of love, and all mitzvos of action are rooted in Love of G-d, is because only action expresses the full creativity of our present reality. In the context of the future, when pleasure replaces action as the focus of existence, taking pleasure while being physically inactive is itself an act of love.

Thus, refraining from physical acts of creativity on Shabbos, although calling for restraint rather than action, gives a sense of expressing Love of G-d, because this is modeling the future state of pleasure in the post-Redemption world. –Ed.]

SIX

SEE TALMUD *BERACHOS* (34B): "Rav Yehuda said, a person should never ask for his needs in the first three blessings, nor in the last three blessings, only in the middle ones. [The standing prayer (*Amidah; Shmoneh Esrei*) has nineteen blessings, the first three of which are praise to G-d and the last three of which are thanksgiving. The middle thirteen are devoted to requests for one's needs. –Ed.] Because Rabbi Chanina said, the first blessings are comparable to a servant offering a series of praises to his master, the middle ones are like a servant requesting a bonus from his master, and the last ones are like a servant who has received a bonus from his master, then [in gratitude] takes his leave courteously and departs."

The *Tosfos* commentary, beginning *Al Yishal*, writes: "*Rabbenu Chananel and Rabbenu Hai explained, that this rule* (against asking for needs in the first and last blessings) *applies only to* (the needs of) *an individual, but it is permitted to ask for communal needs. You can prove this because after all, the main content of the last three blessings are requests for communal needs.*"

These words are very difficult to comprehend. If the three final blessings are really requests for needs, and the permission to make those requests is based on their being communal needs, how does the Talmud compare those very blessings to a servant who has received a bonus from his master and is graciously taking leave before departing?

Are not the request of needs (even communal ones) and the (acknowledgment of) receipt of a bonus two utterly contradictory messages?

SEVEN

LET US EXPLAIN CLEARLY the meaning of the blessing known as *Retzeh* (first of the three final blessings) in the standing prayer.

The blessing says *"Show favor to Your nation, Israel, and to their prayers"*, but it is not only a plea and request. To pray with that intention is inaccurate.

The correct definition of the blessing is as follows. The three last blessings are only for the purpose of the student preparing to take leave of the Master. Here we encounter the idea of a special blessing: the *"blessing of taking leave"*.

A bright student who is delivering a benediction upon taking leave from his master/teacher behaves in a clever fashion and *"steals a blessing for himself"*.

Instead of blessing the teacher with all sorts of good things, he blesses him by saying: *"May the master have great satisfaction from me."* This is a nice blessing to offer his teacher, but in a backhanded way it also includes a blessing for himself.

The intention of the blessing of *"Show favor…"* is also along these lines. The main substance is to offer a blessing to the Master upon taking leave, but that parting blessing is organized in the style of "May the master have great satisfaction from me".

This is the difference between *"accept with favor our prayer"* and *"show favor to the prayer of the Jews"*, which seem redundant on the surface.

When we request that G-d *"accept with favor our prayer"*, that is a plea for acceptance of our prayer, but when we ask Him to *"show favor to the prayer of the Jews"*, our intention is to bless Him that He should take satisfaction from our prayer. And certainly, certainly, that includes a blessing for ourselves.

Indeed this is exactly like that clever student who is coy with his teacher and says: "May the master have great satisfaction from me."

This is what Rav Yehuda meant when he said that the last three blessings are comparable to a servant who received a bonus from his master and is now politely taking leave.

Except that the rule that fulfilling the needs of the receiver gives satisfaction to his master is only definitive when applied to the community at large. Because fulfilling the needs of a community of Jews is a definite satisfaction for G-d.

However, when fulfilling the needs of an individual, there is no certainty that this will bring satisfaction to the Master, in which case it reverts to being a simple request for aid that does not belong in the three final blessings.

[EDITOR'S NOTE: This is intended to answer the earlier question that was leveled at *Tosfos*, who proved that it is permissible to ask for communal needs in the last three blessings from the fact that those blessings seem to be mostly requests for communal needs.

The question was: how could they be mostly about communal needs if the stated purpose is to take leave after receiving a bonus from the Master?

The answer is that there is more here than 'permission' to shoehorn communal needs into a leave-taking. This is a positive strategy of blessing G-d with the satisfaction that our communal needs are met, which functions secondarily as a request for meeting those needs.]

EIGHT

THE SAME RULE AND the same standard applies to the request of "Show favor to our repose" in the Shabbos prayer. Here, too, the intention is as noted above.

In the arena of enjoyment and good will, there is always a governing principle of "like the water in front of the face reflects the face" (*Mishlei* 27:19). When we ask for G-d to "show favor to our repose" it implies a blessing to ourselves, that we also find favor and satisfaction in our own Shabbos rest.

NINE

WE CAN NOW CONNECT the end of this lecture with its beginning. At the outset of the lecture, we found this request to "show favor to our repose" problematic.

We asked: what is the meaning of this implication that showing favor is somehow directed more to the aspect of resting on Shabbos than to the general substance of Shabbos?

Furthermore, we find that this request for showing favor is divided into a double format: the second phrase refers to Shabbos in general — (*"And bequeath to us with favor Your holy Shabbos"*), while the first phrase related specifically to the aspect of Shabbos rest in particular (*"Show favor to our rest"*).

Now we can understand this effort to stress and highlight the special connection of G-d's favor to the specific observance of resting on Shabbos.

Because this favor encompasses also our own enjoyment and satisfaction, and that has a particular ability to affect the nature of the Shabbos repose. Although rest is a function of "sit and don't act", when it is accompanied by enjoyment and favor the Torah regards that pleasure as the equivalent of physical action.

[When we ask G-d to show favor, we ask also to expand our own enjoyment of the day. If we enjoy our rest more, it becomes more of an 'active' mitzvah of Shabbos, since pleasure constitutes the main activity of Shabbos, which is designed to be a foretaste of the future world of reward, in which pleasure substitutes for activity as the main focus of existence. – Ed.]

Consequently, rest on Shabbos is taken out of the category of "sit and don't act" as it would be applied in the rest of Torah. And the "keeping" is expressed as part of the same utterance as "remembering".

This in turn gave birth to the amazing new insight, that even the prohibitions of Shabbos are assessed within the context of serving G-d through Love.

TEN

"SHOW FAVOR TO OUR REPOSE."

NINE

I Am for My Beloved as My Beloved Is for Me

INTRODUCTION

SHABBOS SERVES BOTH TO memorialize the Divine Creation of the Universe, and as a remembrance of the Jewish People's Exodus from Egypt.

In a sense, the Creation aspect relates to G-d's experience and the Exodus aspect relates to the experience of the Jews. Commemorating both in the same event testifies to the mutual loving commitment to each other of G-d and the Jewish People.

ONE

THE SANCTITY OF SHABBOS is described as a forerunner to the sanctity of the festivals. It is called *"Techilah l'mikra'ei kodesh"*, "the first proclamation among the national holy days" (*Shemos* 23:12, *Vayikra* 23:3, *Bamidbar* 28:9). Shabbos initiates the concept of the sanctity of time; the other festivals extend this idea forward. Therefore, Shabbos always takes precedence over the holidays in terms of their relative sanctity.

117

This relationship also determines its precedence in the Torah text. When the Torah speaks of the festivals, as a rule it mentions Shabbos first. The sole exception to this rule is the thirty-fourth chapter of *Shemos,* where the festivals are mentioned in their usual order, while Shabbos is mentioned between the holidays of Pesach and Shavuos (*Shemos* 34:21). (See the Torah commentary of the *Ramban.*)

TWO

THE *MAHARAL* TEACHES THAT the nature of the Book of *Devarim,* which is called *Mishna Torah* (the repetition of the Torah), is more in keeping with the character of receiving the Torah — than with the giving of the Torah. Says the *Maharal,* "*Mishna Torah,* the fifth book, is closer to the recipient than are the first four books of the Torah (*Tiferes Yisrael* 43). When one hands an object to another, the beginning of the object is in the hand of the giver while the end of the object is in the hand of the recipient. Since the *Mishna Torah* is at the end of the Torah, it is closer to the recipient."

The *Maharal* proceeds to explain the differences in phraseology between the first (presentation of the) Ten Commandments in *Yisro,* and the second (presentation of the) Ten Commandments in *V'eschanan.* His approach is that the language usage in the Ten Commandments of *V'eschanan* is in the nature of a supplement to the contents of the first version of the Ten Commandments — a supplement that more closely reflects the level of the recipient.

At first blush, this explanation seems relevant only for understanding the dissimilarity between the language of the Book of *Shemos* and the language of the Book of *Devarim.* The problem is that the difference in language also divides between the first and second Tablets.

This seems to suggest that the alterations in language that occur between the two sets of Commandments are not rooted in the distinction the *Maharal* drew between the nature of the Book of *Devarim* and the rest of the Torah.

THREE

IN TRUTH, THE *MAHARAL'S* explanation even accounts for the differences in the two sets of Tablets. The identical relationship that prevails between *Devarim* and the other four books also exists between the second Tablets and the first Tablets.

After all, when the first set of Tablets were given to Moshe they were Divinely inscribed on both sides (*Shemos* 31:18, 32:15), while the second set of Tablets had to be carved by Moshe (*Shemos* 34:1; *Devarim* 10:3). Here we see that the second set of Tablets were more firmly in the grasp of their recipient than were the first set. It is therefore clear that the second Tablets relate to the first Tablets in the same way that *Devarim*, the *Mishna Torah*, relates to the other four books of the Torah.

For this very reason, the Ten Commandments of the second set find their proper place in *Parshas V'eschanan*, which is in the *Mishna Torah* (i.e. *Devarim*). Just as fittingly, the first version of the Ten Commandments was incorporated into *Parshas Yisro*, which is in the Book of *Shemos*.

FOUR

ONE OF THE DIFFERENCES between the stone tablets of *Yisro* and the stone tablets of *V'eschanan* relate to the commandment to keep Shabbos. The origin of Shabbos is ascribed to the process of creation in *Yisro* (*Shemos* 20:11), while the Exodus from Egypt is emphasized in *V'eschanan* (*Devarim* 5:15).

In its role of commemorating the process of creation, Shabbos is closer to the character of the giving of Torah because it was G-d, the giver of Torah, Who rested on the Seventh Day. [Therefore in *Yisro*, the section of Torah that the *Maharal* says is more in keeping with the character of Torah-presentation, the origin of Shabbos is ascribed to the process of creation. – Ed.]

But Shabbos in its role of memorializing the Exodus from Egypt is closer to the character of the receivers of the Torah, because it was they who were liberated from Egyptian bondage. [The origin of Shabbos is therefore ascribed to the Exodus in V'eschanan, which is in that part of the Torah that is more in keeping with the character of the receivers of Torah. –Ed.]

Carefully study the words of the *Ramban* in *Shemos 34*, where he explains why the subject of the holiday-cycle was reviewed there. It is because that is the chapter discussing the presentation of the second set of Commandments. There was a need to reassure the Jewish community that they had not lost their holy stature of "seeing their Divine King" due to the offense of the Golden Calf [which necessitated and preceded the giving of the second set of Commandments].

We might deduce from this *Ramban*, that Chapter 34 is more geared to the new material that appears for the first time in the second edition of the Commandments. From this viewpoint, which is oriented toward the receiver of Torah, the origin of Shabbos belongs primarily to the Exodus. In the context of the Exodus from Egypt, Pesach precedes Shabbos. [Note that both Shabbos and Pesach commemorate the Exodus. –Ed.]

Shabbos is multi-faceted, incorporating both the process of creation and the Exodus from Egypt. It is because Shabbos represents such a consolidation of various facets that makes Shabbos the *techilah l'mikra'ei kodesh* — first among all the occasions of hallowed convocation (i.e. the Holidays).

The chapter whose contents are explicitly and specifically tailored to accord with the second set of Tablets is the exception, the one place where Shabbos is not mentioned first, despite being *techila l'mikra'ei kodesh*. Here its proper place is after the holiday of Pesach, since that introduces the Exodus which Shabbos memorializes.

TEN

PREPARING FOR SHABBOS

INTRODUCTION

WHEN WE PUT SPECIAL food and delicacies aside — during the weekdays — for the Shabbos table we perform a *mitzvah* act of showing honor for Shabbos.

On the other hand, there is an approach that puts off setting aside things for Shabbos until later in the week, to show trust in G-d's Providence.

ONE

THE *B'REISA* TEACHES — "It was said regarding Shamai the Elder that all his days he would eat to honor the Shabbos. If he found a choice animal he would say, 'This one is for Shabbos.' If he came across a superior animal, he would eat the first and set aside the superior one for Shabbos (*Beitzah 16a*). Hillel the Elder had a different approach in that all his actions were dedicated to the purposes of Heaven, as is written in the passage: *'Boruch Hashem yom yom'* — 'Bless Hashem day by day' (*Tehillim 28:20*)."

Let us try to understand this statement that all of Hillel's actions were performed for the sake of Heaven (*Avos 2:12*). Shamai and Hillel are debating whether it is proper to rely on faith with respect to honoring Shabbos. How does dedicating all of one's actions to Hashem relate to that debate? (*Avos* 2:12)

Please study the language of the *Darkei Moshe* as quoted in the *Magen Avrohom: Orach Chaim* 250. His words indicate that this difficulty compelled him to explain the *B'reisa* differently, but his legal conclusion is not accepted by most authorities.

TWO

TO EXPLAIN THE ABOVE *B'reisa*, we must first understand that "dedicating every effort and activity to Heaven" refers to optional activities and interests. It does not deal with the underlying motivation or the purity of thought expected of us when we perform set and explicit *mitzvos*.

Note that the source for "dedicate all your actions to Hashem," is a passage in *Mishlei* (3:6), *"In all your ways know Him."* This verse concludes with, *"And He will set your paths in a straight direction."* It would be redundant to state 'and He will set your paths straight' in relation to the performance of explicit *mitzvos*, since *mitzvos* are already straight paths. Clearly, the verse relates to optional activities, teaching us that acknowledging Hashem in all our ways will help straighten our paths.

THREE

OUR *B'REISA* DESCRIBES THE differing postures of Shamai and Hillel. Shamai emphasizes honoring the Shabbos, while Hillel is concerned with the quality of faith.

Had the *B'reisa* ended here, we would have thought the debate between Shamai and Hillel was over the following question: should one give primacy to honoring the Shabbos or to the quality of faith? To correct this, the *B'reisa* informs us that were this the sole issue, Shamai would give primacy to the quality of faith. But here a different reasoning applies.

After all, Shamai's practice of designating the finest animal for Shabbos is an act of *mitzvah*-fulfillment, giving honor to Shabbos. However, Hillel's practice of eating the fine animal midweek seems like an act of personal choice. It is *"Bless Hashem day by day."* Hillel's intention and attitude — which transforms that meal [appreciating Hashem's midweek blessings and trusting that a still finer animal would become available for Shabbos] into an act of faith.

For Shamai, the decisive advantage is that he can perform an immediate act of *mitzvah,* without having to create a retroactive *mitzvah* through the application of an intention "for the sake of Heaven".

To counter the position of Shamai, the *B'reisa* tells us that Hillel had a different approach, in that all his actions were performed for the sake of Heaven. Hillel disputed Shamai's conclusion that it is preferable to select a course of conduct that is an automatic fulfillment of a *mitzvah.* He relied on the teaching that all of one's actions should be dedicated to Hashem [and trusted in his ability to make the act into a mitzvah by the proper intention. – Ed.].

FOUR

THE WORDING OF THE *B'reisa* was carefully chosen: "Hillel had a different approach ..." Not, as the Talmud might have ordinarily put it, "Hillel said on various occasions ..." or "Hillel customarily conducted himself in such a manner," but "Hillel had a different approach ...," to say that the doctrine, "all your actions should be dedicated to Hashem" was Hillel's decisive credo, the formula upon which he based all his actions.

Without doubt, Shamai also accepts this doctrine, but he considers his form of conduct more appropriate because it does not render his act subject to his level of success in dedicating his actions to Hashem. What we are saying fits very well with the teachings of the "scholars of truth" [Kabbalists – Ed.] concerning the nature of the behavior of both Shamai and Hillel.

ELEVEN

THERE IS NO NIGHT ON SHABBOS

INTRODUCTION

THE GENERAL DIVISION BETWEEN day and night as separate entities does not apply to Shabbos. Shabbos is one long twenty-five
hour stretch of spirituality that transcends the outward manifestations of physical darkness, in essence providing an uninterrupted
experience of uplifting spiritual light.

ONE

A NON-JEW WHO KEEPS Shabbos deserves to die (Talmud *Sanhedrin*
58b). *Rashi's* opinion is that this refers to any act of refraining from
work for a day (*Sanhedrin* 58b, "*Oveid Kochavim Sheshavas*"). *Rambam*, however, says that it only includes a cessation from work with
a religious intent to observe a Sabbath (*Hilchos Melachim* 10).

The source of this prohibition is the verse, "*Day and night they
shall not cease* (work)." This was said in reference to G-d's covenant
with Noah. This derivation is difficult to explain according to the
Rambam. After all, the literal meaning of the verse applies to cessation from work in the sense of the physical act of work stoppage.
There is no context at all for discussing the institution of a religious

125

Sabbath. If so, how can we deduce from here a prohibition limited to the cessation from work by a non-Jew with a religious intent to observe a Sabbath? This question has been widely asked.

TWO

IT SEEMS TO ME that there is a second, implicit dispute here between *Rashi* and *Rambam*. In *Rashi's* view the phrase *"they shall not cease (work)"* was speaking of Noah and his sons [who are being told not to stop working –Ed.] (see *Rashi* on *Sanhedrin* 58b). The *"day and night"* mentioned in the verse would then only represent a time frame for this prohibition. Only a work vacation of a full day and night would constitute an illegal 'cessation'. If so, this is an explicit law against a non-Jew taking a day of rest.

However, in the view of *Rambam*, the subject of the phrase *"they shall not cease (work)"* (*Bereishis* 8:22) is the aforementioned *"day and night"*. In other words, the cycle of day and night shall never be interrupted in all eternity. ['They' is not a reference to the people but to 'day and night' i.e. day and night will never break their natural cycle. –Ed.]

Now, the Torah repeats throughout the Six Days of Creation that *"it was evening and it was morning"*. But on the Seventh Day the existence of night is not mentioned at all. (It is a custom among the holy Jewish People to wish a "good Shabbos" both by day and by night, as opposed to the other days of the week where they distinguish between day and night by saying "good day" and "good night.")

THREE

THUS, A NON-JEW WHO creates a religion and institutes a day of idleness for twenty-four hours as a holy Sabbath rest is negating the natural cycle of day and night. Because in the description of a Sabbath that is recorded in the first Sabbath of Creation there is no mention of the cycle of day and night.

[The distinction between day and night implies a work schedule. Daytime offers the convenience of light to make work more possible. Night brings darkness as an aid to sleep, to get rested for tomorrow's work. The day-night cycle is a system of working by day and sleeping by night. Shabbos declares a twenty-four hour period of rest with no work at all during that time. In that sense, Shabbos shuts down the day-night working system built into Creation. – Ed.]

This, then, is how we derive from *"they shall not cease* (work)*"* the prohibition for a non-Jew to take a day of rest, specifically for the sake of a religious Sabbath. Because only through such a day of rest can it be said that the cycle of day and night has been negated. (See *Chemdas Yisrael: Ner Mitzvah* 58.)

[In brief, if *"they shall not cease work"* means people should not stop working, any form of work stoppage is prohibited. If it means the day-night system of work-by-day-rest-by-night should not stop, only a religious act of declaring a particular day of rest is seen as undoing that schedule.

The inspirational message here, beyond the textual and legal analysis, is that Shabbos is more than a day off from work; it is abandoning the cycles of the natural world and entering a new spiritual reality. This is a supernatural ability and experience given only to the Jew who has committed to eventually transforming this world into a spiritual world of reward, not work. — Ed.]

TWELVE

PUNISHING SHABBOS VIOLATORS

INTRODUCTION

PUNISHING PUBLIC VIOLATORS OF Shabbos [with two witnesses] was given over to the authority of Jewish courts.

Just as the Jew is G-d's agent in publicizing G-d's creation of the world by resting on the Seventh Day as He did, the Jew helps repair and set right the world by punishing those who failed to teach the world through keeping Shabbos publicly—as G-d punishes those who violate it privately.

ONE

"KEEP THE SABBATH BECAUSE it is holy for you, violators will surely die, because whoever does work on it, that soul shall be cut off (Koress) *from within its nation" (Shemos 31:14).* [This punishment known as Koress is translated literally as "cutting off" the soul, but is explained by the Talmud to refer to premature death.—Ed.]

This verse screams for an explanation even on its most surface level. After all, many crimes in the Torah get the death penalty (with witnesses) despite the fact that there is no cutting-off of the soul (*Koress*) for that violation (without witnesses). Similarly, some prohibitions carry the penalty of cutting off the soul (*Koress*) with no capital punishment in court. What was it that caused the Torah to pair the death penalty for Shabbos violation (with witnesses) together with the *Koress* punishment (without witnesses)?

Furthermore, the Torah actually says *"because* whoever does work on the Shabbos, that soul shall be cut off,"* indicating that the *Koress* punishment is the foundation for the court-administered capital punishment. The Torah explicitly mentions *Koress* as the basis for the capital punishment.

We are confronted with an inescapably amazing surprise, that the stoning of a Shabbos violator is different from all other court-administered inflictions of capital punishment in the Torah. Whereas other capital punishment verdicts in the Torah are not dependent on the existence of any other Divine punishment for that same sin, the stoning of a Shabbos violator is built exclusively upon the foundation of the *Koress* penalty found in the same violation (when it was perpetrated without witnesses).

How can we explain this unique linking of a capital punishment (in court) to the existence of a parallel *Koress* punishment (by G-d)?

TWO

THE FUNDAMENTAL POINT IS as follows: Divine Providence follows the rule of "measure for measure". This system of measure-for-measure includes both tracks of Divine payment — the credit track for giving reward, as well as the debit track for inflicting punishment.

However, the debit track of delivering punishment shows an aspect of the measure-for-measure principle which has no parallel in payment of reward on the credit track.

On the credit track, "measure for measure" has only one meaning. The nature of the reward given corresponds to the nature of the *mitzvah* performed. Naturally, this meaning applies equally to the debit track.

On the debit track, however, this approach of "measure for measure" also applies to the function of the punishment as repairing the sin. The repair that grows out of the punishment is parallel to, and essentially duplicates, the positive result achieved had the sinner passed his original test and never sinned.

Every time someone passes a test and rejects the temptation of sin, that builds up the weight of the credit side in the overall balance of good versus evil in the world. Since punishment is essentially the rectification of sin through the system of law, the very same tipping of the scales toward the good that rejecting the sin initially would have accomplished will now emerge from the delivery of punishment by Divine justice.

THREE

THUS, THE APPROACH OF "measure for measure" on the debit side, the side of delivering punishment, has two meanings: (a) The suffering in the punishment fits the evil nature of the crime. (b) The corrective quality accomplished by the punishment duplicates the good that would have been generated by rejecting the sin.

This parallel between the repair achieved by the punishments of the Torah and the positive effect achieved by rejecting the sin to begin with, is completely beyond our grasp. This is one of the hidden secrets of the Torah. But as it relates to the punishment of a Shabbos violator, the Torah allows us a glimpse of one particular aspect of this parallel.

Our ability to achieve the same rectification by punishing a Shabbos violator and the betterment that results from keeping Shabbos to begin with is founded in our ability to emulate G-d — when we keep Shabbos on one hand, or when we execute the penalty imposed on the Shabbos violator on the other hand.

After all, G-d decreed (so to speak) a reprieve from work on Himself on the Seventh Day and He imposed upon us the obligation to imitate Him and refrain from work on the Seventh Day, as is explained in the Torah several times (*Shemos* 20:11, 31:17).

The same rule and standard applies to the punishment of the Shabbos violator. By punishing the Shabbos violator (through our court system) we are emulating G-d, we are executing Him by human hands just as he would have received *Koress* from Above (had he sinned without witnesses).

The special element that we find in the punishment of a Shabbos violator is the fact that it includes the repair we achieve by emulating G-d, a remedial equivalent of the good that could have been done by rejecting the sin of Shabbos violation. This is what the Torah revealed to us by showing that the stoning of the Shabbos violator is dependent upon the fact that there is a *Koress* punishment for violating without witnesses.

[EDITOR'S NOTE: It might be helpful to some to phrase this another way as well:

When G-d punishes a person, He not only delivers a deserved penalty, He also sees to it that whatever the world lost by the *mitzvah* not having been done or by the prohibition being violated will now be replaced in the course of the punishing.

To accomplish this requires the punishment to be doubly "measure for measure". Not only a penalty mirroring the violation but also a repair that has the same content as the original mitzvah would have had if observed properly.

Now all *mitzvos* of Shabbos are based on feeling and acting this day just as the Creator does, looking around at Creation with satisfaction at its completeness and certifying that no further creative work is required.

When a person violates Shabbos, beyond the illegality of the act there is a rejection of the Creator's sabbatical outlook and behavior.

When punishment is in our hands, through Bais Din, we are tasked with not only penalizing but also repairing.

Thus, we must punish for Shabbos by doing an act below that mirrors the act G-d would have done if the sin had been left in His hands. So our capital punishment is deliberately linked to G-d's cutting short a person's life had he done the same thing without witnesses.]

THIRTEEN

THE THREE SHABBOS PRAYERS

INTRODUCTION

THE NIGHT OF SHABBOS is a time for bearing witness about G-d based on our knowledge. The day of Shabbos is a time for bearing witness about G-d based on what we have actually seen. This is because daytime, in daylight, is a time for seeing.

The Shabbos meals, symbolizing the Mann [Divine food that sustained the Israelites in the desert], represent three stages. Testimony of Creation from knowledge, testimony of Creation from seeing, and testimony that predicts the coming of a great Future World.

The three Shabbos prayers follow a similar, but not identical, progression, representing in sequence: the Shabbos of Creation, the Shabbos of Sinai and the Shabbos of the Future World.

ONE

THE CENTRAL STATEMENT OF the Shabbos *Mincha* is that, *"You are One (unique: the only One) and Your Name is One, and who compares to Your nation Israel as the one (unique) nation on earth?"* [Here the oneness of G-d is stated in the present tense. The time of Mincha and the third Shabbos meal portend the Messianic period which proclaims the total unity of G-d and the Jewish nation. – Ed.]

135

There is a Halachic view that one may fulfill the requirement of the third meal on Shabbos without breaking bread and making the *hamotzi* blessing (as required in the first two meals) (*Shulchan Aruch, Orach Chaim* 291:5).

Our question is this. The requirement of three meals on Shabbos is based on the repetition of the word 'today', 'hayom', in the retelling of the story of the *Mann* (the food G-d provided during the desert journey) (*Shabbos* 117b and *Shemos* 16:25). It would seem that the three meals would share similar requirements and be equal to each other (*Tosfos, Berachos* 49b).

Furthermore, the Shabbos *Shemoneh Esrei* prayers each carry a different theme. The first is *Ata kidashta* — "You sanctified" — referring to the Sabbath of Creation. The second is *Yismach Moshe* — "Moshe rejoices" — recalling the Sabbath of the Revelation of Torah. The third is *Attah Echad* — "You are One" — which speaks of the Sabbath of the Messianic Era, "the day that is totally Shabbos" (*Levush, Orach Chaim* 292a).

We see that in the progression of the three Sabbaths, the last, the Sabbath of the Messianic Era, is the culmination of history, the highest and defining event of creation. We also know that a person who ate the third meal prior to saying the *Mincha* prayer has not fulfilled his obligation (*Orach Chaim* 291:5). This shows that the final meal is intrinsically bound to the *Mincha* (third) prayer of Shabbos, and must take place during the same time frame. If the third prayer represents the pinnacle of the three-part Shabbos progression from creation to completion, i.e. the Messianic Era, why is the meal accompanying the third prayer diminished in comparison to the first two meals?

TWO

THE ANSWER LIES IN the uniqueness of the morning *Kiddush* of Shabbos. This *Kiddush* stands out in contrast to all other utterances that require a recital over a cup of wine. Ordinarily, each text of a blessing recited over wine is phrased according to the theme of that blessing.

Only the daytime *Kiddush* of Shabbos morning has no reference at all to the substance of what is being celebrated by this cup of wine. All we recite over this cup is a simple blessing for the pleasure of drinking wine [i.e. the same blessing we make over wine any time we drink it, Borai Pri Hagafen – Ed.].

The hidden insight here is best revealed by using an analytic approach that proceeds from the branches to the root. Let us begin with one of these branches.

THREE

THE *RASHBA* FAMOUSLY EXPLAINED the blend between the revealed and hidden (references to G-d) in the blessings upon *mitzvos* (Rashba, *Sheilos U'teshuvos*, Section 5:52). The opening phrase of these blessings is: *"Blessed are You* (G-d)*"*. This is in the second person, addressing G-d directly. They continue by saying *"… Who sanctified us with His commandments… "* in the third person [i.e. addressing an imaginary person and referring to G-d as a third entity, not a party to the conversation – Ed.].

The reason is because G-d is known in terms of His actions but hidden in terms of His essence. Therefore all blessings are constructed by grafting the revealed and hidden (aspects of G-d) together.

This fits well where there is no repetition and duplication. Then there at least exists a division between the revealed and the hidden, with each in its assigned place. The revealed relationship, addressing G-d as "You", is connected with the concept of blessing, as in "Blessed are You …" The hidden relationship, referring to G-d as "He" in the third person, is connected with the concept of sanctity, as in "Who has sanctified us with His commandments."

[Blessing is a tangible physical concept that we can see and experience. Consequently, we relate to G-d in a direct way when discussing blessing, even though "Blessed are You" is our blessing to G-d or our acknowledgment of His blessedness. Sanctity, on the other hand, is an intangible echo of G-d's essence. In that context, we refer to G-d in a hidden way, even when we speak of His giving us sanctity. – Ed.]

In the *Kiddush* of Shabbos, we find real duplication in the course of this merging of the revealed and the hidden.

Early in the Shabbos *Kiddush* it says *"… and His holy Shabbos with love and goodwill He bequeathed to us"*, while the later portion reads: *"… and Your holy Shabbos with love and goodwill You bequeathed to us."* It begins with the hidden third person usage and concludes with the revealed second person usage. In fact, the two phrases are repetitive, saying the identical thing with the only difference being this change in the form of address. This calls for an explanation: what is this duplication in the merging of the hidden and revealed (aspects of G-d) in the *Kiddush* of Shabbos?

FOUR

THE ENTIRE TORAH IS called a testimony (see *Rashi* on *Shemos* 25:16; see also *Gur Aryeh*). There are general and specific applications of this concept. While the entire Torah is a testimony in a general way, the specific application of the term "testimony" relates particularly to the two Tablets of the Covenant (*Shemos* 31:18). They are given an individual title as the "Two Tablets of Testimony".

Let us explain in clear language the substance of the general aspect of testimony encompassing the entire Torah and the specific aspect limited to the Tablets.

We must know an important principle: 'Testimony' is one of the major wheels on which the carriage of history works its way through the events of each generation until the End of Days. Prophecy revealed to us that "you (the Jewish People) are my witnesses and I am G-d" (*Yeshayahu* 23:12), which our Sages explain to mean: "When am I G-d? Only when you are my witnesses. If you do not serve as my witnesses, I am not (recognized as) G-d." (See *Yalkut Shimoni* and *Sifrei Devarim* 35:5)

Since the power of testimony is so vital to the system of sanctity in the cosmos, the structure of testimony in the realm of sanctity must encompass all the forms of testimony which exist in the reality of our world. (Indeed the inverse is more accurate. The concept of testimony in civil and criminal law draws its spiritual substance from the sanctified essence of the cosmic testimony. As was said about Torah matters in general: "All of Your words are one unity, but we do not know how to interpret them correctly.") (See *Megillah* 13a.)

FIVE

THE TORAH PRESENTS TWO systems for generating valid testimony. "And he is a witness, either he saw or he knows" (*Vayikra* 5:1).

There is testimony based on seeing and testimony based on knowing. The Sages explained: "*Saw*" is a reference to (witnesses who say) "He lent him money in front of us", "*Knows*" refers to (witnesses who say) "He admitted to him in front of us (that he owes the money)" (see *Shevuos* 33b). Thus, hearing from a reliable source constitutes 'knowing', but 'seeing' is only achieved by sensory contact with the actual event.

Maimonides wrote in the Laws of the Fundamentals of Torah (8:1): "*Moshe, our teacher, was not trusted by the Jewish People because of signs and miracles etc. But because our own eyes, not a stranger's, saw etc. As the Torah says, 'Behold, I am coming to you in the thickness of a cloud so that the nation should hear when I speak to you, so that they will trust you, Moshe, forever'*" (*Shemos* 19:9).

The entire Torah was heard by us from a reliable source (Moshe), which constitutes a testimony based on knowing. By contrast, his prophecy at the Mount Sinai gathering is described as "our own eyes, not a stranger's, saw", a testimony based on seeing.

Here, then, is the presentation of a truth in clear language, a truth as powerfully deep as it is massively simple. The general concept of testimony which includes the entire Torah is a manifestation of the phrase "...*or he knows*..." that is cited in the laws of testimony. On the other hand, the specific testimony expressed by the Two Tablets of the Covenant is a manifestation of the phrase "...*either he saw*..." that is cited in the laws of testimony.

[The presentation of the Torah as a total body of knowledge and law is testified to by the Jewish People in two ways. We *saw* the Tablets come down as the end product of G-d's prophecy to Moshe at Sinai. We *know* the rest of Torah, because it was taught to us by the prophet whose authenticity was established at Sinai. –Ed.]

SIX

ALL THIS APPLIES ONLY to the general concept of testimony through Torah and *mitzvos*. But there is one *mitzvah* in the Torah which, in and of itself, within its own boundaries, is defined as testimony. The name of this *mitzvah* is Shabbos.

We recite *"And they* (all the parts of Creation) *were completed..."* (in the Friday night liturgy) in a standing position, because the law requires witnesses to deliver testimony while standing (*Tur, Orach Chaim* 278). Also, we recite *"And they were completed..."* in pairs, because a matter is only considered an established fact when there are two witnesses. (See earlier, Lecture 4, where this valuable principle is explained at length.)

Since the sanctity of Shabbos is said to express testimony, it must include the entire reality of testimony, in both of its aforementioned manifestations. It must feature both an aspect of 'seeing' and an aspect of 'knowing'. Because observation and knowledge are the two pillars of testimony in this world.

Indeed we must pose this question: Where is the source in the text for the role of Shabbos — Shabbos per se, not as one element in the larger body of Torah — as testimony? There must be an explicit verse in the Torah — explicit enough for youngsters to read it with their teachers. The answer is as follows.

Moshe told the Jewish People in the segment dealing with the *Mann*: *"See that G-d has given you the Sabbath, therefore He is giving you on the sixth day* (Friday) *a two-day supply of bread"* (*Shemos* 16:29). [This 'seeing' of Shabbos makes us into the witnesses who can deliver testimony.]

Why is there no similar event that Moshe could point to, an event he could identify as a proof that G-d had bestowed upon the Jews the *mitzvah* of, say, *tzitzis*, or the like?

SEVEN

SHABBOS IS CALLED TESTIMONY. To express the sanctity of Shabbos there must be a testimony through seeing and a testimony through knowing within the framework of Shabbos itself. Therefore, there had to be an event demonstrating Shabbos before the very eyes of the six hundred thousand Jews who left Egypt and stood at Mount Sinai.

In fact, in the above-quoted verse delivered by Moshe to the Jewish People in presenting the *Mann*, there is a revelation of both the testimony through seeing and the testimony through knowing.

This is what the Torah states: *"See* that G-d has given you the Sabbath, therefore He is giving you bread for two days (on Fridays)." This 'seeing' is a combination of two separate phenomena: the double portion of bread falling on the sixth day, and the fact that there was no rotting or insect infestation on the Seventh Day. Consequently, this 'seeing' is actually completed on the morning of Shabbos. (See *Pesachim* 105, also *Orach Chaim* 271: *Poskim*.) Then, the lack of rot or infestation proves retroactively that the double portion of bread on Friday was a preparation for Shabbos.

Thus, the new 'seeing' which took place on Shabbos morning served as a 'knowing' for the eve of Shabbos as well (*Shemos* 16:6–7). Anything that is clarified retroactively has to be defined as something learned through 'knowing' because the physical contact of seeing is no longer present.

EIGHT

THIS IS ILLUMINATED BY the words of the Shabbos morning *Shacharis* prayer. There it stresses the fact that Shabbos is mentioned both in the Tablets and in the Torah. "And they (the Tablets) had the sanctity of Shabbos inscribed upon them, as it is also written in Your Torah."

What elevation is expressed by Shabbos being mentioned in both the Tablets and the Torah? The above provides the answer.

There is a distinction between the Torah and the Tablets — where Torah is "testimony-by-knowing" while the Tablets are "testimony-by-seeing". We find this distinction reflected in the testimony of Shabbos.

The testimony of Shabbos includes an element of "testimony-by-seeing" that parallels the essence of the Tablets; it also includes an element of "testimony-by-knowing" that parallels the essence of the Torah. This duality shows that Shabbos is indeed "equivalent to the entire Torah". All the aspects of testimony in Torah in general, exist also in the sanctity of Shabbos in particular. Understand this well.

NINE

THIS IS WHY WE distinguish within the sanctity of Shabbos between the honor we show to Shabbos during the day and the honor we show to Shabbos at night. The distinction is so strong that we even have a *Halacha* that if one cannot do both, one takes priority. *"In a choice between the honor of Shabbos Night and the honor of Shabbos Day, the honor of daytime takes precedence."*

Were it not for the element of testimony in Shabbos, we would not have two separate categories of "the honor by day and the honor at night". Because day and night relate equally to the sanctity of Shabbos. However, Shabbos is called testimony. And the existence of testimony in this world has two facets, testimony by seeing and testimony by knowing. It is inevitable that Shabbos should incorporate both these facets within itself, as well.

From the story of the *Mann* we see that these two facets correspond to the difference between day and night. The verse says: "In the morning you will see and in the evening you will know." Seeing the *Mann* in the morning created a retroactive knowledge about the events of the night, as was explained earlier. The advantage of the honor shown to Shabbos Day over the honor shown to Shabbos night is rooted in the advantage of seeing over knowing.

TEN

IT IS ESTABLISHED *HALACHA* that the *Kiddush* (sanctification of Shabbos over wine) recited on Shabbos morning is only a Rabbinic obligation (*Orach Chaim: Magen Avraham* 289). The *Ran* explains that since the honor of Shabbos Day takes precedence over the night, the Sages strove to assign a particularized *Kiddush* for the honor of Shabbos Day. The general, inclusive *Kiddush* for the entire Shabbos, which begins at night and extends through the day, is perforce recited at night, because that is when Shabbos begins (*Ran* on *Rif, Pesachim* 106). But since the honor of the day is really greater, it was thought important that the day be acknowledged at least through having its own *Kiddush*. [Ironically, as Rav Hutner goes on to explain, the day *Kiddush* has no room left to make particular points about the sanctity of the day, since everything was already covered in the night *Kiddush*. –Ed]

We can deduce that the Torah requirement to recite *Kiddush* is a general one encompassing the night and day into one unit. [The person making Kiddush at night is really declaring the sanctity of the entire 24-hour Shabbos ahead of him. –Ed.] But the Sages came along and instituted a special recitation to highlight the priority of honoring the Shabbos Day (*Shulchan Aruch, Orach Chaim* 171:8).

This decodes for us the implicit message in the duplicate phrasing of the Shabbos *Kiddush* blessing, which merges the hidden third person usage (referring to G-d) and the revealed second person usage, as presented earlier in Segment 3.

First it says *"… and His holy Shabbos with love and goodwill He bequeathed to us"*, while later it reads: *"… and Your holy Shabbos with love and goodwill You bequeathed to us."* It begins with the hidden third person usage and concludes with the revealed second person usage.

The explanation is as above. Since the Torah obligation is one *Kiddush* which includes both the night and day of Shabbos equally, it must cover both aspects.

Now, here is the rule. Things that are seen are expressed in the direct phrasing of the second person usage, while things which are known appear in the indirect phrasing of the third person usage. Sensory contact with another is reflected in "you" (i.e. I see you). Intellectual awareness of another is reflected in "him" (i.e. I understand him). When we try to accentuate both, things that are known and things that are seen, that effect is achieved by a duality of expression, referring to both "you" and "him".

Thus, the selfsame expression is repeated but with a difference. Its main substance is the mere repetition of the statement, except with a shift in the mode of address. The statement undergoes a change from the hidden, indirect usage of third person to the direct, revealed usage of the second person. We begin by saying "His holy Shabbos He bequeathed to us" and end by saying "Your holy Shabbos You bequeathed to us."

[The night of Shabbos represents the things that we 'know' about Creation, because we cannot see in the dark. We can only celebrate, and testify to, the part that is known rather than seen. In recognition of that, we say we know that "His holy Shabbos He bequeathed to us." The day of Shabbos brings light and, with it, all that we 'see' in Creation. Then we say we can see that "Your holy Shabbos You bequeathed to us."

By using both expressions in the *Kiddush* recited at the beginning of Shabbos, we sanctify both the night and day of Shabbos; we testify to all that is known, and all that is seen. – Ed.]

ELEVEN

THIS EXPLAINS THE UNIQUENESS of the *Kiddush* done Shabbos morning. Of all the observances that call for a cup of wine it is the only one that includes no mention of its purpose. It is recited in the simplified form of a blessing on the enjoyment (of the wine). This is the question raised earlier in Segment 3.

Now we understand. This special *Kiddush* was instituted for Shabbos morning because of the priority for showing honor to the day of Shabbos over showing honor to the night of Shabbos. This priority reflects the advantage of seeing over just knowing. Both the seeing and the knowing were really already included in the Torah-required Kiddush of Shabbos evening. Yet, on top of this comes the Rabbinic enactment to make a separate *Kiddush* when the sanctity of the Shabbos Day makes its actual arrival.

Therefore, the *Kiddush* for Shabbos morning offers no new addition of substantive phrasing. Everything has been expressed already in the *Kiddush* of last night… this new *Kiddush* is only a reminder of something already established the previous evening.

TWELVE

AS AN OUTGROWTH OF this insight, we make the following Halachic determination: Where something prevented a person from reciting *Kiddush* on the evening of Shabbos, the *Halacha* says that the initial (longer version of) *Kiddush* may be recited at any time during the day (i.e. as soon as the person is able). In our view, such an individual should not make another *Kiddush* afterwards in an effort to do the special *Kiddush* of Shabbos morning. [Once he recited the long Kiddush generally reserved for the night, in the morning, there is no need at a later time to make the usual Shabbos Day Kiddush, as well. – Ed.]

The entire purpose of making *Kiddush* on Shabbos morning is to reaffirm that the sanctity of the Shabbos Day was already celebrated in the *Kiddush* of Shabbos evening. Thus, if he makes the initial

Kiddush — that is usually recited at night — during the day, there is no place for a new recital of the daytime *Kiddush*.

THIRTEEN

WE NOW RETURN TO our opening words. Many Halachic authorities say that there is no obligation to eat bread in the third meal of the Shabbos Queen. This provoked a powerful question concerning the contrast between the sequence of the Shabbos prayers and the sequence of the Shabbos meals.

Why do we find that the hierarchy of the prayers hits its peak at the time of *Mincha* while in the sequence of festive Shabbos meals, the meal eaten in late afternoon, *Mincha* time, actually goes down a notch in relation to the previous two meals?

The basis of this question was a preliminary point. The source for the obligation to eat three festive meals on Shabbos is from the three times that the verse says "Today" when discussing the *Mann*. If the source is identical for all three, how can we differentiate between these meals by treating one more lightly than its companions?

The obligation to eat bread in Shabbos meals is to be similar to the eating of *Mann*, which the Torah calls 'bread' (*Shemos* 16:15). The opinion of these Halachic authorities is that the idea of "bread-similar-to-*Mann*" (*Beis Yosef, Orach Chaim* 284, in the name of the *Smag*) is not to actually simulate the *Mann* itself but to achieve a parallel to the way the *Mann* functions within the sanctity of Shabbos. The role of *Mann* within the sanctity of Shabbos is limited to two areas, the honor of Shabbos Day and the honor of Shabbos night, as explained.

Although the obligation for three Shabbos meals is derived from the three times it says 'Today' in the Torah segment about the *Mann*, the requirement to simulate the eating of the *Mann* itself only applies to the first two meals of Shabbos. These are the meals representing the honor of Shabbos night and the honor of Shabbos Day, where the *Mann* effected substantive results.

[This underscores the testimonial effect of Shabbos night and Shabbos Day. Shabbos night represents what we 'know' about Creation. To express this, the *Mann* did not rot overnight. When the Jews saw this, they 'knew' the *Mann* was prepared for Shabbos. Shabbos Day represents what we 'see' in Creation. To express this, the *Mann* arrived on Friday in double portions. When the Jews saw this, they 'saw' that the *Mann* was prepared for Shabbos. – Ed.]

However, the further division of Shabbos Day into a morning segment (*Shacharis*) and a late-afternoon segment (*Mincha*) has no corresponding distinction within the lessons of the *Mann*. Therefore, the late afternoon meal does not simulate the eating of the *Mann*, and there is no special reason to require eating bread.

FOURTEEN

IN THE SEQUENCE OF the prayers, *Mincha* (late afternoon) is the pinnacle. Yet in the sequence of festive meals, *Mincha* time brings a diminution from the level of the earlier meals. After all, we relieve it of the obligation to eat bread. But after absorbing the material in this lecture, we find here the hidden gem (that explains the above contrast).

Clearly the trustworthiness required for promises about the future (to be believed, and kept) is immeasurably greater than the trustworthiness required for relating events from the past. This is true in relation to the general standard of trustworthiness.

By contrast, when it comes to the trustworthiness required for the delivery of testimony, there is no place at all for being reliable about the future, since the concept of delivering testimony applies only to (relating events from) the past.

Thus, it turns out that precisely because the level of trustworthiness required for the future is so exalted, it is excluded from the issue of honesty in testimony — which is limited to being honest about events that have already transpired.

[This idea is not fully explained. Testimony affects the past, so it ignores the question of a person's track record in keeping promises about the future. That is obviously true. But how does this show that the exaltedness of honesty about the future is what prevents it from relating to testimony?

Perhaps the idea is that testimony is limited to current physical reality, an intrinsically lower realm than the future, improved world. Promises extend into that nobler region. Honesty in the nobler realm is by definition more exalted than truth-telling within the framework of present reality. – Ed.]

We can now absorb the light inherent in the third meal of the Shabbos Queen. It is precisely because of the exaltedness of the time of *Mincha* on Shabbos that the function of the *Mann* is not discernible.

The function of the *Mann* within the sanctity of Shabbos is in the arena of Shabbos serving as testimony. Since the prayer of *Mincha* time on Shabbos is "You are One and Your Name is One", which is the future-vision of "That day" of redemption (*Zechariah* 14:9), there is no role for this time as testimony, since the honesty expressed here is honesty concerning the future.

This is its glory, but that very exaltedness excludes it from the realm of testimony. This time of day is therefore relieved of the obligation to consume bread in its festive meal.

FIFTEEN

WE HAVE NOW SUCCEEDED in arriving at the point of illumination emanating from the sanctity of the Third Meal of the Shabbos Queen.

SIXTEEN

"YOU (G-D) ARE ONE and Your Name is One."

FOURTEEN

UNDERSTANDING THE CREATOR AS THE ARTIST

INTRODUCTION

T HE BEAUTY OF CREATION bespeaks a Creator Who created beauty as an instrument for sanctity.

There is an aspect of G-d's work as Creator known as "the Artist". This refers to the process of creating smaller or lower creatures that convey a sense of larger or higher things. Foremost among these is man who is formed in 'the image of G-d'.

The 'extra soul' of Shabbos is such a miniaturization, giving a glimpse of the fusion of body and soul in the Future World. In a more general way, the complete environment of Shabbos is a miniature version of the entire Future World.

ONE

THERE IS A REQUIREMENT to eat festive meals on Shabbos. The Shabbos meal. Our first sense of this is that the essence of Shabbos generates an obligation for festive meals.

The Talmud (*Baitzah* 16a) expresses a second sense. On Shabbos we receive an "extra soul". *Rashi* explains this to mean an "expansive heart for eating and drinking". This shows that the Shabbos meal is not merely an obligation arising from the occasion. Indeed, Shabbos creates a new energy with which to enjoy a festive meal.

How do we understand this concept of new capacities for festivity being born from an "extra soul"?

TWO

CHANNAH SAID (IN *SAMUEL 1*, Ch. 2) there is *"no protector (tzur-*Heb.) *like our Lord"*. The Sages (Talmud *Berachos* 10a) offer an alternate reading: "There is no artist (*tzayar*-Heb.) like our Lord. A person draws a picture but it has no life. G-d draws a picture and it has a spirit of life."

If someone created a complete thing and we described his handiwork as making a picture, that would belittle his achievement. In speaking of G-d's work we certainly would not use belittling descriptions. How can we say that the Creator of all existence is drawing pictures [when He fashions a living thing]?

THREE

WE HAVE A TRADITION that this represents one of G-d's self-defined roles, referred to as "artist (*tzayar*)". This role incorporates the making of all the miniatures that exist in the world. All of creation, including Torah and *mitzvos*, employs this concept of miniatures.

In building the Tabernacle (*Mishkan*) we find this referred to explicitly by the Sages. When the verse says *"standing boards of cedar"* (*Shemos* 26:15), it expresses the immanence of the Divine Presence. The Sages said of this: "You with your ornaments and Me in My glory" (*Shemos Rabbah* 35:6). The *"standing boards of cedar"* below are just a miniature version of the *"seraphs standing"* before G-d in Heaven (*Yeshayahu* 6:2).

On the one hand, *"indeed the sky and the heavens above the sky cannot contain You"* (*Melachim I* 8:27). Yet when G-d wishes, He can speak from between the poles of the Ark (*Bereishis Rabbah* 4:3). Between the poles of the Ark is not qualitatively different from what exists in the sky and the heavens. It's the same thing, just in miniature.

FOUR

THE FIRST TWO MINIATURES that we encounter explicitly in the Torah are as follows. First, the creation of man "in the image (*tzelem*) of G-d" (*Bereishis* 1:27) on Friday. The word "*tzelem*" comes from "*tzel*" meaning 'shadow'. A shadow is no more than a picture of a thing, not the thing itself.

In fact, we often say a person is a "small world". By 'small' we mean the same essence in miniature.

The second miniature is Shabbos, since every Shabbos is described as a "facsimile of the Future World, *Mei'ein Olam Habah*". As our Sages teach, when the psalm says "*a tune, a Song for Shabbos*" it refers to the Future World, "the time that is completely Shabbos." This is totally based on the concept of miniatures. Yes, the role of "*there is no artist like our Lord*" creates the possibility to fashion a 'facsimile of the Future World'. This is in the nature of a portrait; the essence of the thing is there, but in a miniature form.

(It emerges that the Friday and Saturday of Creation produce the two miniatures — man and Shabbos — around which all of creation revolves.)

FIVE

THIS PHENOMENON OF 'PORTRAITURE' is present in the creation of the "extra soul" of Shabbos, as follows.

The phrase in the *Asher Yatzar* blessing of "*He manufactures wonderfully*" is explained by Rabbi Moshe Isserles (*Ram"o*) as a reference to the wonder of linking the physical and the spiritual to create a human being.

When two things are tied together, often there is an outside force, a third element, binding them to each other. As in the Talmudic phrases: "There is no *egged* (cluster) less than three (*Succah* 13a); no *chavila* (package) less than three; no *shayara* (caravan) less than three" (*Eruvin* 16b). Or as Shlomo says in *Koheles*, "*The threefold cord will not quickly unravel*" (4:12).

The soul and the body, whose connection is defined by the phrase "*He manufactures wonderfully*", have no third force functioning as a binder. A component within the soul itself is the hinge enabling it to merge with the body as one unit.

Ramban explains G-d's decree of death upon Adam (and his descendants) as follows. Before the sin, that portion of the soul which unifies it with the body was fully functional. After the sin, some of the light of the soul was extinguished. As a result, the soul only stays connected to the body for a scant few years (*Ramban Bereishis* 2:17).

The 'extra soul' of Shabbos is a facsimile-of-a-facsimile of that portion of the soul that binds body and spirit together. On Shabbos the connection of body and soul becomes strengthened. This is a facsimile of "*the time that is completely Shabbos*", when the unification of body and soul will once again be a permanent one.

SIX

IN OUR CURRENT EARTHBOUND existence, the activity that holds body and soul together is eating and drinking. To express on our human level a strengthening of the connection between body and soul, we must increase our eating and drinking. Adding special foods in honor of Shabbos strengthens the link between body and soul. This in turn fashions a facsimile of the ultimate connection of body and soul which is '*the time that is completely Shabbos*' (*Tamid* 7:44). Eating is bound up in the spiritual essence of Shabbos.

[The purpose of eating more on Shabbos is less the act itself of enjoying the food and more the process of bringing body and soul together, offering a glimpse into our future existence when that bond will be permanent and death will be eliminated. Ed.]

Indeed, increased eating and drinking is the very function that defines the 'extra soul' of Shabbos, i.e. the extra link between body and soul. This is the depth of *Rashi's* words explaining the 'extra soul' to be 'an expansive heart for eating and drinking'. We spend every Shabbos enveloped in a miniature reality of *'the time that is completely Shabbos'*.

Our festive Shabbos meals, our beautiful Shabbos clothes, our glowing Shabbos faces, our *Lecha Dodi* Song ("Come, my beloved, let us greet the Shabbos bride …"), our Shabbos melodies — all of these shine with the inner illumination of *"There is no artist like our Lord"*.

SEVEN

THE TALMUD (*CHULLIN* 90B) teaches that 'the Sages spoke in exaggerations'. On first glance, this is not understandable. When we want to belittle the significance of a particular story, we say "It's an exaggeration!" Why would the Sages choose a form of expression that often makes people look at a thing less seriously?

This too is based on the concept of *"There is no artist like our Lord"*. For example: the actual movement of the sun is up in the heavens. An image of this movement is captured on earth in the form of a shadow. The movement identifiable on earth is only an extremely tiny sliver of the actual movement at its source in the heavens.

Thus, the words of the Sages are sometimes forced to take the form of exaggerations. Otherwise, their truth would only be relative. It would be a truth limited to the picture of the thing, the shadow of the thing, the facsimile of the thing. The Sages are able to look at the shadow of any thing and glean from it the true sense of the thing. They are naturally aware that the thing itself is many times greater than its shadow.

We only grasp the shadow, so the words of the Sages seem like an exaggeration. But the phenomena they discuss, when viewed at their source, are fully as broad as the exaggerated statement that the words of the Sages indicate. A precise statement in the context of the world above is an exaggeration in the context of this world below.

FIFTEEN

TWO CONSECUTIVE SABBATHS

INTRODUCTION

THERE IS A LINK BETWEEN observing Shabbos properly and the arrival of the Redemption. This is because our perfect adaptation to the miniature version of the Future World entitles us to experience the complete Future World.

A perfect Shabbos is one in which the entire seven-day week is defined strictly in terms of its relation to Shabbos.

Moshe is the one who brings us Shabbos because his superior prophecy traces all created things to their true spiritual source.

The idea of the perfect Shabbos anticipates a world that is transformed into an environment that is totally and eternally Shabbos.

ONE

THE PURPOSE OF THIS lecture is to expand upon its predecessor (Chapter 14), showing the extent and power of G-d's role as *"There is no artist like our Lord"*. (See Talmud *Berachos* 10a)

TWO

IT SAYS IN THE Torah reading of *Ki Sisa* (*Shemos* 31:13): *"And you should speak to the children of Israel to just keep my Sabbaths..."*

What is unique about this version compared with the other presentations of Shabbos which preceded it? And what differentiates it from the chapter of *"And the children of Israel must keep the Sabbath ...",* which follows shortly afterwards?

Furthermore, this particular rendition of Shabbos is the one in which the Sages (Talmud *Baitzah* 16a) see this implicit message: "G-d said to Moshe, 'I have a good present in My treasure house and its name is Shabbos. I want to give it to the Jews. Go and notify them'" (*Shabbos* 10b).

These words are astounding. There had been many previous chapters dealing with Shabbos. Suddenly Shabbos is called 'a good present in My treasure house'? Now?

THREE

WHAT IS NEW IN contrast to previous mentionings of Shabbos is this plural form: *"Keep My **Sabbaths**".* This distinction of using the plural was captured by our Sages, who declared: "If the Jews would keep two consecutive Sabbaths they would become redeemed immediately." (Talmud *Shabbos* 118b)

This calls for an explanation. What qualitative advantage is there in keeping two Sabbaths over keeping one?

FOUR

THE PHRASE 'REDEEMED IMMEDIATELY' has the ring of our previously established principle that 'the picture evokes its subject'. That is, Shabbos is a portrait and a facsimile of the future (redeemed) world. [When this portrait is at its sharpest, it evokes its subject, bringing the redeemed world to immediate reality. – Ed.] Thus, immediate redemption comes when there is greater equivalence between the portrait (Shabbos in the present) and the subject portrayed (i.e. the Future World).

(We refer here to the 'immediate' quality of the response, indicative of a natural reaction that is being triggered, rather than the payment of a reward which would be reserved until the end of the process.)

Let us explain the special quality of 'two consecutive Sabbaths', and how it creates this greater symmetry between Shabbos and the future redeemed world.

FIVE

HALACHA DIVIDES THE SIX weekdays into two groups. The first three days of the week are attached to the previous Shabbos and the last three are preparatory to the coming Shabbos. The ability of Shabbos to extend its influence into the weekdays and embrace them is divided into two sequences, one before Shabbos and one after Shabbos.

To actualize these two sequences, which surround the Shabbos in its complete mode, we require two Sabbaths in a row. The first three weekdays are an extension of a properly observed Shabbos beforehand and the last three a prelude to a properly observed Shabbos afterward. This is the unique element introduced by the observance of two Sabbaths. It provides a clearly defined presentation of Shabbos with all its subdivisions, consequences and offshoots.

SIX

ONLY THIS SCENARIO BRINGS 'immediate redemption'. It incorporates the weekdays as fully related to Shabbos, providing a clear facsimile of "the time that is all Shabbos" (Mishna *Tamid* 7:4).

The power of weekdays is lessened when they are bracketed between two properly observed Sabbaths. They are then thoroughly subordinated to Shabbos. This tableau is so close to the reality of the future redeemed world that it has the power to tow that reality in its wake, and consequently 'they are redeemed immediately'.

SEVEN

THE IDEA OF BEING 'redeemed immediately' is derived by the Sages from a verse in *Yeshayahu* (56:4), "Thus said G-d to the barren men who keep My Sabbaths ...", which is immediately followed by "... and I will bring him to My holy mountain."

Everything in the prophets is hinted at in the *Chumash* (Talmud *Taanis* 9a). It would seem the original hint is in the verse commanding us to "just keep My Sabbaths", which precedes a full chapter describing how 'the children of Israel will keep the Shabbos'. [In other words, if we would just keep two Sabbaths now, then all of Israel will immediately keep the Shabbos in "the time that is all Shabbos". – Ed.] "Sabbaths," specifically in the plural form.

Only this definition of Shabbos can be said to be hidden in the 'treasure house'. The redemption is referred to as 'a day of vengeance that is in My heart' (*Yeshayahu* 63:4), which the Sages (Midrash *Shochar Tov* on *Tehillim* 9:1) explain to mean that 'the heart of G-d does not reveal it to the mouth (i.e. it is not revealed in prophecy)'. Because this level known as 'My Sabbaths' is uniquely related to redemption, it is said to be in 'My treasure house'. Hidden, not revealed.

EIGHT

WE CONTINUE OUR ANALYSIS by noting the language of the verse we have been studying: "*And you should speak to the children of Israel to just keep My Sabbaths ...*" The focus on "you" (Moshe) stands out here. The Torah is replete with instructions to Moshe, such as "speak to the children of Israel ..." or "and say ...", but here it says that "you" should speak.

This is mirrored in the way the Sages reported the implicit message: "G-d said to Moshe, 'Moshe, I have a good present ...'" Once again, the stress is on the special selection of Moshe as G-d's agent to deliver this gift.

NINE

APPARENTLY, THE BESTOWAL OF this spiritual height known as "My Sabbaths" is particularly suitable to the persona of Moshe. We will explain that special connection as follows.

TEN

"AND THEY BROUGHT THE (unassembled) *Tabernacle* (*Mishkan*) *to Moshe."* (*Shemos* 39:33) *Rashi* explains (in the name of *Midrash Tanchuma*) that no one was able to lift the Tabernacle into position because the boards were too heavy. Only Moshe was able to lift it.

Why was this the case? Because Moshe had been told earlier: "And you should erect the Tabernacle according to its structure as you were shown on the mountain." (Mt. Sinai.) Again, we see this fundamental principle being applied, that the portrait is very close to its subject [as will be explained shortly – Ed.].

Although the manufacture of all the components of the Tabernacle was done by Bezalel, the actual installation could only be accomplished by Moshe. Why was this so important?

ELEVEN

"ACCORDING TO ITS STRUCTURE as you were shown on the mountain" means Moses was shown how the Tabernacle below serves as a portrayal of things that exist in Heaven above. He was shown the extent of that correlation, to its highest heights.

Moshe knew all the little hints of the Tabernacle, how they paralleled the objects they represent. For example, the Midrash says that the *"standing boards of cedar"* (*Shemos* 26:15) in the Tabernacle are a parallel to the *"seraphs standing before Him"* (*Shemos Rabbah* 35:6) in Heaven.

Each object in the Tabernacle is a link to something above it, which in turn links to something higher, and Moshe understood it all. Through him every portrait was brought closer to and connected to what it portrayed, and every hint was brought closer to what it suggested.

TWELVE

IN FACT, THIS IS the simple understanding of the phrase "an illuminated mirror". [This phrase in Talmud *Yevamos* 49b describes the uniqueness of Moshe's prophecy. Other prophets see visions in an unlighted mirror, while Moshe's is illuminated. The Aramaic word used is 'aspaklaria', which seems to come directly from the Latin verb 'speculari', to observe, and the Latin adjective *specularis,* of a mirror. The first reference to *aspaklaria* is in the Mishna (*Kelim* 30:2), where *Bartenura* interprets it as a mirror, while the Rambam explains it as a magnifying glass. Here we are assuming that it is a mirror. – Ed.] Even the smallest grasp of this level of prophecy is beyond our capacity. Still, we are obligated to try to understand the meaning of the words.

There is vision through a glass window and there is vision using a mirror. One is not like the other. Through a window one sees the object itself, but in a mirror one sees a reflection, not the actual object. Seeing the object itself and seeing it in a mirror are contradictory propositions.

Here is the uniqueness of Moshe's prophecy: "An illuminated mirror." He is seeing in a mirror, and yet the thing is illuminated. He sees the portrait and through that arrives at a clear conception of the object being portrayed.

It is utterly appropriate for Moshe, due to his unique level of prophecy, to be the one to present to the Jews the gift of "My Sabbaths". That is why G-d says that "you" should deliver the message. [Because Moshe saw objects in this world and knew exactly what they signify in the higher worlds, he could bring us Shabbos observance that fully coincides with the 'time that is all Shabbos'. – Ed.]

THIRTEEN

THE SECOND PART OF the verse says all this is *"so you will know that I am G-d Who makes you holy"* (*Shemos* 31:13). Why is this said in reference to Shabbos specifically? In what way is this different from all the *mitzvos*, of which we say that G-d has sanctified us with His commandments? [In general, we say that having and doing mitzvos is a result of our special holiness. Yet, in Shabbos we are being told of some unique holiness that it demonstrates. –Ed.]

FOURTEEN

OUR OBLIGATIONS ARE DIVIDED into two categories. The first includes instructions (to do certain things) and prohibitions (not to do certain things).

The second includes optional affairs of personal choice. These are not defined as either mandatory or forbidden. Such matters call for making sure that 'all your acts should be for the sake of Heaven' (Mishna *Avos* 2:12), which we derive from the verse: *"In all your ways you shall know Him"* (*Mishlei* 3:6). By 'knowing' we mean 'connecting'. A person should connect his bodily needs to Heavenly matters and tie them to spiritual things. The instruction to 'know Him' encompasses all of the needs that a Jew has in life.

When it comes to Shabbos we find a special level. Every pleasure one enjoys on Shabbos has intrinsic religious significance; it is part of performing the *mitzvah* of *"oneg Shabbos"*, experiencing enjoyment on (or of) Shabbos.

Here again Shabbos brings a great closeness between the portrait and the state it portrays. The experience of our Shabbos, where all pleasure is turned into *mitzvah*, is very evocative of the future 'time that is all Shabbos', where the concept of secular or neutral areas of life will no longer exist. Truly a time that is **ALL** Shabbos.

Therefore, while in other areas of life "In all your ways you *shall* know Him" is an instruction to approach them a certain way (i.e.

make an effort to know Him), on Shabbos we read it as a simple statement of fact: "You shall know him" by definition.

"So you *know* that I am G-d Who makes you holy."

[This is to answer the point raised in Section 13 above. This verse concludes by saying that keeping Shabbos will enable you to 'know' that G-d sanctifies the Jews, more so than the performance of other commandments. By observing Shabbos in the sense of 'Sabbaths', where our portrayal of the future world comes as close as possible to *that* ultimate reality, we gain a greater connection to *that* time and state of being. – Ed.]

In other *mitzvos* we say (in the blessing) 'that He has sanctified us with His *mitzvos* (and commanded us to…)'. The sanctification is limited to that particular matter and its *mitzvah*. On *Shabbos*, however, it says that through its performance we will know that G-d is the one 'Who makes you holy' in a general way. [Shabbos portrays, and through that portrayal evokes, a state of the world that is **ALL** holy, i.e. a general state of sanctification not limited to one particular *mitzvah*. – Ed.]

FIFTEEN

LET US CONTINUE EXPLAINING the verse. It goes on to say, *"that it (Shabbos) is a sign [so that you know that I am G-d Who makes you holy]"*. Yet this 'sign' is not the same as the sign mentioned in the following chapter that deals with Shabbos. In that chapter, which begins *"And the children of Israel shall keep the Sabbath"*, the 'sign' is mentioned in relation to events from the past. It is a *"sign that G-d created the world in six days and desisted from creation on the Sabbath."*

In our chapter, however, the 'sign' also relates to the future, so that we know that it is G-d Who makes us holy (*Shemos* 31:13).

Once again, this is to be understood in the sense of 'they would be redeemed immediately'. [Since the observance of Shabbos as a full portrayal of the redeemed world has the potential to trigger redemption, this 'sign' is actually an omen for a future redemption. – Ed.]

This very sense of Shabbos inspired the author of the *Lecha Dodi* Song to greet the Shabbos by including the phrase: *'Sof ma'aseh be'machshava techilah,'* 'The end of the manufacture (Creation) is (foreseen) in the initial plan.' Past and future merge in the experience of Shabbos.

SIXTEEN

WE ARE NOW PREPARED to answer the earlier question we raised concerning the opinion of the *Ge'onim*. They cited a source for the idea that a Shabbos violator is considered to have rejected the entire Torah, even though he has only committed one transgression of one prohibition. They say it is derived from the designation of Shabbos as a 'sign'. The violator of Shabbos is seen as denying the 'sign'.

This seems astounding. Doesn't it also say that circumcision and wearing *Tefillin* (phylacteries) are each a 'sign' as well? Yet one who refrains from performing one of those *mitzvos* is not considered to have rejected the entire Torah.

Our explanation provides the answer. The *mitzvah* of Shabbos has the quality of being a miniature portrait of the future redeemed world. A person who violates this *mitzvah* is seen as rejecting the entire vision of redeeming the world through Torah and *mitzvos*. This is the nature of Shabbos: it tows its 'portrayed subject' in its wake.

[Although circumcision and phylacteries are each identified as a 'sign', they are not signs of the entire enterprise of bringing the world to redemption through Torah. Denying those signs is not seen as rejecting the project of redeeming the world through the performance of G-d's commandments. – Ed.]

SEVENTEEN

OUR SAGES SAY (TALMUD *Shabbos* 118b) that "whoever keeps Shabbos with all its detailed rules (*halachos*), even if he worships idols as did the generation of Enosh, will be forgiven". How does Shabbos accomplish forgiveness for idolatry?

Shabbos is very close to the image of *'the time that is completely Shabbos'*, a time of which the prophet said that 'the idols will be completely destroyed' (*Yeshayah* 2:18). Observing Shabbos properly brings a person close to that redeemed state which accomplishes the negation of all idolatry. This serves as a counterweight to his earlier sin of idol worship. (See also *Bais Yosef* at the beginning of *Tur Hilchos Shabbos*.)

EIGHTEEN

THIS ILLUMINATES FOR US the words of Rabbi Yehoshua Leib Diskin, who explains that the chapter dealing with Shabbos written into the Torah immediately before the story of the Golden Calf is a form of prescribing the repair before describing the sin itself.

[The observance of Shabbos, especially in this fully realized form of 'two Sabbaths', triggers a greater connection to the reality of a redeemed world. That redemption includes the complete elimination of any aspect of idolatry. Thus, Shabbos is both the cure and the antidote for the sin of the Golden Calf. – Ed.]

NINETEEN

THE MIDRASH (*YALKUT* ON *Parshas Ki Sisa*) on the words *"that I am G-d Who makes you holy"* adds this comment: "Who makes you holy — in the future (world) yet to come."

[This confirms the principle described here, that Shabbos not only portrays the future reality of this world in the 'time that is all Shabbos' but actually has the power to bring that reality closer.

G-d, by giving us the Shabbos, is making us holier not only in our present state, He is also bringing us, incrementally, to that state of holiness which is our promised future in *'the time that is completely Shabbos'*. – Ed.]

SIXTEEN

SHABBOS, A FACSIMILE OF THE FUTURE WORLD

INTRODUCTION

JUST AS IT IS important to hope for the Messiah, it is important to hope for the arrival of Shabbos, which is a miniature Messianic world. Acts of preparing for Shabbos and greeting its arrival are the physical expression of our hoping.

Teacher and student greet Shabbos together to show that teaching the next generation is the way to build the future.

King David's kingdom in his lifetime was a miniature version of the Messiah's kingdom of the future, similar to Shabbos being a facsimile of the Future World.

ONE

"SHAKE OFF YOUR DUST and rise up high,
Don your splendorous garb, my nation,
By the hand of Bethlehem's son-of-Yishai,
Bring nearer to my soul its salvation."

(*Lecha Dodi* Song, Friday night liturgy)

A Shabbos Song mentioning the soul's 'salvation' certainly fits with the previous two chapters demonstrating the unique relationship between Shabbos and the ultimate Redemption.

This relationship is not merely a reward for *mitzvah* performance. The Talmud (*Shabbos* 118b) says when the Jews observe two consecutive Sabbaths *"they will be redeemed immediately"*. However, the relationship between performing a *mitzvah* and receiving its reward is not one of 'immediately', because the system of *"G-d withholds His reaction"* applies to both punishment and reward. (As the Talmud says in *Eruvin* 22a, *"He withholds His reaction"* to righteous people as well as to evildoers.)

Instead, the relationship between Shabbos and the Redemption follows the special rule that the portrait is linked to that which is portrayed. This bond is the source of 'immediately'. The Talmudic phrase speaks of being 'redeemed' immediately, without being more specific.

Yet the poet (who wrote *Lecha Dodi*) would not settle for that; he insisted on adding the detail that redemption must come about "by the hand of Bethlehem's son-of-Yishai."

TWO

IN WHICH DIRECTION IS this detail pointing?

THREE

LET US EXPAND OUR discussion of the portrait and the portrayed — and the relationship between them. We have been concentrating on Shabbos as a portrait of Redemption. Now we are ready to meet a linkage of a portrait and its subject that is even more advanced.

Clearly, the greatness of David's kingdom in the past is only a dim reflection-of-a-reflection of the kingdom of the Messianic King, may he be revealed soon and in our lifetimes.

Any existing thing that reflects in miniature form a reality that exists in a far greater form is included in the Song of Chanah (the mother of Samuel the Prophet) who said (according to the alternate reading spelled out in Talmud *Berachos* 10a): *"There is no artist like our L-rd."* Why was this concept revealed specifically through Chanah?

The Messianic King draws his power from the anointing (of David) that took place within the present reality of our world. The Messianic King will not require a new anointing. He is descended from David. And a king who is the son of another king does not require anointing, since his father's anointing serves him as well. (Talmud *Horayos* 11b)

The anointing that functioned in its time to establish the kingdom of David will establish the kingdom of the Messianic King. The greatest example of a miniature (or portrait) portraying something greater is the kingdom of David foreshadowing the Messianic Kingdom of the future. This portrait is only a reflection-of-a-reflection of that which it portrays. Still, this act (of anointing) done to the body of the reflection-of-a-reflection is the very one that extends and produces the Messianic kingdom of the End of Days. [Editors Note: This should not be taken to imply that the Messianic King is much greater than David himself, only that his kingdom will be greater in the sense of presiding over a redeemed world.]

We have often repeated that the highlight of Samuel's prophecy is the anointing of David as king, which incorporates the anointing of the Messianic King. Hence, Samuel the Prophet is the key to the most powerful link between portrait and portrayed.

The existence of Samuel the Prophet devolved and entered this world through the prayer of Channah. Consequently, the most appropriate venue for revealing the conduct known as *"There is no artist like our L-rd"* is at the point when Samuel the Prophet was born. Indeed, the book would be lacking its main section if the Song of Channah would fail to include this characterization.

[Both the *Targum* and *Rashi* explain Channah's Song to include many references to David's kingdom. In fact, Talmud *Megillah* 14a lists Channah as a prophet, seeing in her Song a prophecy that David's kingdom would be "extended" because the anointing was done in a special way. That certainly supports this analysis. – Ed.]

The poet therefore greets Shabbos by mentioning that the Redemption comes through the Kingdom of the House of David. Since Shabbos portrays a great spiritual concept through a miniature, it is appropriate to refer to the ultimate miniature: the Kingdom of David, which is a small replica of the Messianic Kingdom.

FOUR

ALL THESE WORDS ONLY approach the first layer of understanding of this matter. There is depth beyond this depth.

We have spoken here (Chapter 15) about the presentation of Shabbos in the reading of *Ki Sisa*; we explained some of the distinctions between the first and last verse in that chapter. This time we will address another difference.

In the first verse (*Shemos* 31:13) it says Shabbos is "*a sign for your generations*". (The entire verse is: "*And you should speak to the children of Israel to just keep my Sabbaths because it is a sign between Me and you for your generations, so that you will know that I am G-d Who makes you holy.*") In the latter verse (*ibid.* 31:16) it says that keeping Shabbos is for "*their generations*". ("*And the children of Israel should keep the Shabbos to make the Shabbos for their generations as an eternal covenant.*")

FIVE

WE FIND IN THE Talmud (*Shabbos* 119a) that Rabbi Chanina would say "Come, let us go out and greet Shabbos". See *Rambam* (*Laws of*

Shabbos 30:2) who quotes this as a *Halacha*, adding that scholars and their students would go out to the field together to greet Shabbos. This seems astonishing: why connect the relationship of teachers and students to the idea of greeting Shabbos?

[The citation referring to Rabbi Chanina does not explicitly mention that his students were present. He was not alone, because he addresses somebody: "Come, let us go…" Add to that the earlier (*Shabbos* 25b) description of Rabbi Yehuda-bar-Illai greeting Shabbos, which *Rambam* uses as a source for some of the details in this *Halacha*. That story specifically mentions students. *Rambam's* saying that students were a part of this process seems well-founded in the sources. The question is: what is the connection? Why should greeting Shabbos be an activity that is best engaged in with a group consisting of scholars and students together? – Ed.]

SIX

IN *SHULCHAN ARUCH* (*Orach Chaim* 250:1) the *Halacha* clearly dictates that the preparations of Shabbos on *Erev Shabbos* (Friday) begin on Friday morning. The Talmud (*Shabbos* 117b) derives this law from the verse: "*And they shall prepare what they are bringing* (i.e. the *Mann* they are collecting and bringing home should be prepared for Shabbos)." (*Shemos* 16:5) This implies that the preparation is done immediately after bringing home the *Mann*. Since the double portion of *Mann* would arrive first thing Friday morning, the preparation for Shabbos begins at that time.

This is obviously not an obligation to be energetic in promptly performing the *mitzvah* of preparation for Shabbos, similar to Abraham getting up early in the morning to fulfill G-d's command (*Bereishis* 22:3). This is a specialized *Halacha* concerning Shabbos, making it clear that this particular concept applies only to the preparations for Shabbos on *Erev Shabbos*.

This is not a law of *zerizus*, of haste and intensity. What else is it?

SEVEN

[THERE IS A GENERAL *halacha* to perform all *mitzvos* energetically with *zerizus*. In this case, there seems to be an extra responsibility to start preparing for Shabbos first thing Friday morning. –Ed.] We find the idea of preparation for all *mitzvos*, such as the law in Talmud *Shabbos* (10a) concerning a special garment for prayer, which we derive from the verse *"Prepare to face your L-rd, O Israel"* (*Amos* 4:12). Similarly, we saw that our great teachers strove constantly to prepare themselves before doing good deeds.

Still, the preparations for Shabbos done on Friday, *Erev Shabbos*, have a new and different face. As *Rambam* said above: one should 'sit and look forward with dignity to greeting the face of Shabbos as if he were going out to meet a king'. [The point is that this is a concept not found in other preparations for *mitzvos*. We are greeting the Shabbos in a personal way, as if a king is coming. This is more than the mere anticipation of a prospective *mitzvah*. –Ed.]

This 'looking forward' to the arrival of the Shabbos Queen belongs to the same class of activity as 'hoping for Redemption' (*Shabbos* 31a), except that it is applied to Shabbos instead of the ultimate Redemption. As every Shabbos is a facsimile of *'the time that is completely Shabbos'*, anticipation for Shabbos is a facsimile of the general hope that we will see the complete redemption.

Once again, we are establishing the portrait as a detailed replica of its subject. This is the key to the idea that true preparation for Shabbos must take place on Friday, *Erev Shabbos*, because this preparation is an expression through action of the anticipation for Shabbos.

General anticipation is a responsibility of the heart. But the preparation (of food and the like) is a *mitzvah* of physical action that expresses this anticipation.

Based on this, we say that the double portion of *Mann* falling on Friday, *Erev Shabbos*, was a Divine act of anticipation for Shabbos. [By sending food for Shabbos a day in advance, G-d is performing an act of looking forward to Shabbos and assuring that it will be observed comfortably. –Ed.]

In observing Shabbos we establish ourselves as imitators of G-d's resting on the Seventh Day. Similarly, we imitate Divine behavior by beginning to do the act of anticipating Shabbos (i.e. food preparation) immediately upon collecting the *Mann*. This is why we say that food preparation should be as close as possible to the *Mann* being brought in to the house. [Our act of anticipation for Shabbos, food preparation, proceeds seamlessly out of G-d's act of anticipation for Shabbos; in that G-d dropped on the earth tomorrow's *Mann* today. –Ed.]

Thus, the preparations of *Erev Shabbos* are not just a process of achieving '*readiness*' in time for Shabbos's arrival, they express an '*expectation*' of that arrival.

EIGHT

WE FREQUENTLY MENTION THE Mishna in *Eduyos* (2:9) that says that the 'End' (i.e. the Redemption) is contingent upon the number of generations. [Some predetermined number of generations must live before the Redemption can arrive. –Ed.] This is derived from the verse predicting the Exodus from Egypt: "*Then the fourth generation shall return here*" (*Bereishis* 15:16).

We recently found some words of the *Vilna Gaon* that were new to us. After the Torah was given, the counting of the generations toward Redemption changed. It was only before the giving of the Torah that the counting was done by generations of birth. Now, we measure the generations through the handing down of the Torah from teacher to student.

This new insight of the *Vilna Gaon* explains why the *mitzvah* to teach Torah to students was expressed in the text as "*And you should make them clearly known to your children*" (*Devarim* 6:7), with the Sages explaining that 'children' is a reference to students, because students are like one's children (*Sifri* on *Devarim* 6:7).

Why should the Torah set us on a roundabout path, by saying 'children' to convey 'students'? Why not command us directly to "make them clearly known to your students"? The answer lies in the words of the *Vilna Gaon*. The Torah's purpose is to stress through this language that teaching students creates the reality of a new generation being established, just like the birth of a son to a father.

NINE

LET US NOW MERGE these two premises. (1) Greeting Shabbos is a miniature facsimile of awaiting the ultimate Redemption.(2) The relationship between a teacher and a student brings Redemption closer by adding a new link in the chain of the 'number of generations'.

It is therefore especially appropriate for a teacher and his student to greet Shabbos together, because this anticipation of Shabbos (which contains elements of anticipation of the final Redemption) is brought closer to its ultimate reality by that connection.

We clarified earlier (Chapter 15) that the presentation concerning Shabbos in *Ki Sisa* was told to Moshe to deliver to the Jews on a level that relates to his own service, which is why it says *"And You should speak to the children of Israel"*.

[Moshe's prophecy was unique in its understanding of how each function that we perform in this world relates directly to greater Heavenly realities. Since Shabbos is designed to mirror the state of the post-Messianic world, it calls for a Moshe to deliver that gift to the Jews, because he can prophetically see how the entire process unfolds. – Ed.]

We can now appreciate the sweetness of the verse which said that this is a sign 'for your generations'. It is a statement from the first Rabbi/teacher to his students declaring that Shabbos is a sign 'for your generations'. You and I, teacher and student, together, shall initiate the counting of the generations. Through that counting there will emerge and accrue with each passing Shabbos — the "time that is completely Shabbos".

TEN

ONE MORE THING MUST be said. David devoted his life to the building of the Sanctuary. As he testified in *Psalms* (132:3,4,5), "*I won't enter into the confines of my home... I won't give sleep to my eyes... until I find* (a place for G-d's house)..." Our Sages taught us that this is why there is a Psalm which begins "*A tune, a Song, for the inauguration of the House by David*" (*Tehillim* 30:1). Although it was Solomon and not David who built that House, it was called by David's name because he devoted his life to its eventual construction (The House refers to the *Bais Hamikdash*, the Sanctuary). (*Midrash Tanchuma, Naso*, 13)

The conceptual structure of this is as follows. The Sanctuary can only be built as the product of anticipation. So much so that the one who provides that anticipation contributes more to the partnership than the one who does the physical building. Therefore the Sanctuary is divided into two aspects. The existence of King David represents the aspect of anticipation for the Sanctuary, while Solomon represents the aspect of the building process itself.

King David also represents the greatest hope for, and anticipation of, Redemption. Therefore, it is so fitting that in the prayer for greeting Shabbos, and in *Lecha Dodi* which is the beautiful hymn for this greeting, we should mention the most passionate anticipator of Redemption, Bethlehem's son-of-Yishai.

SEVENTEEN

SHABBOS, THE CORONATION OF G-D AS KING

INTRODUCTION

THE PROCESS OF CREATION reached its climax on the Sixth Day when mankind was created and G-d was crowned King over Man. The concept of kingship for G-d is only meaningful when His subjects have intellect and choice. This was confirmed on the Seventh Day when G-d rested, proving that Creation was fully accomplished. Thus Shabbos provides retroactive insight into the entire journey Creation took from conception to completion.

The Jews receive Shabbos not as a random gift, but as a deserved gift. Since the Jews are committed to bringing G-d's world to the fulfillment of His purpose, the original act of Creation was 'for them'.

The activity of waiting in anticipation of Shabbos to greet its arrival links the weeklong process of G-d's Creation with the ultimate purpose as expressed in Shabbos.

ONE

'REMEMBER' AND 'KEEP' WERE stated as one
The Unique Lord spoke and we heard
G-d is One, His Name standing alone
In renown, in glory and praising word.

(*Lecha Dodi* Song, Friday night liturgy)

This idea, that the commandments to remember and to keep Shabbos were somehow spoken simultaneously, is a pillar of the sanctity of Shabbos. Still, the holiness of Shabbos has other such pillars. Why is this pillar singled out to be mentioned when greeting the arrival of Shabbos?

To explain this, we must establish a number of fundamental principles: When we say that *'remember'* and *'keep'* were spoken simultaneously, the point is not limited to the Divine expression of those two words. These words are shorthand for the entire Shabbos commandment. The entire commandment beginning with *'Remember'* (in *Shemos* 20:8-11) was said at the same time as the entire commandment beginning with *'Keep'* (in *Devarim* 5:12-15). In other words, the two commandments are essentially one.

There is a very deep message here, one which serves to dispel a potentially erroneous conception of Shabbos that might have taken hold.

There is a special phrase concerning Shabbos: *"G-d did not give it to the nations of the lands"*. This phrase is used (in the Shabbos morning liturgy) without any introductory statement. By contrast, on Yom Tov we don't say *"and You gave us* (the holiday) ...*"* until we first say *"You chose us from among all the peoples"*.

On a surface level, one might have explained this as follows. The first event that Shabbos celebrates (i.e. Creation) occurred when Jews were not yet present in the world. Therefore, both Creation and Shabbos relate to the entire world. This constitutes an outstanding endorsement of the Jews when G-d chose only them to receive a gift that intrinsically relates to all nations equally.

By contrast, each Yom Tov is built on a unique historic event which happened to the Jews alone. [Therefore, there is no special mention of the 'gift' not being given to non-Jews. The prayer merely notes in a general way that G-d chose the Jews from among the nations and that He gave them the gift of that particular Yom Tov. – Ed.]

This would indeed be an erroneous conception. Yes, it is technically true that the event which brings Shabbos about (i.e. Creation) took place in the absence of Jews in the world. Still, the fact is that this very event, Creation, was undertaken exclusively and specifically on behalf of the Jewish People.

This is the profound meaning of the inclusion of *'remember'* and *'keep'* in one unifying commandment. The commandment of remembering Shabbos cites as its basis the fact that G-d created the world in six days. The commandment of keeping Shabbos asserts that it commemorates the redemption of the Jews from Egypt. The deeper idea of saying them both at once is to include these two reasons as one.

In a legal sense we say that "anyone obligated to keep is also obligated to remember" (*Shevuos* 20b) (as a result of the two instructions having been issued simultaneously). Similarly, we must say that whatever is true of the Redemption from Egypt (as it relates to Shabbos) is similarly true of the Creation of the world (as it relates to Shabbos). Just as the Redemption from Egypt is specific to the People of Israel, so too is the Creation of the universe intrinsically specific to the People of Israel.

TWO

THE TALMUD (*SHABBOS* 119A) teaches that the great scholars would greet Shabbos with the words: *"Come, let us go out to greet the Shabbos Queen."* It seems that until the *Lecha Dodi* song was composed, the text of greeting Shabbos varied according to the custom of individuals. The public acknowledged the arrival of Shabbos either by a direct text of accepting the Shabbos [such as "I hereby accept the Shabbos upon myself" uttered sometime before sundown – Ed.] or by reciting the Psalm of *"A tune, a song, for the day of Shabbos"*.

When the recital of the *Lecha Dodi* became a communal custom [about 350 years ago – Ed.], our current type of *Kabbalas Shabbos* prayer became the universally accepted mode of welcoming the Shabbos. What was unique about the approach of saying "Let us go out and greet the Shabbos Queen" more than other forms of accepting the onset of Shabbos?

[Why was this the province of the great scholars rather than ordinary folk? And why was it important to create the *Lecha Dodi* song to capture that approach—don't the words *"Lecha Dodi likras kallah"* mean "Let us go, my friend, to greet the bride," making it the universal approach for all Jews? – Ed.]

There is another unique element of the *Lecha Dodi* that calls for an explanation. This is not a song about Shabbos; instead, it is a song specifically geared to the process of greeting Shabbos, and particularly to the approach of "Let us go, my friend, to greet ..."

THREE

WE RETURN TO WHAT we established in Segment 1, that Shabbos is not something that did not originally belong to the Jews, but was given to them later. On the contrary, even Shabbos as founded in Creation relates essentially and originally to the Jewish People. All this is included in the reason the commandments to *'remember'* and to *'keep'* were issued simultaneously, as was previously explained.

There still remains a need to better explain how the events of Shabbos (i.e. Creation) were directed exclusively to the Jewish People, even though those events preceded by thousands of years the emergence of the Jews as a people.

FOUR

THE SONG THAT THE Levites sang on Friday begins with *"G-d reigned as King..."* (*Tehillim* 93). The reason for this (as explained in Talmud *Rosh Hashana* 31a) is because on the sixth day Man was created, and it is man who crowns G-d as king over Himself. As we know, Shabbos is referred to as the Shabbos Queen (*Baba*

Kama 32b). What is the difference between the majesty of Shabbos as expressed in the title of Shabbos Queen, and the kingship shown on Friday through the awareness of *"G-d reigned as king…"*?

The answer is as follows. The meaning of the word "Shabbos" is not as it is commonly translated: "Rest." [As in "a day of rest". –Ed.] Rest is tranquility. Tranquility is passive. An absence of activity. "Shabbos" is an active verb that entails going opposite to one's previous direction.

Prior to Shabbos, the direction of all of one's energies had been from inside to outside. Now we take back all these energies which had been radiating outwards and return them inside, to their source. "Shabbos" from *"shav"*, means to return. To go back to the place where one was before. Taking a trip in an opposite direction to one's previous travels.

The purpose of every venture can be deduced from its conclusion. *"G-d reigned as king"* comes at the end of the Creation process, representing its purpose. In truth, we only know this because after Friday comes Shabbos, and Shabbos means returning to where one began. This announces that forward progress has ended, confirming that *"G-d reigned as king"* is the conclusion of the Creation process. In the conclusion lies the purpose. Thus, Shabbos clarifies that the kingship of G-d is the purpose of all Creation. This is the majesty of the Shabbos Queen.

In the Shabbos morning prayer we say that *"on the Seventh Day He elevated Himself to sit upon His throne of honor"*. *"Elevated"* indicates a step upward from the means to the goal. Shabbos is a time in which the goal, the purpose of Creation has already been clarified. Consequently, it is called a time of elevation.

The entire majesty of the Shabbos Queen is to confirm that "G-d reigns as king" is the purpose of Creation. The one who said that *"G-d reigns as king"* was Adam, the first man. Thus, the goal of Creation was to reach that true man who is called "Adam" (*Yevamos* 61a). Since only the Jewish People are called "Adam" as a nation, then Shabbos was in fact originally created for the Jews, intentionally and specifically.

This explains what we said earlier. Any element found in the Redemption from Egypt (as it pertains to Shabbos) can already be found in Creation itself (as it pertains to Shabbos). Both were designated for that nation of whom it can be said: "*You are called Adam (true man).*"

FIVE

THE *BARAISA* (TALMUD ROSH *Hashana* 31a) says: On the first day (of each week) they (the Levites) would say (in the Bais Hamikdash, when bringing the daily morning Tamid offering)… On the second day they would say… etcetera. On the day of Shabbos they would say, "*A tune, a Song for the day of Shabbos*", for the day that is all Shabbos.

We must understand why, when discussing the songs that the Levites recited along with the Temple offerings, our Sages appended the commentary that when King David says that he is singing a song for the Shabbos Day, he is referring to "a day that is all Shabbos".

Furthermore, even in the choice of songs that the Levites apply to each day, we find a distinction between the approach to individual days of the week and Shabbos. On weekdays, the song discusses matters pertaining to that which was created on that day (as the Talmud in Rosh Hashana *ibid.* explains). However, on Shabbos it was not enough to sing about what occurred on the Seventh Day of Creation. [Instead, the Shabbos Song speaks about the world as a whole including elements pertaining to Messianic times, '*the time that is completely Shabbos*'. – Ed.]

This is particularly troublesome when we consider that the Shabbos morning liturgy says in the blessings of *Shema*: "*This is the Song of praise that applies to the Seventh Day, for on that day the Lord desisted from all His work.*" [The question then is: why in the morning liturgy is it sufficient to praise Shabbos as the day upon which G-d refrained from work, yet in the song of the Levites it is necessary to seek broader themes—the entirety of Creation and the sweep of history? – Ed.]

SIX

WE SAY EVERY DAY: *"Today is the… day, upon which the Levites used to say in the Bais Hamikdash such and such."* It seems to me that there is a common error concerning this.

Why add the fact that this song was said by the Levites in the Temple? People assume that it is to show that we expect to accomplish with this a real performance of that song in the sense of, *"And our lips shall compensate for the* (offerings of) *cows"* (Hoshea 14:3). [It is possible to achieve the equivalent of bringing an actual Temple offering at a time when the Temple is not standing, such as today, by reciting a description of that offering. This is derived from the above-quoted verse that lips can compensate for cows. Here, too, one might assume that reciting these songs would be counted as if we had sung those very songs in the Temple today. – Ed.]

However, this somehow does not seem reasonable. After all, the song in the Temple was delivered during the morning *Tamid* offering, and we do not find an effort to achieve "And our lips shall compensate for the cows" for the *Tamid* itself (we do not describe the *Tamid* in the morning *Shacharis* liturgy). Why would they suddenly trouble to achieve this effect in relation to the song that accompanied the *Tamid*?

SEVEN

CELEBRATORY SONG (*SHIRA*) IS recited over a miracle (*Erchin* 10b). Either a miracle that involves the collapse of wicked people or a miracle that involves the salvation of righteous people. The definition of a miracle is — something that defies the limitations of Nature.

Now, it is self-evident that creating an entire system of Nature is the greatest miracle against 'Nature'. [Without G-d's laws of Nature there is no Nature. If opposing the laws on a particular occasion is worthy of celebration as a miracle, because Nature has taken such hold that countering it is miraculous, then putting it in place to that degree of reality is certainly the most powerful and noteworthy achievement of all. – Ed.]

Why do we not find a celebratory song, a *Shira*, for the creation of Nature, which is itself the miracle of all miracles? The answer is that a *Shira* calls for something new. Without newness there can be no celebratory song. While it is indeed true that the creation of Nature is the greatest miracle, (relative to us) this is an old miracle. It does not carry with itself an element of newness (or renewal), and therefore it is not eligible for celebratory song.

The question then is: what about the principle that G-d "*constantly renews each moment the handiwork of Creation*"? Looking at the world from the perspective of constant renewal, then the miracle of establishing Nature is never old or stale. [Why not have a celebratory song each day for all of Creation, based on the newness of the miracle of each day's renewal of Creation? – Ed.]

The answer is that the Torah itself prevented us from establishing a celebratory song for this renewal. This is because this facet of daily renewal is rooted in the Name of G-d known as *Havaya*. The *Halachic* texts teach us that it means "*He gives life and creates all that exists in each and every instant*" (*Orach Chaim* 5).

When it comes to this special Name, the Torah uses the world "*le'olam*" (*Shemos* 3:15) meaning forever, but writes it as 'le'alaim' (*Pesachim* 50a) meaning to keep hidden. From this we derive that the name which is written as *Havaya* we actually read as *Adnus* (Master/Creator).

[Because of the tradition of being extra-careful to avoid any enunciation of G-d's name outside of reading Torah texts or reciting blessings and prayers, and because of the tradition not to overtly spell out the four-letter name of *Havaya*, we are not reproducing either the spelling or exact pronunciation. Those who pray regularly will recognize that there is one name of G-d that is spelled one way but is pronounced an entirely different way. – Ed.]

That Name is never sounded verbally, because G-d said "I am not read the way I am written" (*Sotah* 38a). So, too, the quality of "He renews each day the handiwork of Creation" which is the message of the Name of *Havaya*, exists only as a hidden piece of knowledge (in our minds but not our mouths). Hiddenness and celebratory song are mutually contradictory.

[Thus, the Torah's message to keep that element of G-d's Creation as hidden knowledge eliminates the possibility of reciting a celebratory song over the wonder of His daily renewal of Creation. – Ed.]

EIGHT

THIS APPLIES EVERY PLACE in the world. One place stands as an exception to this rule, namely the Bais Hamikdash, the Sanctuary. That is the one place where *that* Name of G-d is pronounced as it is written. Apparently, in the Bais Hamikdash the quality of "He renews each day the handiwork of Creation" is so illuminated, so clear and so apparent that we can express it openly. Since the hiddenness does not apply in the Temple, the mouth can be open with *Shira*, celebratory song, for the Creation itself.

We stress this point when we introduce our recital of the Daily Song, which is actually a celebration of Creation itself for that day. We find it necessary to explain that what we are reciting is *"the song that the Levites would sing in the Bais Hamikdash"*. In other words, we are only repeating what they said. We are not capable of saying anything on our own (about Creation itself). All we can do (outside the Temple) is to repeat (what was recited in the Temple).

NINE

HOWEVER, ON THE SEVENTH Day, what was created was the Revelation that G-d's Kingship is the purpose of the entire Creation. And — *just think!* — this purpose is the ultimate in hiddenness.

We see, for instance, in the Rosh Hashana prayer, that a great deal must happen before we finally arrive at the phrase *"And You shall reign…"*. First we need to accomplish that *"the corruption in the world shall have its mouth sealed"*. Then we need that there should be an opening of the mouth for *"those who hope for You"*. Only then can we say: *"And You shall reign…"*

As long as all the cities of the world are firmly settled upon their foundations and only *"those who hope for You"* find that their mouths are blocked, [because for many reasons we are unable to rebuild the Jerusalem Temple and offer sacrifices on its altar – Ed.] then the dominion of G-d is obstructed by seven locks.

We noted earlier that things that are hidden from view cannot be the subjects of celebratory song. Therefore it is not possible to say a celebratory song about Shabbos (in the context of our present-day reality).

If despite this we encounter a Psalm that says *"A tune, a Song for the day of Shabbos,"* it must be referring (not to our contemporary observance of Shabbos but rather to) *"the day that is all Shabbos"*, that future time in which G-d's kingship over us will be revealed and visible.

TEN

WE SPOKE (IN THE previous chapters) at length about the fact that Shabbos is tightly bound up with the reality that it symbolizes. Since every Shabbos represents in miniature an image of *"the time that is all Shabbos"*, it becomes possible for us to recite the song that applies to that future time.

Let us now return to our first questions. What makes the text of *"Come, let us go out and greet the Shabbos Queen"* more powerful than an ordinary text of greeting Shabbos? It is that this phrase clarifies and stresses that Shabbos is something specific to, and designed for, the community of the Jewish People.

Why is this so? Because when someone greets the arrival of Shabbos through a direct text of accepting the observance or by reciting *"A tune, a Song for the day of Shabbos"*, then the "receiving of Shabbos" and the advent of Shabbos happen simultaneously. Thus, the ordinary text of receiving Shabbos has no mention of *Erev Shabbos*. By contrast, the text of *"Come, let us go out to greet the Shabbos"* indicates that it is being recited on the sixth day, *Erev Shabbos*. Shabbos itself is clearly still standing 'outside' if a person is announcing 'Come, let us go out to greet Shabbos.'

This way of accepting Shabbos by saying 'Come, let us go out…' is that form of acceptance that enfolds the eve of Shabbos, *Erev Shabbos*, into the Shabbos itself.

Put another way, it merges the *"G-d Who reigned as King"* of *Erev Shabbos* with the kingship of Shabbos. Here, in fact, we can detect, beneath the surface, the essential concept of the exclusive connection between Shabbos and the Jewish People (representing Adam, who was created on Erev Shabbos.).

Thus, when we greet Shabbos with the Song of *Lecha Dodi* (embodying the approach known as "Come, let us go out and greet the Shabbos Queen"), we express and then explain that what makes this form of greeting special is found in the fact that 'Remember and Keep are stated as one'.

Because it is that very 'unified commandment' which incorporates the concept of how Shabbos is essentially identified with the Jewish People.

['*Remember*' represents Shabbos as a celebration of Creation and '*Keep*' represents Shabbos as a celebration of the Jews emerging from Egypt to reestablish the true Adam. By bringing the Jews in, the Torah clarified that the original Shabbos of Creation is inseparable from the Jewish People who were redeemed from Egypt in order to achieve the purpose of the original Creation. – Ed.]

This identification of Shabbos with the Jewish People is the defining theme of *Lecha Dodi*. Naturally, then, the stanza of *'Remember and Keep stated as one"* is woven in beauty and grace into the Shabbos greeting of *Lecha Dodi*.

ELEVEN

ALL THIS REFERS TO the first unique element of *Lecha Dodi*; namely, that it goes out of its way to include the fact that *'Remember'* and *'Keep'* were delivered simultaneously as a unified commandment.

Now we are prepared to explain the second innovation of *Lecha Dodi*. That is, the fact that it designates a celebratory Song for the specific purpose of greeting Shabbos.

TWELVE

WE SAID EARLIER THAT each day of the Six Days of Creation has its individual song (in the Holy Temple). Through the activity of 'accepting/greeting the Sabbath' which is done on Friday, *Erev Shabbos*, there is introduced a dual identity for the sixth day of the week. Because the sixth day is evaluated on two levels.

First, it is the sixth day in the process of Creation. Second, it functions also as the day of *Erev Shabbos*. Consequently, we deal with the sixth day in a legal sense as two different days that were fused into one inclusive day. As a result, it becomes necessary to assign to the sixth day two separate celebratory songs.

One Song celebrates the day's identity as the sixth day: *'G-d reigned as King…'* [that the Levites recited in the Holy Temple, and that we repeat in their name –Ed.]. The second Song celebrates the day's identity as *'Erev Shabbos'*, the day on which Shabbos is greeted and accepted. This personality of the sixth day also calls for its own special Song. The name of that Song is '*Lecha Dodi…*'

One of our scholarly friends appended a very nice observation to this discussion. The Talmud in *Erchin* (11a) identifies *Shira*, celebratory song, as a service of G-d using a Name. *Rashi* comments that this is because the Name of G-d is mentioned in these songs.

What does the fact that G-d's Name happens to be mentioned have to do with the essence of celebratory song?

The answer must be as above. The power of the Levites to recite the 'Song of the Day' is a direct result of their unique power in the arena of expressing the Name of G-d, the fact that they articulate it verbally as it is written. This is amazing.

[Their being given permission to pronounce the hidden Name of G-d is taken as an indication that they may celebrate in song elements of Creation that are usually too hidden to be expressed openly, as explained above. Thus, the unique power of their music and poetry in celebrating Creation is related to their enunciation of The Name in those songs. – Ed.]

EIGHTEEN

FULFILLING G-D'S
ULTIMATE PURPOSE

INTRODUCTION

NON-JEWS HAVE THE CAPACITY to emulate G-d and behave in ways He has modeled for mankind. Yet only Jews are permitted to emulate G-d by resting on Shabbos. This is because the Jews have accepted the role of fulfilling His ultimate purpose, entitling them to emulate Him on a higher level.

Thus Shabbos and the Jews are intertwined. The Jews teach the message of Shabbos to the world, and Shabbos elevates the Jew to a higher level of emulating G-d.

The Jew therefore greets Shabbos with a song on his lips, because Shabbos brings him to a higher self-realization.

ONE

COME, MY FRIEND, TO greet the bride
Welcome the face of Shabbos inside.

(*Lecha Dodi* Song, Friday night liturgy)

We have elsewhere explained that the '*Lecha Dodi*' Song represents the third level in a series of three levels which arrive, one on top of the other, in the course of our greeting Shabbos.

The first level is the basic obligation to greet Shabbos. The second is the custom of the scholars in the Talmud who would go outdoors to greet Shabbos. The third level is the celebratory song (*Shira*) of greeting Shabbos by going outside.

In this presentation, we will examine these three levels.

TWO

THE TALMUD SAYS IN *Berachos* (49a): 'We do not seal a blessing with two (themes)'.

[Some blessings are just a simple declarative statement such as 'Blessed are You, Hashem, our Lord, King of the universe, who brings bread out of the earth'. There are also longer blessings that discourse at length on a subject, like the blessings on food after a meal, *Birchas Hamazon*. These are 'sealed' by a final declaration, such as the ending of the first blessing after food: 'Blessed are You, Hashem, Who feeds all.' The Talmud expresses a principle that such sealing statements must be limited to one theme only. – Ed.]

Therefore, we cannot seal a blessing with the praise that G-d is 'the savior of Israel and the builder of Jerusalem'. Because this constitutes sealing a blessing with two separate themes.

In that context, the Talmud asks: how do we seal the second blessing after food with the phrase blessing G-d 'for the Land and for the nutrition'? They reply that it means 'for the land that gives forth nutrition'. Then they ask, what about the phrase (used in the Yom Tov liturgy and *Kiddush* over wine) that G-d 'sanctifies the Jewish People and the holidays'? They answer: 'The Jewish People who sanctify the holidays'. Then they question the phrase (used when *Yom Tov* overlaps Shabbos) that G-d 'sanctifies the Shabbos, the Jewish People and the holidays'. The previous answer sufficed to explain the combination of sanctifying the Jewish People and the holidays. What do we do with this added complication of 'sanctifying Shabbos and the Jewish People…'?

The Talmud answers (see the *Rif, Berachos* 49a): 'They each depend on the other.' [In other words, the Jewish People and Shabbos are concepts that are mutually dependent. –Ed.] Rabbenu Yonah in his commentary on the *RIF* explains this to mean that the sanctity of the Jewish People grows out of the sanctity of Shabbos. Other *Rishonim* (Early Commentators) make the point even more sharply. They say that if not for Shabbos there would be no Jewish People.

This is something we need to do some pondering about. After all, the Talmud explains that we do not seal a blessing with two separate themes because *"We do not make mitzvos into bundles and bundles"* (see *Rashi, Sotah* 8a). The reason we do not do multiple *mitzvos* in a single act ('bundles and bundles') is 'so they should not appear to be a burden'. In other words, one *mitzvah* is all it takes to fill all the space inside a person; there is no room to pack in another one (at the same time).

This is somewhat similar to the Talmudic injunction that when 'the teacher is occupied with one volume of the Talmud, don't ask him questions from another volume'. This means that when a person is engaged in one Torah subject, it fills him completely, leaving no room for another subject. This is true of Torah; the equivalent concept concerning *mitzvos* is the above mentioned *"We do not make mitzvos into bundles and bundles"*. [Yet despite this concern not to bundle unrelated *mitzvos* and have them intrude on each other's space, we are comfortable bundling Shabbos and the Jewish People into one blessing. –Ed.]

Apparently, then, we are saying that the sanctity of Shabbos and the sanctity of the Jewish People are so thoroughly unified that one does not interfere with the other when they occupy the same space.

THREE

WE WILL NOW DISCUSS this from two perspectives.

One of the 613 *mitzvos* is *"And you should go in His ways"* (*Devarim* 28:9) (which our Sages interpret as 'You should be like

Him' by emulating G-d's activities, such as helping the unfortunate). Naturally, since the entire Torah was directed to the Jewish People, this instruction does not apply to non-Jews who are trying to keep the Noahide obligations. [Note: The *sheva mitzvos b'nei Noach* are seven obligations that form the foundation of an expansive set of behavioral instructions to the nations of the world. – Ed.]

That is only true of the '*mitzvah*' designation. But in terms of a 'higher virtue' (Rabbenu Yonah establishes the distinction between behaviors categorized as '*mitzvah*' or as 'higher virtue') (see *Sha'arei Teshuvah* 3:17), there is no question that the value of 'You should emulate Him' is open to anybody.

'You should emulate (i.e. be like) Him' is more than a codified obligation that you must behave a certain way. After all, you cannot instruct a person to be something that he is not. Therefore, saying 'You should be like Him' is first and foremost a confirmation of the fact that a human being is a facsimile of G-d. And certainly a non-Jew is also in the category of a facsimile of G-d.

The *Rambam* established a deeply-rooted principle. We are only taught about G-d's practices and systems when they are relevant to us as role models for 'You should be like (emulate) Him' (*Shabbos* 133b). Any practices which we are not obligated to emulate [or, we are unable to emulate – Ed.] are totally irrelevant to us, and we are told nothing about such matters.

The Torah revealed and taught that there is a system by which G-d 'refrains from work'. When a human practices this type of vacation he is acting in emulation of G-d. (Indeed it is explicit in a verse of the Torah itself that when we rest on Shabbos we do that in emulation of G-d not creating on that day, completely independent of the general injunction to 'be like Him') (*Shemos* 20:11).

How, then, can we explain the general prohibition against trying to 'be like Him' when it comes to taking a reprieve from work? The

Torah says *"Day and night they* (the universe) *may not cease work"* (*Bereishis* 8:22), and the law is that *"A non-Jew who observes a day of Shabbos rest deserves to die"* (*Sanhedrin* 58b).

This proves that there are gradations in the concept that Man is in some way a facsimile of G-d. There is a first floor of being a facsimile of G-d, and on top of that there is a second floor… etc.

On the first level there is no concept of 'You should be like Him' in relation to taking a respite from work. But the higher level does apply 'You should emulate Him' in the arena of desisting from work.

Thus, the revelation that G-d does have a practice of desisting from work has an application in the service of 'You should be like Him' (because otherwise it would not have been revealed). On that upper level, the rule of 'Day and night they may not cease work' does not apply. It is on that upper storey, a level superseding the universal level that all men share as facsimiles of G-d, where we find the sanctity of the Jewish People.

Thus, the sanctity of Shabbos [limited to those people who are exempted from the prohibition of 'Day and night they may not cease work' – Ed.] and the sanctity of the Jewish People can be found in the very same location.

Our understanding of time in the arena of sanctity is not the same as our understanding of time in ordinary activities. When it comes to sanctity there exists a concept of specialized time. (Holy times are not determined by taking testimony from witnesses as to when an event occurred and then memorializing that event by declaring the time holy. Instead, it is the holiness of the time that produces such events i.e. the Holidays.)

There are times (i.e. days in the calendar) which are pre-designated for various spiritual experiences, times for joy, times for mourning, times for repentance, times for awe, times for all the spiritual movements that exist in the soul. Every movement within the human soul has a parallel in a designated time (prepared by its nature to be most suitable for that kind of spirituality).

If indeed a particular spiritual phenomenon is found to have no parallel in a designated time, then that proves that this spiritual phenomenon has no hold on the human soul. Whatever we do not find in time is not present in the soul. Whatever is not in the soul, we will not find in the realm of time.

In relation to events described in the Torah, time and soul stand facing each other in a precise parallel. If there was not a special time designated for taking a respite from work, then the soul would never be able to accommodate the upper level of man-as-facsimile-of-G-d, the level that requires a reprieve from work.

This is what Rabbenu Yonah means when he says that the sanctity of Shabbos and the sanctity of the Jewish People are not considered two separate themes at the end of a blessing because they add up to one single concept. The concept is the same in both, differing only in the arenas where it is manifested. One is manifested in time and the other is manifested in the spirit.

Since the type of sanctity is the same, the difference in location does not turn these two concepts into two separate themes. Mentioning the sanctity of Shabbos and the sanctity of the Jewish People together does not constitute sealing a blessing with two disparate themes.

FOUR

"AND THE HEAVENS AND the earth and all their component parts were completed" (*Bereishis* 2:1). On this verse in *Bereishis*, the Midrash says as follows. *Rabbi Levi said, until this point it is 'The honor of the Lord is in concealing matters': from this point on, it is 'The honor of kings is enhanced by analyzing matters'* (*Mishlei* 25:2) (*Bereishis Rabbah* 89a).

What does this mean? From 'In the beginning' through 'and the heavens ... were completed' there is a continuous coming-into-being of something from nothing, a phenomenon which is completely removed from our ability to comprehend. Hence it is described as 'the honor of the Lord'.

The very essence of creation *ex nihilo* (out-of-nothing) belongs to godliness [only G-d is able to create something out of nothing, which is precisely how He created the universe and its contents. –Ed.]. Thus, its honor is the honor of godliness, which takes the form of 'hiding matters'.

However, from 'and the heavens ... were completed' and further, there is now a chain of developments of something-from-something. This is the management of Creation that belongs to kingship, and the honor that stems from such administration is 'the honor of kings', founded upon 'analyzing matters'.

In this distinction between 'hidden matters' and 'analyzing matters' there lies interwoven a second distinction which touches upon one of the basic foundations of Judaism, as will be explained.

FIVE

WE HAVE A DISPUTE with one of the great 'scholars of Torah' who lived almost in our own time.

He asks how could non-Jews, Sons of Noah, have been commanded to observe *mitzvos* without first being asked if they agreed to accept them. When it comes to the 613 *mitzvos* (i.e. obligations) of the Jews, we find an entire discussion (between G-d and the Jews) complete with questions and answers about whether the Jews want to receive those commandments or not (*Shemos* 19:3). Without their agreeing they could never have received the *mitzvos*. (So how could non-Jews be commanded to observe their seven obligations without having agreed in advance to accept them?)

He solves this by quoting the Mishna that 'the Jewish People are especially beloved' (*Avos* 83:14). He interprets this to mean that the

Jews must be asked to agree as a special courtesy which is extended to them because of their being especially beloved. When someone wants to be close to a person, they are careful to consult with him about any (joint) plans. The non-Jews, on the other hand, are not sufficiently beloved to be entitled to that courtesy.

We are in disagreement, 'at war', with such a view. First, we must repeat the words of the Vilna Gaon in interpreting the verse: *"For kingdom (melucha) belongs to G-d and He reigns (with memshala) over the nations"* (*Tehillim* 22:29).

He explains that the difference between kingship (*melucha*) and reign (*memshala*) is that reign exists even when the subject does not wish to be ruled. Kingship is only when there is a judgment and a will on the part of the subject agreeing to accept the rule of that king. *"If you do not coronate me, I am not your king at all."* This is well-known (see *Be'ur HaGra* on *Mishlei* 27).

SIX

WE AGAIN REFER TO the difference between 'the honor of G-dliness' and 'the honor of kingship'. The precondition of requiring 'the knowing consent of those over whom one is a king' only applies to kingship (and its honor), but the honor of G-dliness can be achieved even against the will of the person over whom one is ruling.

[G-d rules as G-d even over those who prefer not to be ruled by Him, and this rulership brings a measure of honor that goes under the heading of 'the honor of G-dliness'. When G-d rules over those who desire His rule, they crown Him as their king, enabling Him to receive a new kind of honor, 'the honor of kingship'. – Ed.]

Thus, from the entire Creation preceding the phrase 'And it was completed', the world does not produce any honor of the sort that is demanded of the Jewish People. What is asked of the Jews is 'the honor of kingship' and until that point all honor goes under the heading of 'the honor of G-dliness' (inasmuch as there was no one who could intentionally crown G-d as his King).

In this context, we need to study the question that Rabbi Abraham Ibn Ezra reports being asked by Rabbi Yehuda Halevi.

Rabbi Yehuda Halevi asked: Since the Creation of the world precedes the Exodus from Egypt, when the Creator begins speaking about Himself, shouldn't He rather have introduced Himself by referring to His act of Creation than by referring to His bringing about the Exodus from Egypt? It should have said (as the introductory phrase of the Ten Commandments) as follows: "I am Hashem, your Lord, Who created you ..." (Why, instead, does it say *"I am Hashem, your Lord, Who took you out from Egypt... "*?) (See Ibn Ezra on Shemos 20:1–2).

The truth is as stated above. The commandment of *"I am Hashem, your Lord"* (*Shemos* 20b) constitutes the *mitzvah* of accepting the Kingship of G-d, as explained by Nachmanides. Our acceptance of the Kingship of G-d does not grow out of the fact that He created us, but from His redeeming us in Egypt. (In fact, in *The Kuzari*, written by Rabbi Judah Halevi, it seems that he never intended this as a real question but as an opportunity to discuss this principle with us.) Consequently, the beginning of the Revelation of 'the honor of kingship' for G-d in this world is the advent of Shabbos (See *Kuzari* A:25).

[Once the Torah says *"And it (Creation) was completed"*, then the purpose of the world for the achievement of holiness as facilitated by the Jewish People becomes clear. As explained earlier, Shabbos exists because the Jews exist. At that time, there is a sense of a world that will voluntarily crown G-d as its King. This brings about 'the honor of kingship'. –Ed.]

To prove this, let us imagine that in Creation, immediately after Friday came the next Sunday, with no intervening day of Shabbos. Certainly, the second Sunday would have shifted over into G-d managing the world on the basis of something-from-something.

Still, every Sunday would have a connection to the first Sunday, and every Monday would have a connection to the first Monday, so on and so forth. The proof is from the Song of the Day, where we see that the song designated for each day is crafted (see Talmud *Rosh Hashana* 31a) as a reflection of what happened on that day during the Six Days of Creation.

What would have inevitably resulted from such a scenario would be that there was no day of pure kingship, because as long as there is only (the process of) Creation there can be no honor of kingship.

[Now that there is a Shabbos, we have a moment that takes us beyond the process of Creation into the world of *"And it was completed"*. In a world in which the purpose of Creation is clarified, the existence of the Jewish People becomes inevitable. Once there are Jews there can be kingship. – Ed.]

Shabbos is the first day in which there was a revelation of pure 'honor of kingship'. This is the key to the origins of the *Kabbalas Shabbos* service with which we greet Shabbos. Shabbos is the first day of kingship in the world, and kingship requires acceptance.

[Just as G-d can only be a King if the people are willing, Shabbos, which celebrates His kingship, is greeted willingly by those who observe its laws. By greeting the Shabbos with a special service, the Jews are in essence declaring their willingness for G-d to be their king, thus giving Him the 'honor of kingship'. – Ed.]

Here we see yet again how the sanctity of the Jewish People stands face-to-face in a full-fledged parallel with the sanctity of Shabbos. The only people who have the power to accept (G-d's kingship and, consequently, the arrival of Shabbos) are the Jews.

When we see one kingship that corresponds to another kingship, there must be an acceptance of one to correspond to the acceptance of the other.

SEVEN

'COME, MY FRIEND, TO *greet the bride; welcome the face of Shabbos inside*' (from *Lecha Dodi*). This song is saying: Let the soul that is suited to receive, meet the time that is also suited to receive.

[The Jewish soul receives G-d willingly, bringing Him into the world as King. The time at the beginning of Shabbos is a time of reception as well, because the world that was physically created over a span of six days is now receiving the holiness that comes with clarity of purpose concerning G-d's kingship of the world. Thus, the receiving soul of the Jew meets the receiving time of Shabbos's arrival. – Ed.]

This idea enhances our appreciation of the receiving of the Torah at Mount Sinai; namely, the fact that it was not only received with words (*"We will do and we will hear"*) but also required actions to assist its reception (i.e. immersion in a *mikvah*).

[The time when the Torah was given was also a time of reception in the world, similar to the time of reception when Shabbos arrives. There, too, the Jewish soul set out to receive the Torah, another case of the receiving soul matching up with the receiving time.

The physical acts of preparation for that reception enhance the experience. They show that the physical world which is the vessel for the new spirituality being received from G-d is bestirring itself to accept the authority of G-d that is expressed in this gift. – Ed.]

In like fashion, we find that when it comes to receiving the Shabbos there is an advantage to doing so with a physical act (of getting dressed in special clothes and going out to the field to welcome its arrival).

EIGHT

NOW COMES THE THIRD level, the fact that the service of *Kabbalas Shabbos*, the greeting of Shabbos, was turned into a celebratory song.

The *Ohr Zarua* (one of the early commentators) says that singing special songs (*zemiros*) on Saturday night after Shabbos (*Motzoei*

Shabbos) is derived from the words of Lavan. Lavan said to Jacob, had I known you were leaving my house I would have *"sent you away with songs"* (*Bereishis* 31:27). Similarly, when we escort Shabbos out of this world, we escort it with songs (see *Sheloh*, Amsterdam Edition, page 135, in the name of *Tola'as Yaakov*).

The rule is that a guest cannot be honored more upon his departure than he was honored upon arrival. Therefore, there must be a celebratory song in the process of greeting the Shabbos when it arrives.

[This segment is somewhat under-explained, almost cryptic. The logic of deriving an obligation for song in greeting from the obligation for song in parting is strong. But it seems to be independent of the previous discussion.

We suggest that its meaning is as follows. There can be no joy in the departure of Shabbos just as there is no joy in Jacob leaving town, an event that leaves the town poorer, as *Rashi* explains in his commentary concerning when Jacob left the Land of Israel. Obviously, the joyful singing is to celebrate retroactively the fact that we had this opportunity to visit, also, the fact that the visit leaves the place enriched to some extent, as Rabbi Hutner explained in public on Purim 5731.

Therefore, the celebration at departure cannot exceed the celebration upon arrival. Both are really celebrating the arrival, so that obviously the time of arrival is the main celebration. The Torah teaches us the principle of singing for the visit by explicitly mentioning the song at departure, to show us that the visit is transforming; it is moving.

Thus, the Song of greeting Shabbos is the first level. The second level was moving the body to greet Shabbos, the movement is a signal for receiving and acceptance. The third level is singing as an expression of 'being moved', showing that the spiritual gift had the effect of moving the body and making one into a holier person. — Ed.]

The soul sings as it recognizes its own image in the mirror of time [as explained earlier that all movements in the soul have corresponding movements in time, and that the arrival of Shabbos is the reflection in time of the capacity in the Jewish soul to willingly accept G-d as a crowned King – Ed.].

NINE

IN THE PROPHETS (*NEVIIM*) and Holy Writings (*Kesuvim*) we often find a title referring to G-d: *"King of Glory."* This unique phrasing is to stress that we are referring to the 'honor of kingship' rather than the honor of G-dliness which has a hidden quality (*"haster davar"* — a matter for concealment).

When, during the reign of King Solomon, the Temple was built and it became necessary to carry the Ark into the Holy of Holies, we find (see Talmud *Shabbos* 30a) that they prayed in the following language: *"Gates, lift up your heads, and lift the entranceways of the world, so that the King of Glory may enter"* (*Tehillim* 24:7). This language was carefully chosen. Because the entire essence of Torah which is placed inside the Ark must be "accepted" by the Jewish People, as explained above, therefore at this juncture they called G-d by the title of "King of Glory".

[This is the ultimate 'honor of kingship', when the Jewish People accept the Torah and G-d's kingship of their own volition. – Ed.]

NINETEEN

PREPARING FOR SHABBOS

INTRODUCTION

THE PROPER SEQUENCE FOR preparing on Friday for Shabbos is to wash one's face and then dress in special Shabbos clothing.

This is because the Sixth Day is the bridge between the Creation of the weekdays and the Resting of Shabbos. It is still one of the weekdays but it also marks the completion of Creation that allows for the subsequent Rest.

Washing the face allows a transition from weekday grime to a clean, restful tranquility. Then we may dress in the clothes of Shabbos.

ONE

FIRST, I WOULD LIKE to joyfully inform the assemblage that the essence of what we spoke here last week (Chapter 18) ... I have found to be virtually explicit in a verse of the Torah: *"Just keep my Sabbaths ... so that you know that I am G-d Who sanctifies you"* (*Shemos* 31:13).

Here we have an open verse saying that the sanctity of Shabbos has an effect on our knowledge of the sanctity of the Jewish People. This is all that we were trying to bring out in our previous address.

TWO

THIS EXPERIENCE IS A good example of the words of the *Vilna Gaon*. He said that although the sequence of Torah study begins with the simple exposition of the text and works its way deeper and deeper into greater levels of understanding, still in all, at the very end you come back to the simple text. The paradox is that by the time you work your way back to the exposition of the text, you find that the simple text is not so simplistic. (See *Ruach Eliyahu* I, 57–58.)

[This is not the sort of insight you would be likely to have the first time you read that you should keep Shabbos so that you know that G-d sanctifies the Jews. You would read it to mean that working on matters of holiness will remind you that G-d made holiness your agenda.

Later, after expending much effort to understand that the spirituality of Shabbos actually expands a Jew's capacity to understand the essential sanctity of being the nation that crowns G-d in the world, you can revisit the text and see that it says more than you thought. It says that the keeping of Shabbos will help you 'know' your holiness as a Jew. –Ed.]

THREE

IN THE *SHULCHAN ARUCH* we learn that the time for donning Shabbos clothes is right after washing one's face in honor of Shabbos. The source cited for this is the text of the Talmud (*Shabbos* 25b): "*Such was the practice of Rabbi Yehuda b. Illai. He would bring before him a tub full of water and would wash his hands, his face and his feet. He would then wrap himself in satin garments that had tzitzis… he was similar in appearance to an angel of the G-d of Hosts.*" Certainly this is a valid source. But it still does not explain the proximity between donning the garments of Shabbos and washing one's face.

Let us, then, analyze the basic facts described here in the Talmud. First, that he wore satin garments with *tzitzis*. This is saying that *tzitzis* provide an enhancement to the Shabbos garments.

This enhancement has an exalted character, which we will now work to explain. After all, when else should we discuss exalted matters, if not at the moment of greeting Shabbos?

FOUR

THIS SUBJECT BEGINS BY introducing the words of the Jerusalem Talmud that the *RA"N* brings in his commentary to Talmud *Nedarim* (25a) (while discussing the law that promises delivered in exaggerated terms are presumed to be invalid).

The Jerusalem Talmud says: *"Nothing in Creation is square"* (*Nedarim* 3, *halacha* 2). Among the many creatures which came into existence in the Six Days of Creation, not a single one appeared in the form of a square. In fact, in Creation there is a tendency toward roundness, and the circle is the geometric form that is the polar opposite of the square [since it has no corners or angles at all –Ed.].

We have repeated here the statement of Rabbi Levi (in *Midrash Bereishis Rabbah* 89). He says that the entire description of Creation from *'In the beginning… '* until *'And it was completed …'* goes into the category of *'The honor of the Lord is in concealing matters'.* From *'And it was completed…'* forward (i.e. the rest of the Torah) goes into the category of *'The honor of kings is enhanced by analyzing matters'* (*Mishlei* 25:2). What emerges is that the nature of G-d's honor undergoes a transformation with the advent of (the first) Shabbos.

[Since *'And it was completed…'* (*Bereishis* 2:1) signals the end of the Creation process and the beginning of the spiritual tranquility we call Shabbos, and that is the fault line between the mysterious honor of being the Lord of Creation and the comprehensible honor of being the King of the World, it is accurate to say that Shabbos brings a new type of Divine honor into the world. –Ed.]

We also know that our Sages described clothing as bringing

honor to a person (Talmud *Shabbos* 113a). The function of clothing is to stamp upon its wearer a seal of honor.

In this context, we can absorb this concept of being obligated to wear new garments for Shabbos. A change in the nature of honor (which comes with the arrival of Shabbos) demands a change of clothing (which reflects honor).

We know that the requirement to put *tzitzis* on a garment comes when it has four corners. Four corners is a type of image that was not available during the Six Days of Creation, because 'nothing in Creation is square'. The honor that accrues from a garment with four corners belongs exclusively to the category of 'the honor of kings', and not to the category of 'the honor of the Lord'.

A garment having *tzitzis* enhances the notion of special garments worn for the sake of Shabbos. This is why Rabbi Yehuda used to don satin garments with *tzitzis* on them to greet Shabbos.

FIVE

WE KNOW THAT G-D undertook the major things Himself in bringing about the Exodus from Egypt, as the Haggadah says: *"I, G-d, not an angel; I, not a* seraph*"* (*Shemos* 12:12; also see Haggadah of Pesach). It is self-understood that although this is considered extraordinary Divine behavior in relation to the Exodus, it certainly is ordinary behavior when we refer to the Six Days of Creation.

This is because when it comes to creating something from nothing, there is no possibility of employing an angel. An angel is by definition an agent. [And there can be no agent at a time when G-d is engaging in a process that begins with "nothing". – Ed.]

Incidentally, the makeup of the word 'malach' for angel comes about as follows. Oftentimes we find an angel speaking in first person about himself as if he were the King. That is obviously impossible. So a word was constructed that takes the letters of 'melech', meaning king, and adds the letter *"Aleph"* as a reference to G-d Who is the first (like *Aleph* is the first letter) and Who is One (like the numerical value of *Aleph*). This shows that the words of the angel are undertaken on the behalf of the First of the First, G-d Himself.

He is now able to speak as if he were the king, because he is an agent of the true King. And the servant of a king is a (sort of) king (see *Shevuos* 47b). Be that as it may, we see that the existence of angels belongs to the type of honor that begins after the stage of *"And it was completed…"*

Now, after Rabbi Yehuda b. Illai had donned his Shabbos clothes, consisting of satin garments that had *tzitzis*, this entire concept of the new kind of honor which Shabbos engenders was recognizable on his face. At that point, it was the appropriate time for it to be said of him that he *"had the appearance of an angel of the G-d of Hosts"*.

SIX

THIS IS ONE PORTION of today's presentation. The other part of today's presentation will explain the unique element in the nature of Friday.

The Talmud says that the scholars used to greet Shabbos with the phrase: *"Come, bride. Come, bride."* The *Maharsha* commentary explains the seemingly repetitious language. It is because a bride is brought in twice. First, she is brought to the wedding canopy. Then, she is brought into the home of her new husband. This insight of the *Maharsha* is built upon the unique element in the nature of Friday (*Maharsha, Chidushei Aggados*, on *Baba Kama* 32b). We will explain this as follows.

There is an aspect of preparing for Shabbos that inheres in Friday, as indicated above. We need to avoid an error in understanding this principle. Every *mitzvah* has an adjunct concept of 'preparing for a *mitzvah*', and the same is true of prayer. When someone puts on a nice jacket for *Shmoneh Esrei* (the standing prayer of eighteen blessings, three times daily), that is also called a preparation for a *mitzvah*. The Talmud (*Shabbos* 10b) derives this from the verse, *"Prepare to greet your Lord, O Israel"* (*Amos* 4:12). It is therefore natural to assume that since Friday comes before Shabbos, the preparations on Friday for Shabbos are in the category of preparing for a *mitzvah*, similar to such preparations for all *mitzvos*.

The truth is that the existence of Friday serves as a spur for the arrival of Shabbos. [If the only intrinsic holiness is contained in Shabbos itself, then whatever we do on Friday to prepare for Shabbos only acquires holiness as an auxiliary extension of Shabbos. The fact is otherwise. Friday has its own source of holiness. In fact, to some extent it is the holiness of Friday that opens the door to the possibility of Shabbos, in effect serving as a prompter for Shabbos to arrive. –Ed.]

There is an open verse to this effect, *'go to a teacher and read it'*. The verse says: *"See that G-d gave you the Sabbath, therefore He gives you on the sixth day enough bread for two days"* (*Shemos* 15:29). The verse is explicitly stating that the proof (you can 'see') of the gift of Shabbos is Friday. This shows that the preparation for Shabbos that takes place on Friday represents an intrinsic holiness of Friday.

On the other hand, the inner connection of Shabbos to Friday creates the fact that Friday's preparations are for Shabbos.

[Here we are trying to balance two contrary indications in the verse. It shows that Friday teaches the world a message of its own. Yet, Friday's teachings and preparations are not for itself but for Shabbos. The answer is that both are true. Friday has an intrinsic holiness as a time devoted to opening the world to a certain truth. Then it is Shabbos that arrives as the embodiment of that truth. –Ed.]

An open proof for this is from the *Halacha* stating that the Friday preparations for Shabbos should begin first thing in the morning (*Orach Chaim, Reish* 250). This is certainly not an application of the general concept that one should be energetic in the performance of *mitzvos*, doing them without delay, as derived from the fact that

"Abraham woke up early in the morning" (*Pesachim* 4a) to perform the circumcision on his son (*Bereishis* 22:3).

Instead, the occupation of preparing for Shabbos is an expression of the intrinsic holiness of the time of Friday itself. Furthermore, this rule that the preparations should begin first thing Friday morning is derived from the statement, *"(And it shall be on the sixth day) that they will prepare what they will bring* (i.e. the *Mann* that they collect in the morning and bring into their tents)... " (*Shabbos* 117b). Our Sages explained, that just as the bringing is done in the morning, the preparing should be done in the morning (see *Rashi* from *V'Haychinu*). We see from this that the preparation undertaken on Friday stems from the same spiritual source as the basic obligation of observing Shabbos itself.

[Since the *Mann* for Shabbos falls on Friday, we see this as the arrival of the essence of Shabbos. What we do then is to begin to cook this *Mann* on Friday, that is an expression of the holiness of Friday. Consequently, we see that these two sanctities are united at the source. – Ed.]

There is an interesting observation by some very early commentators, who note that we make a blessing over two loaves of bread at our Shabbos meal to memorialize the two loaves that fell for the Jews in the desert, despite the fact that the two loaves never fell on Shabbos but on Friday (*Orach Chaim, Reish Siman* 274). The answer is that Shabbos is the culmination of the spiritual essence that created the need for that *Mann* falling on Friday.

SEVEN

FRIDAY IS A TIME with two faces. On one hand, Friday belongs to the side of Creation (the Six Days) that is before "And it was completed..." As a result of this it belongs to the type of glory known as 'the honor of G-dliness'.

It is also true to say that with Friday comes the beginnings of obligations pertaining to Shabbos. In that respect it belongs to the type of glory known as 'the honor of kings'. This is what King David said: *"Your throne is prepared from back then"* (*Tehillim* 93:2). 'Prepared' means that it was ready beforehand.

On Shabbos itself it says: *"On the Seventh Day He went up and sat on His throne of honor."* Just as the existence of Friday creates a requirement for a Shabbos to follow it, so the presence of a throne of honor creates a requirement that the King will eventually sit down. This is the intention of the *Maharsha* when he says that on Friday we consider Shabbos to be an *arusa* (a woman entering under the canopy, not yet fully married and about to enter her husband's house).

The meaning of *arusa* is that there is a level of commitment that obligates the man to complete the process of marriage. As the Mishna teaches, from that time forward we give the man and woman a certain time period in which to prepare for marriage and at the conclusion of that time they are obligated to marry (*Kesuvos* 57a).

In the same way, the presence of Friday creates an obligation, a demand, for Shabbos to arrive. Friday is an *arusa*. And an *arusa* is brought in twice. Once under the canopy and once into the house of her husband.

EIGHT

BECAUSE OF THIS DUAL character of the sanctity of time that is embodied in Friday, the *Halacha* must establish systems to accommodate both facets. Therefore the *Halacha* institutes the practice of washing one's face on Friday, which already represents a change within the person's body to reflect the newfound honor associated with Shabbos. [This is seen as an act intrinsic to Friday's own sanctity. – Ed.]

This immediately stimulates a recognition of the facet of Friday which reflects the essence of Shabbos. At that point, it becomes time to put on the Shabbos clothes.

TWENTY

THE HOLY LIGHT OF CREATION

INTRODUCTION

THE HOLY LIGHT OF the beginning of Creation was hidden away until our arrival at the Future World. Because Shabbos contains elements of the Future World, it absorbs some of this special light.

This is why the *Havdalah* (Separation) ceremony at the end of Shabbos involves a fire. Fire signifies our separation from the holy light of the Future World and our return to the lesser light that prevails in the current state of the world.

Torah also contains the concealed light of the Future World. This light is reserved for righteous Torah scholars in the Future World.

[The original chapter, as published in the *Pachad Yitzchak*, begins with an ellipse to indicate that it is missing a piece at the beginning. The content of that segment becomes obvious at the end of the chapter, when Rav Hutner concludes his answer to that opening question. We will add the missing information in brackets to aid clarity and flow. – Ed.]

ONE

[THE TALMUD IN *PESACHIM* 104a gives a long list of *havdolos* (areas where G-d established divisions between people or things in the world) that must be recited as part of the separation/*Havdalah* blessing at the conclusion of Shabbos. These include His separation 'between holy and mundane, between light and darkness, between Israel and the nations'.

However, the most natural candidate, His separation 'between the day of Shabbos and the six days of action', does not appear on the list. Yes, we do mention it right before the end of the blessing. But this, the Talmud explains, is only to fulfill the requirement of saying something right before the signoff of the blessing that is ...] ... similar to the signoff itself.

[Longer blessings have an introductory clause, "Blessed are You..." an intermediate section which is the main message of the blessing, and a signoff that also begins "Blessed are You..." There is a rule that the signoff cannot be too different from the phrase said right beforehand.

Sometimes, if a blessing has gone far afield in its main section and wishes to sign off with one specific detail, it will include one phrase that bridges between the main section and the signoff. It is called *"me'eyn chasima,"* a phrase 'similar to the signoff'.

Here, too, the main blessing is celebrating the series of separations that G-d has built into His world. The signoff is *"Blessed are You, G-d, Who separated the holy from the mundane."* The mention of separating Shabbos from the other days is the phrase 'similar to the signoff', but is not part of the main message of the blessing. – Ed.]

Certainly, it would be appropriate for us to call attention to this unusual setup. The fact is that in the performance of the *mitzvah* to proclaim the separation of Shabbos, that very separation is only mentioned in an auxiliary role. It is secondary to all those other forms of separation that have nothing to do with this time of the departure of Shabbos. How can this be?

On top of this, we are confronted by something very astounding. We know that the obligation to make *Kiddush* (to acknowledge the sanctity of Shabbos in honor of its arrival) and *Havdalah* for Shabbos are derived from the selfsame source. Both are learned from the instruction to "Remember the day of Shabbos to proclaim it holy", which is interpreted by our Sages to mean: "Remember it upon arrival, remember it upon departure."

If someone were to mention in *Kiddush* all the types of holiness mentioned in the Torah, but he would refrain from including the sanctity of Shabbos on that list, he would certainly not have fulfilled his obligation of *Kiddush*. Then, why is the remembrance of the departure of Shabbos performed differently than the remembrance of the arrival of Shabbos?

TWO

THE FUNDAMENTAL FACT HERE is the uniqueness of the character of the *Havdalah* of Shabbos (at its end) in contrast to the *Kiddush* of Shabbos (at its beginning).

Of course, holy recitals are found throughout the Torah, so sanctification through speech is not something new. However, *Havdalah* is different, because nowhere in the Torah do we find a (requirement for a) recital to pronounce a separation. Any time the Torah tells us to separate, it refers to actual behaviors of (avoidance or) separation in practice. This very fact testifies like a hundred witnesses that the separation/*Havdalah* of Shabbos has its own unique approach.

THREE

IN TRUTH, WE FIND (the roots of) this approach in the Torah's depiction of the first day of Creation, where it says: *"And G-d saw the light, that it was good, and He separated between the light and the darkness"* (*Bereishis* 1:4).

Rashi explains that He saw the world was not worthy of using this light, so He separated it and placed it into storage for the Future World. Here we see "separation" being explained in the sense of placing something into storage. Clearly, such a separation is intrinsically different from other types of separation, which do not have this element of storage.

After all, the usual sense of the word 'separation' refers to keeping two entities from mixing, but it does not deal with the essence of each individual entity. Separation by placing something into storage is making a statement that this one entity being separated from its counterpart has no place at all in the current state of our world.

Indeed, the very presence of this entity in our contemporary world would constitute an incompatible mixture. Therefore, the act of separation can only be accomplished by placing that entity into storage [until such time as the world becomes capable of absorbing it into daily reality – Ed.]. This is the source of the special separation/ *Havdalah* of Shabbos. After all, that very light of the first day of Creation was placed into storage until the end of days, "the time that is all Shabbos". And each individual Shabbos serves as a 'facsimile' of that time (*Berachos* 57b).

We must then conclude that every Shabbos incorporates within itself a facsimile of that holy light that is in storage until the future. At the moment that Shabbos passes, the time comes for a 'facsimile of storage' proportionate to the degree of 'facsimile' in the light that was present in Shabbos. Because this process of placing that light into storage is designated by the Torah as separation/*Havdalah*, we employ that same language and say that there is an obligation to recite a '*Havdalah*' for Shabbos (when it ends).

FOUR

IMAGINE A PERSON SITTING in *Gan Eden* (Heaven) and enjoying the fruit of his labors in this world. The condition of the soul in a state of receiving reward is utterly different than its condition while experiencing a state of stress and effort. The period of effort and the period of reward are deeply contrasting.

If one were to suddenly jump from a state of reward and bounty into the midst of a state of effort and stress, the confidence and serenity of receiving reward would endanger the ambition and passion required for continued effort and stress.

This is because the illumination of the period of bounty is of a quality that the ordinary world is not worthy of using. Therefore this person (who jumped from reward back into work) would have to place in storage the confidence and serenity of receiving reward, so that it does not cause damage to, and leave a flaw in, the service of effort and stress that is called for in daily life.

FIVE

THE VERY SAME CONCEPT, to the very same degree, applies in reference to the departure of Shabbos. Shabbos is a facsimile of the *"time that is all Shabbos"*, the period of reward, where the requirement for human effort to sustain oneself will be eliminated. Certainly, it is a grave danger to try to introduce the illumination of this 'facsimile' into the six days of action, stress and effort. Because the world of action which exists during those six days is not worthy of utilizing the illumination from this 'facsimile'.

Therefore, the time of the departure of Shabbos requires the placing into storage (of that light). That process of storing it is the spiritual service of the heart which accompanies the physical *mitzvah* of *Havdalah* after Shabbos. For this reason, this act of separation is the only one that uses words; it is also the only one that is fulfilled by the mouth. All the categories of separation whose purpose is only to prevent the mixing of two distinct essences, have no relationship to the verbal, since separating does not affect each individual essence [beyond protecting it from falling into a hodgepodge –Ed.].

The separation/*Havdalah* of Shabbos differs in that it impacts upon the basic essence that is being separated.

[As explained, the *Havdalah* ceremony does not merely record the fact that Shabbos is distinguished from the rest of the week, it actually functions as a tool in a process of self-education and self-regulation. It enables the person to shift out of the relaxed, obligation-free framework of Shabbos, which simulates the conditions of a redeemed post-Messianic world, and to readjust to the grind of the current reality which demands extensive effort for survival and achievement. Thus, the *Havdalah* can be said to be acting on Shabbos per se, working to put its light back into storage until such time as it can prevail. – Ed.]

In this respect, the *Havdalah* that is recited at the departure of Shabbos is similar to the *Kiddush* that is recited upon the arrival of Shabbos. Hence, both are performed orally.

SIX

THE *MISHNA BERURA*, CITES a legal question: Is it possible to satisfy the basic Torah requirement of *Kiddush* [the mitzvah of declaring the sanctity of Shabbos, generally performed over wine after returning from the synagogue on Friday night – Ed.] by saying "Good Shabbos"? After all, these are words which mention the fact that it is Shabbos.

The *Mishna Berura* argues that this is not a legitimate question, because *Rambam* says explicitly that *Kiddush* on Shabbos must include a praise of G-d, and the saying of "Good Shabbos" has no element of praise.

It is obvious that this obligation of including praise for G-d would also apply to *Havdalah*. *Havdalah* is the mention of Shabbos on its way out, just as *Kiddush* is the mention of Shabbos on the way in. Now, the praise that is required by the *mitzvah* of *Kiddush* can certainly only be fulfilled if mentioned in conjunction with the sanctity of Shabbos; for example, to say that that G-d is the "One Who sanctifies Shabbos". In that way, the declaration of the day's sanctity is delivered in a praising manner.

However, if someone were to declare words of praise that had no relevance to the sanctification of the Shabbos Day, the praise would clearly not be connected with the mention of Shabbos.

Consequently, there would be no way to accomplish the *mitzvah* of *Havdalah* after Shabbos while mentioning the day of Shabbos, because the Torah does not record any act of *Havdalah* [i.e. leaving or moving away from Shabbos at its conclusion – Ed.] by G-d at the end of the first Shabbos. Since no praise of G-d in reference to *Havdalah* could be recited, there would have been no way to perform this obligation at all. The only way that we succeed at offering praise to G-d in the text of *Havdalah* is by praising Him for separating light from darkness.

This is because the source of the *Havdalah* of Shabbos is in the separating G-d did in the first day of Creation. The result is that we are able to fulfill both the obligation to praise G-d while mentioning Shabbos as it leaves, and the basic obligation of mentioning Shabbos as it leaves, by virtue of mentioning the act of separating the light from the darkness.

This is what our Sages meant when they said that mentioning the separation of the Seventh Day from the six days of action in the *Havdalah* text is not counted [as one of the basic separations that the blessing is celebrating – Ed.].

When they add that its purpose is to serve as "something similar to the signoff of the blessing", they mean that its fundamental purpose is to show that the obligation to celebrate the separation/ *Havdalah* of Shabbos may be satisfied by mentioning the separation of the light from the darkness.

SEVEN

THE ABOVE DISCUSSION CAN give us a good sense and understanding of the obligation for kindling a candle in *Havdalah*. *"The heart of the wise man makes his mouth intelligent, and on his lips it adds valuable things."*

After all, we never find that the time at which a thing was created by a person should become a time for obligating one to make a blessing for that invention. [Yet, there is a tradition that we celebrate fire after Shabbos because it was discovered by Adam at that time –Ed.]

The reason is as we have indicated. The stowing away of the light of the World of Reward caused the formation of the light of the World of Action, which is the light of Adam, the first man. As a result, the candle must be part of the *Havdalah* ceremony after Shabbos (*Pesachim* 104).

Additional thoughts...

THE YOM TOV ASPECTS OF PURIM AND CHANUKAH
(AS THEY RELATE TO SHABBOS)

This is Chapter 8, Section II of *Pachad Yitzchak,*
originally published in *Chanukah in a New Light*

TEN

THE TORAH CLEARLY STATES that a person who observes Shabbos (*Shemos* 7:10,11) is emulating the behavior of Hashem who scheduled Himself for "relaxation" on the seventh day (*Rashi, Shemos* 20:11 also *Mechilta*). The ordinary impression is that since G-d *"rested"* only on Shabbos (*Bereishis* 2:7), this emulation applies only to Shabbos and not to *Yom Tov*. There is no indication that Hashem also *"rested"* on *Yom Tov*.

SHABBOS: A DAY OF CREATIVITY

THIS PERCEPTION IS FAR from the truth. In truth, just as Shabbos *"rest"* relates to the fact that Hashem *"rested,"* so too is our *Yom Tov* *"rest"* based on Hashem *"resting"*. Just as there took place an event called *"resting"* on the seventh day of creation, so too there took place an event called *"resting"* on *Yom Tov*. [In other words, the original event that is being commemorated on a *Yom Tov* day is considered the spiritual equivalent of *"resting"*. The Exodus from Egypt has a quality that is, in relation to G-d, a form of *"rest"*. Consequently, the anniversary of that day, the *Yom Tov* of Pesach is a day of *"rest"* for Jews – Ed.]

219

Since we are speaking of basics, it is necessary to clarify this with the utmost of clarity. The definition of Shabbos *"rest"* does not imply that the seventh day was a day on which creativity did not take place, to the contrary a new reality was created on Shabbos that is not tied to the 'Ten Divine Sayings of Creation' (*Avos* 5:21).

REWARD AND RECOMPENSE IN THE END OF DAYS

JUST AS THERE ARE laws of choice and worship which govern the world during the six days of creation (*"hayom la'a'sosom"* (*Devarim* 7:11), *"today we are obligated to do them i.e. the Commandments, and tomorrow we will receive our reward,"*), in the same way there were created on the seventh day all of the laws that govern the world in the period of reward and recompense which will take place in the End of Days. That which distinguishes these two types of creation can be found in the source of their coming into being. The rules that govern us during ordinary periods, the time of *"today to do them,"* were enacted by the Ten Utterances during the six days of creation.

In contradistinction, the rules that govern the period of reward and recompense of the End of Days were created through the act of sanctification of the seventh day concerning which the Torah says, *"vayikadesh," "and G-d sanctified the seventh day"* (*Bereishis* 2:3). (This is the subtle meaning of the *Ramban* who defined *"vayeka- desh oso," "and G-d sanctified the seventh day,"* in that the seventh day contains the *neshama yeseira,* an expanded soul. (See *Ramban Torah Commentary, Bereishis* 2:3). Just as something new was cre- ated as the result of G-d's creative expression during the six days of creation, so too was something new created with the sanctification of the seventh day.

The *"rest"* and cessation of the seventh day entail abandoning the rules which govern ambition and labor in favor of the laws which govern the world of reward and punishment.

A DEEPER UNDERSTANDING OF SHABBOS "REST"

THIS IS THE MEANING of what we said previously, that the *"rest"* of Shabbos (our avoidance of the mundane) does not imply that nothing was created on the seventh day. The very opposite is the case. The essence of Shabbos *"rest"* and inactivity tells us that on the seventh day a new reality was created, an existence of *"rest"* and tranquility. This reality was not created in the same manner as were the laws of nature that were established during the six days of creation. This reality is a new existence that was created through *"vayikadesh," "and G-d sanctified the seventh day"* (study *Pachad Yitzchak Pesach* 64 Section 4 since that lecture and this lecture complement each other).

THE LAWS OF THE END OF DAYS

HENCE, WE LEARN THAT the *"rest"* and repose of Sabbath involves a departure from the laws that govern the present reality; it involves an entry into a new regime, the regime of the laws of the End of Days. In order to reach the era of the End of Days we must create a unique people who are suited and motivated to arrive at the End of Days. Those individuals who share the goals, objectives and yearning of *Shabbos* are those who belong to *K'lal Yisrael*. Consequently, any time that the dominion of the present laws of nature are suspended for the needs of *K'lal Yisrael* (i.e., the miracles of the Exodus, receiving the Torah at Sinai, and the special protective clouds in the Desert), we encounter an abandonment of the present reality in favor of utilizing the system of nature designed for the End of Days. We have previously learned that this type of transition is the essence of the *"rest"* and tranquility of Shabbos. From this we derive the cessation and *"rest"* that fosters the sanctity of *Yom Tov*.

WHY ISN'T SHABBOS A *MO'ED*?

WE ARE NOW ABLE to understand the words of our Sages who stated that Shabbos is not called a *mo'ed* — a festival, a designated day (*Eruchin* 10b). Let us explain. The sanctity of Shabbos calls for the suspension of the present laws of nature in anticipation of our future redemption and the reality that will apply then. The sanctity of *Yom Tov* calls for the suspension of the existing laws of nature in favor of those activities that bring about the era of the End of Days. The root of the word *mo'ed*, festival, is from *yiud*, a promised event (see *Malbim* on *Vayikra* 16:21 and *Melachim A* 8:5). The sanctity of Shabbos involves the suspension of the present in anticipation of the future. Shabbos is therefore not connected with the word *mo'ed*. The sanctity of *Yom Tov*, however calls for the suspension of the present in the face of the promise of the future. This sanctification is therefore called *mo'ed*, (a designated day). (The above analysis relates exclusively to festivals which involve a prohibition of labor. The special depth concealed in *Rosh Chodesh*, the New Moon, which entitles it to be called a *mo'ed*, is explained at length elsewhere). The following is the general principle. The suspension of the present in anticipation of the End of Days is characterized as cessation and *"rest"*. We therefore find that the Exodus from Egypt, the revelation of Torah, and the emergence of Clouds of Glory (the description of Pesach, Shavuos and Succos) are also days of cessation and *"rest"* in the world of Hashem.

Just as we emulate G-d through the cessation and *"rest"* of Shabbos by doing that which G-d Himself did i.e., He also ceased and *"rested"* from Creation, so too, we emulate G-d on the festivals, because for Him those miraculous days that we commemorate were days of cessation and *"rest"*.

ELEVEN

THE SUSPENSION OF THE present in anticipation of the future has two aspects. The first is the suspension of physical activities, which is felt by our senses, the second is the suspension of thoughts that express themselves through deeds, a process grasped only by the mind.

The first example is to be found in the events of Pesach, Shavuos and Succos. Clearly the splitting of the Reed Sea, the revelation of Torah and the Clouds of Glory involved abrogating the natural order. This change was felt by the organs, it represents a physical suspension of the laws of the present in anticipation of the promise of the future. An example of the second type of suspension are the events of Chanukah and Purim. The redemptions from Haman and Antiochus did not materialize through a change in the deeds of G-d; what did happen is that the combination of events were woven into one tapestry which outlined a program through which the events of the present are organized toward a future goal.

In all of the above, G-d's *"thoughts are detected through His deeds"*. We certainly see in the events of Chanukah and Purim elements of the suspension of the present in anticipation of the future, because these events resulted in the creation of days of joy for the Jewish People. Without such a suspension, no events can give birth to a fixed time of joy. But this suspension belongs to the second category, in that His thoughts are recognized through His deeds. This is a conceptual suspension of the present in anticipation of a future goal. This suspension is not felt in the senses because the senses are incapable of grasping a thought.

Now that we have gathered the elements of this lecture into one logical chain we are ready to return to the beginning.

Through the *mitzvah* of *Hallel* and thanks, Chanukah was designated a *Yom Tov* even though it does not contain the prohibition of labor. Purim, on the other hand, could only be regarded as a *Yom Tov* if it included the prohibition of labor.

Now we see that there is no contradiction. The essence of the *mitzvah* of Chanukah is the renewal of the lights of Israel's redemption from Greece each and every year. This renewal bestows upon each generation an ability to sense and experience the governance by silence which is illuminated by the superior wisdom of Torah. This superiority implies that wisdom comprehends even the thoughts of the teacher — *"these, these are His strengths."*

Therefore, so far as the teacher's thoughts are concerned, it is totally feasible for the Hasmonean Sanhedrin to think of Chanukah as a Yom Tov despite the fact that it does not include the prohibition of labor. From the viewpoint of the wisdom that is capable of understanding the silent thoughts of the teacher, the word Yom Tov applies to the conceptual suspension of the present in favor of the promise of the future. Purim, however, which took place prior to the sealing of the Biblical text describes events which took place during the era of Prophecy. Prophecy can only define tangible events, and a celebration instituted by prophets could only be a *Yom Tov* if it involved the suspension of tangible physical activity in honor of the future.

TWELVE

THE GENERAL PRACTICE OF Jews, which is itself a form of Torah, is to conduct festive banquets in celebration of the days of Chanukah (*Orach Chaim* 279:2). The *Maharshal* added that it is proper to engage in Torah conversation during the Chanukah Banquet (*She'elos Uteshuvos Maharshal* 65). Speaking words of Torah is a practice which is not unique to Chanukah [and would seem to be out of place in this context—Ed.]. However, the heart that absorbed the lights of this lecture will discover in this statement of the *Maharshal* allusions that speak to his spirit. The essence of the custom to make Chaunkah feasts, is rooted in an aspect of the *"Yom Tov"* quality of Chanukah. This is the way in which we celebrate Chanukah as a *Yom Tov*.

When we speak of Chanukah as a *Yom Tov* we know that it is not analogous to other days that are called *Yom Tov* since Chanukah is called *Yom Tov* for one reason alone, its power as regards the wisdom of Torah. Chanukah is called a Yom Tov only as regards to its serving as an event par excellence which demonstrates the reigning system of *"a scholar is of greater weight than a prophet."* For such a day's festivity to be regarded as a festive meal it must be bolstered by a discussion of the wisdom of Torah.

The mouth at a Chanukah Banquet is incapable of savoring the taste of *Yom Tov* unless the meal is accompanied by the taste of words of Torah wisdom.

Maran Ha'ga'on

RAV YITZCHAK HUTNER

Zecher Tzadik Ve'kadosh Livracha

A BIOGRAPHICAL SKETCH

IT IS FRANKLY IMPOSSIBLE for any one person to describe my Rosh Yeshiva, Maran Harav Yitzchok Hutner, *zecher tzaddik ve'kodosh livrachah; mori, ve'rabi, rechev Yisrael uforoshov*. If each disciple were to write a book about him, each would write a different book. This is about the Rav Hutner I knew.

Some biographical background might be of help. We moved to Brooklyn when I was five so that I could attend the Flatbush Yeshiva. Never in my wildest dreams did I believe that I, a graduate of Brooklyn College, working on a doctorate in political science at the New School for Social Research would become a full-time student of Mesivta Rabbi Chaim Berlin and a disciple of Rav Yitzchok Hutner. But the moment I met him, I was drawn to the unbelievable qualities which made him one of the seminal, most influential and successful educators and molders of men in Jewish history. I might add that when I met Rav Hutner I was the executive president of the American Betar, deeply involved in the Irgun and in the struggle to create a Jewish State. Many of my closest friends were secular Jews. Characteristically, in my many conversations with Rav Hutner we never discussed Betar, Jabotinsky or Zionism. He had one agenda; opening my mind to the depth and riches of Jewish ideology and thought.

I recall three occasions on which I asked Rav Hutner clarification on points of Jewish thought or law. On one occasion he said, "What you're saying is *apikorsus*." It's impossible for a Jew to think that way! His message was clear. You have not thought the matter through, nor have you adequately studied the original sources; go and study. On a second occasion he said to me, "*Ven du vest halten der bi, vest shoin alein farshtein.*" When you will mature; when you will grow in Torah stature, you will discover the answer on your own. And on a third occasion, he spent over an hour orally reviewing a lecture he had once delivered on the topic of my question; the true nature and meaning of Midrash; making his points clear as he went along, so that I comprehended each point and followed his logic.

What struck me most, is that despite the fact that the line of students outside his door was always quite long, this giant of Jewish scholarship, ideology and thought would take out an hour and more to clarify an ideological point with a 19 year old student. Despite the fact that I have had the privilege of knowing and hearing many great men, it was he who had the strongest influence on my life because he was prepared to invest of his time, brilliance and energy in me and in scores of students and disciples who saw him as rebbe, Rosh Yeshiva, mentor, advisor, friend, teacher and father figure. Despite over 25 years since his passing, his booming, magnificent voice keeps resonating. I can recall the *tension* in the air as we awaited his lectures; the atmosphere of holiness and trepidation as we sat in his succah, at his seder table, or when we rode the heavens in song following his brilliant Yom Tov lectures. He made Torah come alive; he was the master of *kovod haTorah*; he was majesty. He was the personification of the teaching of our Sages that "*the awe of your teacher should reflect your awe of Heaven.*"

Permit me a few vignettes to describe his acuity and sharpness which were world famous.

When Menachem Begin visited the United States, the Rosh Yeshiva joined other roshei yeshiva in a meeting with Menachem Begin in the home of Rav Moshe Feinstein, *zt"l*. Members of the Israeli Shin Bet security services began to scour the room for possible explosives, devices or weapons; they assuredly didn't expect to find them, but this was routine practice. The Rosh Yeshiva turned to the Shin Bet men and said, "*Im atem michapsim p'tzatzot, timtzeu otam rak b'Igrot Moshe.*" "If you are searching for explosives, you will find them only in the writings of our host, Reb Moshe's compendium of Halachic responsa called *Igros Moshe* — The Correspondence i.e.: the responsa of Rav Moshe Feinstein. Indeed, Haga'on Rav Moshe Feinstein was world famous for his halachic *bombs*, his creative and original solutions to difficult halachic problems.

The Rosh Yeshiva once related the following story to me in a private conversation. Moshe Dayan visited the United States soon after the Israeli cabinet had considered the issue of drafting yeshiva students into the Israeli army. The debate in the cabinet was fierce, and Moshe Dayan carried the day. Despite the fact that Dayan was a secular Jew who was raised on a left-wing kibbutz, the American roshei yeshiva felt it important that they personally convey their appreciation. Because Rav Hutner spoke Israeli Hebrew fluently, he was asked to be the spokesman of the delegation. After Rav Hutner thanked Dayan, he asked Dayan, "what motivated you to champion the right of Israeli yeshiva students to maintain their Torah study vigil?" Said Dayan, "In my childhood home Yom Kippur was like any other day. We ate breakfast and lunch. In high school I was once asked to memorize a poem of Bialik. I chose *Hamatmid* — the Talmud student. Bialik describes the idealism of the Talmud student and then Bialik says, "*Mi ata shamir.*" "To what do you, emery stone compare?" "*Umi ata chalamish.*" "And who are you flint stone?" "*Lifnei na'ar ivri ha'osek baTorah.*" "In comparison to the iron dedication of a Jewish youth who is occupied in Torah study." Dayan continued, "For two thousand years this emery stone, the stone of Torah study preserved the Jewish people; could I be the one who would shatter this stone?"

When Rav Hutner passed on to the '*heavenly yeshiva*' the *yeshiva shel ma'alah* on erev Shabbos, *chof Kislev,* 5741; November 28, 1980, the December 1, 1980 issue of the Jewish Telegraphic Agency Daily Bulletin carried the following notice: "Jerusalem, November 30, Rabbi

Yitzchok Hutner, a leading orthodox educator and Talmudic sage, died here Friday at the age of 74. He was buried the same day, on the Mount of Olives, where his casket was brought on foot by pupils and admirers. Rav Hutner was born in Poland of a distinguished rabbinic family. As a young man he published a learned work on the laws of the Nazir, which earned him the praise of leading Talmudic scholars. Later he settled in the United States with his family and founded the Rabbi Chaim Berlin Yeshiva, one of New York's leading schools of advanced Talmudic studies. Rav Hutner also played a major role in orthodox high school education in the United States." End of JTA report. Was this all the JTA had to say upon the passing of one of the Torah giants of our era? One of the most accomplished towering personalities of world Jewry? Rebbe, teacher and mentor; the *ga'on* and tzaddik, Rav Yitzchok Hutner, *zatzal*? The Rosh Yeshiva of Mesivta Rabbi Chaim Berlin, Kollel Gur Aryeh, Yeshiva Pachad Yitzchok, Kollel Ohr Eliyahu, etc. etc. But the JTA had no file on Rav Hutner since he would not allow his name to be used in any public notice. He had distain for the world of P.R. It was therefore assumed that there would be no eulogies at his funeral, and no obituaries in the secular press on his passing. Rabbi Hutner removed himself from the world of the newspapers; not only because he felt that under the best of circumstances they smacked of *sheker*, of falsehood, but because he wished to teach his students that *emes*, truth, had found its last refuge in the *Bais Medrash*, the yeshiva study hall; in the echo of the thunder of Sinai.

When I inquired at the yeshiva if I might arrange for the publication of a report of his passing in the New York Times, I was told, *"You know that he would not want it."* The Times therefore made no mention of his passing even though his funeral in Jerusalem brought tens of thousands who carried his *aron* by foot to his resting place on the Mount of Olives. Even in relating the following feeble words of subjective evaluation I may be violating his rules. The Rosh Yeshiva did not permit public discussion of himself during his lifetime, certainly not after his passing. I never once heard him introduced, described or praised at a banquet of his own yeshiva or in a yeshiva publication. He wouldn't permit it. But just as he wrote many volumes of Torah thought, his very life is now Torah, and we are obliged to learn from it.

This unusual and gifted man was an extremely private person. Rav Hutner avoided conventions, delivered few public addresses outside the yeshiva, wrote few articles but was famous for his letters. In his early years before he developed a world wide reputation, he was largely known to his self imposed circle of students and disciples. He concentrated his unbelievably rich talents and energies on his students because of his conviction that by literally pouring his rich personality into them, he might succeed in creating authentically deep Torah personalities, that one ingredient which was most needed to nurture and transform the barren and stillborn wasteland of American Jewry. He appreciated that more than anything else, the American Jewish community and the world cried out for a Jewish leadership steeped in the eternal sources of Torah learning and committed to its perpetuation. He was keenly affected by the tragedy of Europe, he had lost his neighborhood, his family, his loved ones in *churban* Europe. He was one of the first to believe that America could produce a native *talmid chacham* who did not fall short of his European antecedents. In this respect Rav Hutner can properly be called America's first authentic Rosh Yeshiva. His time, his scholarship and his energies belonged primarily to his students; even the *mesifta*, which he built from scratch to new proportions took second place to his desire to oversee the development and maturation of each student as an individual. From early morning 'till late at night there was a long line of students outside his room waiting to speak to the Rosh Yeshiva about a point raised in a Talmud Shiur, a question which grew out of his frequent *ma'amorim*, his highly intricate and deep philosophical discourses on Jewish thought and ideology, of which he was the world's recognized master; or on a public or personal issue which required the razor sharp, piercing intellect and concern of the Rosh Yeshiva.

If you did not maintain regular contact, a message inevitably arrived through a fellow student, "The Rosh Yeshiva would like to see you." Most of the discussion matter of these sessions would deal with personal topics. His interest in each student's welfare and progress was unwavering and unceasing. He was a supreme student of the mind. He understood each individual and his own personal needs. He possessed that unusual magical capacity to create an intensely intimate bond of kinship, of fellowship, indeed of love, which gave him the ability to bring out the best in each individual and to motivate each individual to develop his unique potential to the fullest extent possible. Indeed, this was one of his greatest talents; he sized you up and saw right through you. He understood who you were and the true nature of your talents.

I once asked him to meet with an individual to convince him to become a student at Mesivta Rabbi Chaim Berlin, and he replied, "As a principle, I never attempt to convince or ask anyone to become a student in *my* mesivta, only to become a student of Torah."

On another occasion he described the uniqueness of Chaim Berlin. "Our mesivta *is nisht a vorsht fabrik*; we are not a salami factory," you don't come in and then emerge as a carbon copy of everyone else. Everyone was unique. Everyone was special. Each person was endowed by His Creator with a unique face, a unique voice, unique potential, a unique future. And it was his task to make sure that your talents developed and reached their potential. Sitting before him, a student was humbled to think that this great man would devote his personal time to his problems; yet that was his strength. A student felt a mixture of both love and awe. It was difficult to say *No* to the Rosh Yeshiva; it was a combination of his stature, his forceful personality, the conviction that the Rosh Yeshiva genuinely cared and knew what was best for *you*. Because there was nothing in it for *him*. But more. The conviction of each student that this man who with his penetrating eyes, charismatic and larger than life personality, brilliant insights and unceasing interest and concern literally could see into your soul. When you sat before him, he *knew* all there was to know about you; and what you were about.

His public forum was his *Bais Medrash*, the wedding of a student, or the celebration of the holidays. There he was majestic and imposing. When he entered a crowded room, all rose instantly. If the room was so packed that it was impossible for another person to enter, *despite that*, a wide path would nonetheless appear the moment he approached the entrance. This insistence on respect was an educational strategy designed to enhance and raise the honor of Torah. To make Torah so important, that his students would be prepared to devote their entire lives to it. He once said that, "a yeshiva is much more than a place for the study of Torah, *limud hatorah*; it is the place for *kovod haTorah*; for creating the stature and honor of Torah." This magnetic, charismatic man in private was a warm father and friend. It was only when you were alone with him did he make his speeches and tell his jokes and stories. Here he was effervescent, overflowing, warm, generous, humorous, lively. Here too, he could be critical, demanding and insistent. He would spend all the time that was required to explain a difficult Talmudic or halachic point, until the problem vanished, or as generally was the case, until you realized that he had replaced your problem with a much more sophisticated problem because he had enlarged and expanded your perspective, by putting your problem into the context of your potential and your place in the world of eternity.

Beyond his stature as a *gadol baTorah*; a preeminent Talmudist; a leading thinker, a great Jewish philosopher, a statesman who carried the concerns of *K'llal Yisrael* on his shoulders, he was primarily a builder and molder of men. He has been properly called the great planter — not the great builder. He was determined to plant trees which would bear living fruits, which in turn would create new forests. He invested *all* of his energies into the creation of individuals. "A builder," he would say, "assembles materials, and constructs a building in accordance with a set plan and design. He may if he wishes, rush his workers to complete the structure quickly. Not so the planter. He must plant each seedling, nurture each growing tree, and wait patiently until it matures and bears fruit. He must water it, prune it, protect it against disease and the elements each and every day; year in and year out. A man in a hurry is capable of being a successful builder, but he can never be a successful planter." Rav Hutner saw how popular the construction of buildings had become in America. Many men build buildings and institutions, but few are engaged in the tedious work of planting.

Many of my friends at the Orthodox Union who heard the name Rav Hutner spoken with awe by his students wondered why they did not have the opportunity to hear him, to see him, to feel the impact of his personality, as would be *expected* of a great leader of the Torah community. "Why," they asked, "was he so very involved with his students. And why did he relate almost exclusively to the limited circle of the initiated?" The answer lies in his evaluation of the needs and priorities of American Jewry. And probably, with his own estimation of how best to invest his strengths, time, and talents. While *all* Roshei Yeshiva and Gedolim concentrate on their students and yeshivos, Rav Hutner carried this to an extreme. He believed that American Jewry could not survive the gradual normal process of communal development. It has been said by historians that any new settled Diaspora community required a period of approximately 300 years before it was capable of producing native Torah giants. Rav Hutner was driven by a determination to accelerate this process; to push as hard as he could, so that the accomplishment of this goal might be achieved within the span of one generation. Indeed he succeeded. As Torah institutions and communities in Europe went up in flames, he realized that Jewish survival was dependant upon the creation of American born Rashei Yeshiva, *talmidei chachomim, rabonim* and *manhigim*. He was *determined* to create authentic, deeply rooted Jewish leaders. To accomplish this required a force that would compel, that would motivate young students to make a qualitative jump in their commitment and lifestyle within a relatively short period of time. With this in mind, Rav Hutner decided to concentrate his influence on his students as one would *concentrate* the rays of the sun through a focused magnifying glass, so as to create the intensity, commitment and the idealism that was required to achieve this goal.

Examined in historical terms his accomplishment was nothing short of miraculous. Within the span of one generation he was able to take students; many of whom came to him from non-orthodox or lukewarm orthodox backgrounds to the point where they were capable of establishing their own major Torah institutions. Not only did he create scores of such individuals, he created an entire society — a human and social environment; a pressure cooker, whose long term effects on the Jewish community are such that it cannot be imagined that one individual could have accomplished this qualitative and quantitative leap in the short span of one lifetime.

Rav Hutner must be described as a *"one man movement"* — he single-handedly changed the outlook, complexion and character of a broad segment of American Jewry. To examine a list of his students; the numbers of outstanding rabbis, *roshei yeshiva, poskim,* authors of *seforim;* creators and leaders of Torah organizations and educational institutions, is simply astounding.

The key to his success was his ongoing campaign to convince as many students as possible that they could indeed become *gedolei Torah, gedolei Yisrael* or *manhigei Yisrael;* leaders or giants in Torah or in Jewish leadership.

The Vilna Ga'on is reputed to have been requested to give his own formula for developing himself to reach the unbelievable heights he achieved. His famous reply was, "I am called the Vilna Ga'on, which in Yiddish means *'vill nor'* just desire it — just will it; with enough intensity." If you are possessed of sufficient drive and will power you, too, can become a ga'on. Rav Hutner's efforts were directed at creating this motivation and the intense Torah environment in which this motivation could flourish and flower.

While Rav Hutner was uncompromising in setting forth his own standards, principles and styles, he possessed the singular ability to establish strong relationships with a broad spectrum of students of diverse orientations and from a multiplicity of backgrounds.

The Chaim Berlin *Bais Medrash* was anything but monolithic in its student composition. Among its students were many who were active in Bnei Akiva. The Rosh Yeshiva did not insist that they leave the movement until such time that it became clear to *them* that this was in their best interest. For a while, Chaim Berlin was a magnet for students who were registered at the Conservative, Jewish Theological Seminary. On the other hand, many students were sons of famous rabbinic leaders or

Chassidic Rebbes. Some came from foreign countries. One had Neturei Karta leanings. Chaim Berlin attracted a broad spectrum of rugged individualists. Instead of serving as a melting pot, the Rosh Yeshiva nurtured and encouraged the individuality of each person by reinforcing and underlining the special qualities of each. I recall students who loved music, who played instruments, who pursued various secular professions and careers, with the encouragement of the Rosh Yeshiva. This ability to relate to so many diverse individuals representing so disparate a human spectrum; yet have everyone who left his presence feel that the Rosh Yeshiva was *my rebbe, my mentor,* that each enjoyed a unique and special relationship with this special individual. Frankly, if you did not develop that relationship, very often, you left Chaim Berlin. But the number of individuals with whom he developed and retained a close and intimate relationship for twenty, thirty *and more years* after they left the yeshiva is astounding! Each of these individuals felt that he was a *ben yochid;* an only son of the Rosh Yeshiva. Indeed the Rosh Yeshiva had but one child, his daughter Bruria; indeed we were all his sons.

Because of his unique life's work, the world has been enriched with hundreds of rabbis, roshei yeshiva and rebbeim. Chaim Berlin has been called "*the yeshiva of one thousand classrooms.*" Hundreds upon hundreds of Jewish families are miniature Torah kingdoms because *he* gave rise to them. He was one of the most resourceful and successful creators of the foundations of Torah in America. He, among a handful of American Torah giants created the revolution we see before our very eyes. His encouragement of NCSY and the *Ba'al Teshuvah* movement knew no end. Not only did much of the teshuvah movement emanate from his own students, he saw in it a unique phenomenon. When encountering yeshiva or Bais Jacob students who were *ba'alei teshuvah,* he would say that we live in a generation of which it could be said that *Eliyahu Hanavi* is walking among us. Once reflecting on the importance of the unique task of NCSY, he said to me that "*only once in many generations does an individual have the unique opportunity for such mighty accomplishments*". When he heard a rumor that I might give up the leadership of NCSY, he spent an hour impressing on me the urgency of not doing so. I'll never forget the booming sound of his voice. He said to me, "If you're tired *zolst foren in Honolulu arein!*" Travel to Honolulu! "*Zolst leigen oifen beach!*" Lie on the beach! But gather your strength to return to the work you are devoted to.

Rav Hutner's multifaceted family and educational background helps explain his versatility and originality. His father came from a prominent Lithuanian family, among the members of his family are the Ga'on Rav Yosef Zundel Hutner, from Eishoshuk near Vilna; (interestingly, the town from which my father's mother comes). Author of the *Chevel Yosef* and *Bikurei Yosef*; commentaries of the *Shulchan Oruch*. And the Gaon Rav Yehuda Seigel, rav and poseik in Warsaw for fifty years. His mother's family Wiedenfeld, were Chassidim with ties to the dynasty of the Kotzker Rebbe, one of the most extraordinary, original and daring of the Chassidic masters. At age 14 Rav Hutner was sent to the Polish yeshiva in Lomza. As a young prodigy he was figuratively snatched away from Poland to Lithuania to study in the world famed *Mussar* yeshiva of Slabodka, the most prestigious Lithuanian yeshiva, successor to the yeshiva of Volozhin. Despite his youth, he soon stood out as a central figure in the yeshiva and became known as the *Varshaver Illui*; the prodigy from Warsaw. He became the protégé of the world famous Dean, *Der Alter of Slabodka*, Rabbi Nosson Tzvi Finkel, one of the great *Ba'alei Mussar*, a giant exponent of the Mussar movement; as well as the Rosh Yeshiva, the Ga'on Rabbi Moshe Mordechai Epstein.

In 1926 when a branch of the Slabodka Yeshiva was established in Chevron, he moved to what was then Palestine to study in the Chevron Yeshiva. The Arab 1929 pogrom of Chevron which resulted in the death of a number of Chevron Yeshiva students and the closing of the Chevron Yeshiva and its reopening in Jerusalem, was a traumatic event in Rav Hutner's life. Fortunately, he was in Berlin at that particular time. While in Chevron Rav Hutner developed a close relationship with the first Ashkenazic Chief Rabbi of Eretz Yisrael, the great mystic and thinker Rabbi Avrohom Isaac HaCohen Kook. Paradoxically, he was simultaneously close to Rabbi Yosef Chaim Sonnenfeld, the leader of the Old Yishuv.

He returned for a while to Slabodka, and then to Warsaw. When he was in Berlin, he developed a life long friendship with Hagaon Rav Yosef Dov Soloveitchik.

In 1932 he published in Kovna his first major work, *Sefer Toras HaNazir*; an extended study of the laws of the Nazarite in Maimonides' Code, which was published with an introductory laudation, a *haskama*, by Rav Avrohom Duber Kahana Shapiro of Kovna, Rav Kook, and Rav Chaim Ozer Grodzinsky.

From 1930-1935 he returned to Yerushalayim, but visited Europe for a short while in 1933 for his marriage to his wife Masha, the daughter of Michoel Yosef Avrohom Alter, and in 1934 to collate manuscripts of the commentary of Hillel Ben Elyakim to Sifra published anonymously as *Kovetz L'Ho'oros L'Rabbeinu Hillel* published in Jerusalem, 1961; many years later.

In 1934 Rav Hutner finally decided to make his big move, and settled in New York where he joined the faculty of Yeshiva Rabbi Jacob Yosef, known as the mother of American yeshivos. I heard that he attempted to convince their leadership to establish a high school, a *mesifta*, but they refused. He therefore moved on to Yeshiva Chaim Berlin which then only had an elementary yeshiva. In 1939 he became the rosh yeshiva of Yeshiva Rabbi Chaim Berlin, which then rose under his leadership from an elementary yeshiva to one of the major yeshivos of the world with a mesivta, beis medrash and subsequently the Kollel Gur Aryeh, which was then under the leadership of his disciple Haga'on Rav Moshe Aharon Schechter and his son-in-law and disciple Haga'on Rav Yonosson David. In his later years he established the Pachad Yitzchak Yeshiva and Kollel in Jerusalem, which is headed by his son-in-law, Haga'on Rav Yonosson David.

In reviewing what I have said thus far, I feel most inadequate. I have said nothing to describe his unique Torah philosophy, a blending of the Alter of Slabodka, the masters of *mussar*, the Chassidic house of Kotzk, the Sefas Emes, Reb Tzodok HaCohen of Lublin, and the Gaon of Vilna. Rav Hutner was a master of Chassidic thought, but especially of the shining light of Torah ideology, the *Maharal* of Prague. I have said little about his volumes of profound and deep Torah thought called *Pachad Yitzchak*, through which the eyes of a generation have been opened to the depths and profundities of Torah wisdom. Nine volumes of *Pachad Yitzchak; divrei Torah b'inyanei hilchos deyos vechovos halevavos;* have already been published. Shabbos, 1962; Chanukah, 1964; Purim, 1966; Pesach, 1970; Shavuos, 1971; Rosh Hashana, 1974; Yom Kippur, 1978; plus a memorial volume and a magnificent volume of Letters and Writings. Additional volumes on tape and in manuscript, remain to be published.

A lifetime of Torah education notwithstanding, it was Rav Hutner who opened for hundreds of students the unbelievably rich and inspiring world of Torah thought and historiography. His lectures motivated us to begin the personal study of the *Sfas Emes,* of the *Maharal,* and of other giants of Torah thought. He taught his students to be autodidactic, devoted to making Torah study a major ongoing lifelong effort.

Rav Hutner's writings are a strikingly fertile synthesis of Talmudic incisiveness with strong components of Kaballah, chassidic conceptualization, mussar, mysticism and historical analysis, pulsating with a striking overtone of the *Maharal* of Prague. His style is at once lyric, poetic, graceful and highly structured. His thought is creative and original; ranging over the basics of Jewish thought and ideology, so as to give even the most initiated student a feeling of treading new ground on every line. Each paragraph reveals new depths and insights. His writing is philosophy, analysis, structure, *halacha* and poetry all at the same time.

I've also failed to convey the electric atmosphere of the yeshiva on the days prior to Rosh Hashanah, Yom Kippur, Pesach, Shavous, and during Chanukah or Purim, where nearly a thousand students and former students would pack the *bais medrash* to hear his Torah lectures on *hilchos deyos ve'chovos halevavos;* ethics, philosophy, concepts, duties. Nor did I describe how he turned *chol hamoed* Succos and Pesach which then, in America, at least so far as I was concerned, were — almost days like any other day into genuine *Yomim Tovim.* Not only by offering a Torah lecture on each evening of the festival, but by teaching us that the intermediate days are veritably *Yom Tov.* In Chaim Berlin they really were *Yom Tov.*

Among the most emotional moments in my memory is the picture of hundreds of students walking to the yeshiva from their homes, from *all* corners of Brooklyn, in order to sit in a dark room; to participate in the bidding of farewell to a *Yom Tov*. As the *Yom Tov* ebbed, we would hold on to its last golden moments with him leading us in song, and inspiring us with his incisive and pulsating words. An indescribable electric magic filled the room; in the darkness the light that shone was his holy presence.

Nor have I described his eclectic grasp of Torah knowledge; the Rosh Yeshiva spoke an unrevealed number of European languages. He was well versed in many areas of human knowledge; but he would rarely admit you to his world of secular knowledge because the hour demanded singular devotion to Torah, and the rebuilding of the world of Torah which was ground to dust and ashes in *churban* Europe. He taught us that the greatest adventure in life is the ability to break down the prison of the mundane, and to achieve the freedom which comes from the service to the Giver of ultimate freedom.

On one occasion, as I was driving him home, he pounded his cane on the floor of the car and said to me, "*Moshiach kimpt nisht — min darf ehm brengen.*" — Moshiach does not come on his own, we must bring him. And on another occasion he said, "*Moshiach kimpt nisht — min darf ehm brengen mit chutzpah*" Moshiach will not come through mundane, everyday deeds, we must bring him with audacity, with heroism, with chutzpah. My debt to him, together with thousands of his students is deep, abiding and profound. I could never fathom how a person who was among the few towering personalities of this generation could contain himself within the world of his yeshiva, and spend hour after hour after hour listening to the questions — often naïve questions — because some were beginners — of students; and then maintain that relationship for twenty and thirty years afterwards without the relationship dimming in intensity.

On the last Rosh Hashanah he was with us, despite his weakened condition, and his obvious failing health, we all lined up after davening as we had done for thirty Rosh Hashanahs before, after Maariv of the first night; all 500 of us in the beis medrash to wish the Rosh Yeshiva a *leshana tova tikoseivu*. He spent *well over an hour* — standing, greeting each and every one of us. Some of us into our late thirties, forties and fifties. Men, some of whom were grandparents; many whom were students of the mesifta high school, the bais medrash or the kollel. For each he had a special and unique *brocha*; a word, a sentence, a thought that pierced the heart, that added a new dimension to the Day of Judgment. You asked yourself, "He has been in Jerusalem for the past six months; how does he know this, how does he know so much about me? How well he understands what's going on!"

Rav Hutner painted before our eyes the possibility of a new and elevated existence. He wove the tapestry and created the image of a *ben Torah* and inspired each of us to aspire to become one.

His passing leaves a deep wound, a great void. The world suddenly became dry, silent, empty. He was without doubt the most sublime, the most compelling, the most awe inspiring individual I have ever known. To have been able to call him Rebbe, was one of the greatest gifts ever bestowed. To continue to live in his shadow, to continue to fathom his writings, to listen to his tapes, as though he is still with us every day, to weep because he is gone, but to rejoice in the knowledge that he was. I once had the chutzpa when I met him in Jerusalem, to say, "Rebbe, if you will permit me — to thank you for allowing me to be your *talmid*." He planted in us his unique Torah veltanshaung. This continues to be life's greatest heritage.

Books by the Same Author

Living Beyond Time: The Mystery and Meaning of the Jewish Festivals. 446 pages. Sha'ar Press (Artscroll). *$24.99*

The Sacred Trust: Love, Dating and Marriage: The Jewish View. 125 pages. NCSY/OU (Artscroll). *$14.99*

Purim in a New Light: Mystery, Grandeur and Depth, as revealed through the writings of Rabbi Yitzchak Hutner (*Sefer Pachad Yitzchak: Purim*). 243 pages. David Dov Publications. *$23.95*

Chanukah in a New Light: Grandeur, Heroism and Depth, as revealed through the writings of Rabbi Yitzchak Hutner (*Sefer Pachad Yitzchak: Chanukah*). 240 pages. David Dov Publications. *$23.95*

Hidden Lights: Chanukah and the Jewish/Greek Conflict. A thorough and fascinating review of the history, events and background of the Chanukah era. Based on the writings of *Chazal*. 291 pages. David Dov Publications. *$23.95*

Five Glorious Brothers: The Chanukah War as told in the ancient *Sifrei Maccabim.* (*Maccabees I and II*) plus an examination of the Chanukah miracles. 180 pages. David Dov Publications. *$14.99*

AVAILABLE SOON:

Shabbos ♦ Not a Day of Rest: The Majesty, Mystery, and Meaning of Shabbos. This book will surprise, inspire and uplift you. 200 pages. *$22.95* — 2008

These books are available at your local Jewish book store, or can be purchased from **The David Dov Foundation**, 603 Twin Oaks Drive, Lakewood, New Jersey 08701, by mail. There is no additional cost for postage or delivery. Please allow three weeks for delivery.